BASIC LAWS ON THE STRUCTURE

OF THE SOVIET STATE

BASIC LAWS ON THE STRUCTURE

OF THE SOVIET STATE

Translated and Edited by

Harold J. Berman

and

John B. Quigley, Jr.

HARVARD UNIVERSITY PRESS

Cambridge, Massachusetts · 1969

PREFACE

This volume is a collection of basic Soviet legislation defining the political structure of the Soviet state, especially in its legislative, administrative, and judicial aspects. In addition to legislation, we have included the Rules of the Communist Party, which is technically separate from the Soviet state but which under Article 126 of the USSR Constitution is the "leading core" of all state organizations. We use the term "legislation" in the Soviet sense, as including not only acts of a legislature but also administrative decrees of a normative character.

Part One presents, in addition to the USSR and RSFSR constitutions and the Party Rules, legislation prescribing the organization and functioning of the legislative and administrative branches of government. Part Two contains legislation prescribing the organization and functioning of the procuracy, the judicial system (including social, economic, and administrative tribunals), and the legal profession.

Many of the documents included in this collection may be found in translation elsewhere; however, the translations are not uniform and some are not easy to obtain. Although we have consulted other translations, we have in all cases worked from the original sources and have attempted to achieve a uniform set of English equivalents for the language of Soviet legislation. Nine of the documents have not previously been translated.

The collection is intended both for study and for reference, especially in courses in Soviet government, Soviet law, the Soviet economy, and Soviet social institutions.

All documents are given as amended to October 1, 1968.

H. J. B.
J. B. Q.

Cambridge, Massachusetts
October 10, 1968

SUMMARY OF CONTENTS

PART ONE

PART TWO

CONTENTS

PART ONE

1. CONSTITUTION OF THE USSR

2. CONSTITUTION OF THE RSFSR

TRANSLATION NOTES

Translation notes especially applicable to a given document are given in the introductory notes preceding the relevant documents. The notes in this section are of general application.

We have throughout employed the English future imperative (e.g., "a procurator shall direct the activities of...") to render sentences which in Russian are in the present indicative. This is necessitated by the fact that in Russian the present tense is generally used in legislation even though the meaning is prescriptive or normative.

A distinction is made in Soviet terminology between types of legislation enacted by different state agencies. We have translated zakon, which refers to an enactment adopted by a supreme soviet (of the USSR or of a union or autonomous republic), as a "law." The Constitution of the USSR, like the constitutions of the republics, is called osnovnoi zakon, "basic law."

An ukaz, which may be adopted only by the presidium of a supreme soviet in the period between sessions of the particular soviet and is subject to later confirmation by the soviet, is here translated as "edict." A postanovlenie, which refers to normative enactments of councils of ministers is rendered as "decree." (Supreme soviets may also issue decrees, which are not considered "laws" since they do not establish rules of general application. However, supreme courts also issue "decrees" which do establish rules of general application.)

A rasporiazhenie, which is adopted either by a council of ministers or by a local soviet, usually to implement a decree of a council of ministers, is translated "regulation." Prikaz is rendered as "order;" instruktsiia and ukazanie are both rendered as "instruction." All three are used primarily by ministries and departments to govern the activities of agencies and individuals within the ministry or department. A reshenie, which is adopted either by a court or by a local soviet, is translated "decision."

Polozhenie is a term outside the hierarchy of enactments since there are no restrictions as to which agencies may use it. It is an enactment which de-

fines the legal position of a given agency and is translated "statute," in the sense
in which that word is used in English for international instruments setting up
an agency and regulating its scope or authority. The term _ustav_, which has a
similar meaning, is translated "charter."

The Russian word _akt_, which refers collectively to all types of legislative enactments as well as to a variety of other official documents is translated as "act."

SOURCES

Laws and amendments of laws are regularly published in the Gazette (Vedo-mosti) of the USSR Supreme Soviet and in the Gazettes of union-republican supreme soviets. Decrees and amendments of decrees are regularly published in the Collection of Decrees (Sobranie postanovlenii) of the USSR Council of Ministers and the Collections of Decrees of union-republican councils of ministers. Also, important new legislation is frequently printed in full in the journal Sovetskaia iustitsia.

The most recent Russian editions of the twenty-two documents in this collection may be found in the sources listed below. The number of the document is given, followed by the source.

No.

1. Konstitutsia (osnovnoi zakon) Soiuza Sovetskikh Sotsialisticheskikh Respublik, Izdatel'stvo "Iuridicheskaia literatura," Moskva, 1966.

2. Konstitutsia (osnovnoi zakon) Rossiiskoi Sovetskoi Federativnoi Sotsialisticheskoi Respubliki, Izdatel'stvo "Sovetskaia Rossiia," Moskva, 1967.

3. Ustav Kommunisticheskoi Partii Sovetskogo Soiuza, Izdatel'stvo politicheskoi literatury, Moskva, 1966.

4. Ekonomicheskaia gazeta, No. 34, August 1967, p. 7.

5. Polozhenie o vyborakh v Verkhovnyi sovet SSSR, Izdatel'stvo "Izvestiia Sovetov Deputatov Trudiashchikhsia SSSR," Moskva, 1966.

6. Vedomosti Verkhovnogo soveta SSSR, 1967, No. 42, Item 536.

7. Supra, No. 6, 1968, No. 16, Item 131.

8. Sbornik zakonov Azerbaidzhanskoi SSR i ukazov Prezidiuma Verkhovnogo soveta Azerbaidzhanskoi SSR, 1938-1966 gg., Tom I, Izdanie Verkhovnogo soveta Azerbaidzhanskoi SSR, Baku, 1966, p. 184.

9. Sbornik ofitsial'nykh dokumentov (primenitel'no k kursu Sovetskogo gosudarstvennogo prava), pod obshchei redaktsiei professora A. I. Lepeshkina, Izdatel'stvo "Iuridicheskaia literatura," Moskva, 1964, p. 506.

10. Spravochnik narodnogo kontrolera, Izdanie vtoroe, Izdatel'stvo politicheskoi literatury, Moskva, 1965, p. 13.

11. Sbornik zakonov SSSR i ukazov Prezidiuma Verkhovnogo soveta SSSR, 1938-1967 gg., Tom 2, Izdatel'stvo "Izvestiia Sovetov Deputatov Trudiashchikhsia SSSR," Moskva, 1968, p. 573.

12. Supra, No. 11, p. 513.

13. Supra, No. 11, p. 520, plus amendments on p. 802.

14. Sistematicheskoe sobranie zakonov RSFSR, ukazov Prezidiuma Verkhovnogo soveta RSFSR i reshenii Pravitel'stva RSFSR, Tom XIV, Iuridicheskaia komissia pri Sovete ministrov RSFSR, Izdatel'stvo "Iuridicheskaia literatura," Moskva, 1967, p. 637.

15. Polozhenie o vyborakh raionnykh (gorodskikh) narodnykh sudov Ukrainskoi SSR, Izdatel'stvo politicheskoi literatury Ukrainy, Kiev, 1965.

16. Zakonodatel'nye akty po voprosam narodnogo khoziaistva SSSR, Tom I, Gosudarstvennoe izdatel'stvo iuridicheskoi literatury, Moskva, 1961, p. 745.

17. Supra, No. 16, p. 750.

18. Polozhenie o tovarishcheskikh sudakh, Izdatel'stvo "Iuridicheskaia literatura," Moskva, 1967.

19. Supra, No. 14, p. 558.

20. Supra, No. 14, p. 745.

21. Supra, No. 14, p. 811.

22. Supra, No. 14, p. 831.

NOTE ON TERRITORIAL SUBDIVISIONS IN THE USSR

This note outlines the system of territorial subdivisions used in the Soviet Union, as an aid to the reader in understanding terms encountered in the legislation translated below.

The USSR is a federation of fifteen UNION REPUBLICS (soiuznye respubliki). Union republics are organized on a nationality basis, each encompassing the territory inhabited by one or more basic nationality groups. The USSR Constitution grants state sovereignty to union republics, giving them the right to secede from the USSR at will and the right to maintain direct relations with foreign states.

The larger union republics are further subdivided into regions, territories, and autonomous republics.

A REGION (oblast') is the most typical subdivision of a union republic.

A TERRITORY (krai) is similar to a region, except that it is located farther from the center of the USSR and is normally larger in area. Because of its size a territory frequently includes certain subdivisions which a region does not. These are the autonomous region and the administrative region. An AUTONOMOUS REGION (avtonomnaia oblast') is a territorial unit formed for the population of one or several nationality groups and is found in most territories; each autonomous region has five representatives in the Soviet of Nationalities of the USSR Supreme Soviet. An ADMINISTRATIVE REGION (administrativnaia oblast') is an area which, though containing no particular nationality group, constitutes an economic unit and is therefore more easily governed separately from the territory. There are only a few administrative regions in the Soviet Union.

Either a region or a territory may contain subdivisions called national areas or administrative areas. A NATIONAL AREA (natsional'nyi okrug) is a territorial unit formed on a nationality basis but which is too small to merit the status of autonomous region. All national areas are situated in the northern part of the RSFSR; each has one representative in the Soviet of Nationalities of the USSR Supreme Soviet. An ADMINISTRATIVE AREA (administrativnyi okrug), usually called simple "area" is governed separately from the region or territory because of its economic integrity.

An AUTONOMOUS REPUBLIC (avtonomnaia respublika) is a territorial unit inhabited by a population of predominantly one or several nationality groups. Unlike a union republic, an autonomous republic is not granted state sovereignty by the USSR Constitution. Nonetheless, an autonomous republic, unlike a region or territory, has its own constitution, supreme soviet, and supreme court. Each autonomous republic has eleven representatives in the Soviet of Nationalities of the USSR Supreme Soviet and one vice-president in the presidium of the supreme soviet of the union republic in which it is situated.

Below the region, territory, autonomous republic, autonomous region, administrative region, and national area is the district. A DISTRICT (raion) includes a number of population centers plus the rural area around them.

POPULATION CENTERS (naselennye punkty) may be either urban or rural. Urban population centers are the city and the settlement. A CITY (gorod) falls into one of three categories, depending on its size and importance: cities of union-republican rank; cities of regional, territorial, autonomous republic, autonomous region, administrative region, or national area rank; and cities of district rank. Cities in each of these categories are directly subordinate to the respective territorial unit. Larger cities are subdivided into districts (called "city districts" to distinguish them from the ordinary district); in such cities the city district rather than the city itself is the lowest territorial unit, the city district being subordinate to city agencies.

There are four categories of settlements, though not all union republics have all four types. A CITY-TYPE SETTLEMENT (poselok gorodskogo tipa) is a population center which has built up around an industrial enterprise, railroad crossing, hydro-electric station, etc. A WORKER SETTLEMENT (rabochii poselok) is built up around a spa, and a SUMMER-HOME SETTLEMENT (dachnyi poselok) around a group of summer homes.

There is a wide variety of rural population centers, the most common of which is the RURAL LOCALITY (selo). Others referred to in the legislation translated below are the VILLAGE (derevnia), HAMLET (khutor), STANITSA (Cossack settlement) , KISHLAK (settlement in Central Asia), and AUL (pronounced "ahool," a settlement in Central Asia or the Caucasus). A rural soviet (sel'skii sovet) includes one or several rural population centers and the surrounding rural area.

PART ONE

1. CONSTITUTION OF THE USSR

Introductory Note

The Constitution of the Union of Soviet Socialist Republics was adopted by the Eighth Congress of Soviets of the USSR on December 5, 1936. It replaced the all-union constitution which had been enacted on July 6, 1923 and ratified on January 31, 1924, following the formation of the Soviet Union on December 30, 1922. Prior to the formation of the Soviet Union, each of the Soviet republics had adopted its own constitution, the first being that of the Russian Republic, enacted in 1918.

The USSR Constitution has been frequently amended since 1936. However, most of the amendments have related to economic reorganization affecting the structure of the Council of Ministers (Articles 70, 77, and 78) and to changes in territorial-administrative units (Articles 22-27).

Apart from these matters, the major amendments have been the following:

Four new union republics have been added—the Lithuanian, Latvian, Estonian, and Moldavian (Article 13). The Karelian-Finnish Autonomous Republic was made a union republic in 1940 but was returned to the status of an autonomous republic within the RSFSR in 1956.

The right to adopt legislation on court organization and on civil and criminal law and procedure has been transferred from the competence of the USSR to that of the union republics, the all-union authority retaining the right to adopt fundamental principles in those fields; also, the right to adopt fundamental principles on family law has been granted to the all-union authority (Article 14(u), (w)).

New articles have been introduced declaring the right of union republics to have direct relations with foreign states and to have their own military formations (Articles 18-a and 18-b).

Presidents of union-republican supreme courts have been made members of the USSR Supreme Court ex officio, and special courts—which existed for rail and water transport—have been abolished (Article 105). The term of office of people's judges has been extended from three to five years, and provision has

1

been made for election of people's assessors (Article 109).

The seven-hour maximum work day was changed to eight hours in 1947 but restored in 1960. (Article 119). (In fact, the eight-hour work day had been instituted by an edict of the Presidium of the Supreme Soviet in 1940.)

The provision granting the right to a free education for all grades was amended in 1947 to extend only to grade seven. (In fact, tuition fees for higher grades had been introduced by a decree of the Council of People's Commissars in 1940.) In 1956, the original provision was restored. In addition, obligatory education has been extended from the four-year primary school to include eight grades (Article 121).

State aid has been guaranteed for mothers with many children and for unmarried mothers (Article 122).

The Communist Party, which in the 1936 version of the Constitution was defined as "the vanguard of the working people in their struggle to strengthen and develop the socialist system" has been redefined as "the vanguard of the working people in their struggle to build a communist society" (Article 126).

The provision declaring that persons who damage or steal socialist property shall be enemies of the people has been repealed (Article 131).

The minimum age for deputies to the USSR Supreme Soviet has been raised from 18 to 23, and deprivation of electoral rights has been eliminated as a criminal penalty (Article 135).

Finally, the people's commissariats of the USSR have been renamed ministries, and the Council of People's Commissars accordingly renamed the Council of Ministers (cf. Articles 64-78).

A commission was created in 1962 under the chairmanship of N. S. Khrushchev to draft a new constitution for the USSR to reflect its present stage of historical development. In December 1964, the Supreme Soviet elected L. I Brezhnev to replace Khrushchev as chairman of the commission. As of June 1968, no progress report or draft had been published.

Lists of ministries, which appear in a number of articles of the USSR Constitution, are given in the Russian text in alphabetical order. The translators have in all cases followed the order of the Russian listing with the result that alphabetical order is not preserved in English.

The listing of union republics in Article 13 is in descending order of population.

CONSTITUTION (BASIC LAW) OF THE
UNION OF SOVIET SOCIALIST REPUBLICS

(confirmed by the Eighth Congress of Soviets of the
USSR, December 5, 1936, as amended to October 1, 1968)

CHAPTER I

The Social Structure

Article 1.   The Union of Soviet Socialist Republics shall be a socialist state
of workers and peasants.

Article 2.   Soviets of Working People's Deputies, which grew and became
strong as a result of the overthrow of the power of the landlords and capitalists
and the victory of the dictatorship of the proletariat, shall constitute the political foundation of the USSR.

Article 3.   All power in the USSR shall belong to the working people of the city
and country as represented by the Soviets of Working People's Deputies.

Article 4.   The socialist system of economy and socialist ownership of the
instruments and means of production established as a result of the liquidation
of the capitalist system of economy, the abolition of private ownership of the instruments and means of production, and the annihilation of the exploitation of
man by man, shall constitute the economic foundation of the USSR.

Article 5.   Socialist ownership in the USSR shall have either the form of
state ownership (the wealth of the whole people) or the form of cooperative and
collective-farm ownership (ownership on the part of individual collective farms,
ownership on the part of cooperative units).

Article 6.   The land, its minerals, waters, forests, mills, factories, mines,
quarries, rail, water, and air transport, banks, means of communications, large

state-organized agricultural enterprises (state farms, machine-tractor stations, etc.), as well as municipal enterprises and the bulk of the housing in the cities and at industrial sites, shall constitute state ownership, that is, the wealth of the whole people.

Article 7.   Social enterprises in collective farms and cooperative organizations, with their livestock and implements, goods produced by collective farms and cooperative organizations, and also their common buildings, shall constitute social, socialist ownership on the part of collective farms and cooperative organizations.

Each collective-farm household, in addition to its basic income from the social collective-farm economy, shall have for personal use a small plot of household land and in personal ownership a subsidiary husbandry on the household plot, a dwelling house, livestock, poultry, and minor agricultural implements, in accordance with the charter of the agricultural artel.

Article 8.   The land occupied by collective farms shall be secured to them for their use free of charge and for an unlimited time, that is, in perpetuity.

Article 9.   Alongside the socialist system of economy, constituting the predominant form of economy in the USSR, the law shall permit the small-scale private economy of individual peasants and handicraftsmen based on personal labor and precluding the exploitation of the labor of others.

Article 10.   The right of personal ownership on the part of citizens in the income and savings from their labor, in a dwelling house and subsidiary household economy, in household articles, and in articles of personal use and convenience, as well as the right to inherit [objects of] personal ownership of citizens, shall be protected by law.

Article 11.   The economic life of the USSR shall be determined and directed by the state national-economic plan in the interests of increasing social wealth, of steadily raising the material and cultural level of the working people, of fortifying the independence of the USSR, and of strengthening its defense capability.

Article 12.   Labor in the USSR shall be an obligation and a matter of honor for every able-bodied citizen in accordance with the principle: "He who does not work, neither shall he eat."

In the USSR the principle of socialism shall be carried out: "From each according to his ability, to each according to his labor."

CHAPTER II

The State Structure

Article 13. The Union of Soviet Socialist Republics shall be a federal state formed on the basis of a voluntary union of [the following] Soviet Socialist Republics, with equal rights:

Russian Soviet Federated Socialist Republic,

Ukrainian Soviet Socialist Republic,

Belorussian Soviet Socialist Republic,

Uzbek Soviet Socialist Republic,

Kazakh Soviet Socialist Republic,

Georgian Soviet Socialist Republic,

Azerbaijan Soviet Socialist Republic,

Lithuanian Soviet Socialist Republic,

Moldavian Soviet Socialist Republic,

Latvian Soviet Socialist Republic,

Kirghiz Soviet Socialist Republic,

Tajik Soviet Socialist Republic,

Armenian Soviet Socialist Republic,

Turkmen Soviet Socialist Republic,

Estonian Soviet Socialist Republic.

Article 14. The competence of the Union of Soviet Socialist Republics, as represented by its highest agencies of state power and agencies of state administration, shall embrace:

(a) representation of the USSR in international relations; conclusion, ratification, and denunciation of treaties of the USSR with other states; establishment of general procedure governing the relations of union republics with foreign states;

(b) questions of war and peace;

(c) admission of new republics into the USSR;

(d) supervision over the observance of the Constitution of the USSR and en-suring conformity of the Constitutions of the union republics with the Constitution of the USSR;

(e) confirmation of changes of boundaries between union republics;

(f) confirmation of the formation of new autonomous republics and autonomous regions within union republics;

(g) organization of the defense of the USSR, direction of all the Armed Forces of the USSR, establishment of guiding principles governing the organization of the military formations of union republics;

(h) foreign trade on the basis of a state monopoly;

(i) protection of state security;

(j) establishment of national-economic plans of the USSR;

(k) confirmation of a consolidated state budget for the USSR and of the report on its execution, establishment of the taxes and revenues which go to the federal, republican, and local budgets;

(l) administration of banks and industrial and agricultural institutions and enterprises, as well as trade enterprises, of federal rank; general direction of industry and construction of union-republican rank;

(m) administration of transport and communications of all-union importance;

(n) direction of the monetary and credit system;

(o) organization of state insurance;

(p) concluding and granting of loans;

(q) establishment of basic principles of land use as well as the use of minerals, forests, and waters;

(r) establishment of basic principles in the spheres of education and health;

(s) organization of a uniform system of national-economic accounting;

(t) establishment of basic principles of labor legislation;

(u) establishment of basic principles of legislation on the judicial system and judicial procedure, and basic principles of civil and criminal legislation;

(v) legislation on federal citizenship; legislation on rights of foreigners;

(w) establishment of basic principles of legislation on marriage and the family;

(x) issuance of all-union acts of amnesty.

Article 15. The sovereignty of the union republics shall be restricted only within the limits indicated in Article 14 of the Constitution of the USSR. Outside such limits each union republic shall exercise state power independently. The USSR shall protect the sovereign rights of union republics.

Article 16.   Each Union Republic shall have its own constitution, which shall take into account the special features of the republic and which shall be drawn up in full conformity with the Constitution of the USSR.

Article 17.   The right shall be preserved for each Union Republic freely to secede from the USSR.

Article 18.   The territory of union republics may not be changed without their consent.

Article 18-a.   Each Union Republic shall have the right to enter into direct relations with foreign states, to conclude agreements with them, and to exchange diplomatic and consular representatives.

Article 18-b.   Each Union Republic shall have its own republican military formations.

Article 19.   Laws of the USSR shall have the same force in the territory of all the union republics.

Article 20.   In the event that a law of a Union Republic diverges from an all-union law, the all-union law shall prevail.

Article 21.   A single union citizenship shall be established for citizens of the USSR.

Every citizen of a Union Republic shall be a citizen of the USSR.

Article 22.   The Russian Soviet Federated Socialist Republic shall include [the following] autonomous soviet socialist republics: Bashkirian, Buriat, Daghestan, Kabardian-Balkarian, Kalmyk, Karelian, Komi, Mari, Mordovian, North Ossetian, Tartar, Tuva, Udmurt, Chechen-Ingush, Chuvash, Yakut; [and the following] autonomous regions: Adygei, Gorno-Altai, Jewish, Karachai-Cherkess, Khakass.

Article 23.   Repealed.

Article 24.   The Azerbaijan Soviet Socialist Republic shall   include   the Nakhichevan Autonomous Soviet Socialist Republic and the Nagorno-Karabakh autonomous region.

Article 25.   The Georgian Soviet Socialist Republic shall include the Abkhaz

and the Ajar Autonomous Soviet Socialist Republics and the South Ossetian autonomous region.

Article 26. The Uzbek Soviet Socialist Republic shall include the Kara-
Kalpak Autonomous Soviet Socialist Republic.

Article 27. The Tajik Soviet Socialist Republic shall include the Gorno-
Badakhshan autonomous region.

Article 28. Resolution of questions of the regional or territorial administrative-territorial structure of union republics shall lie within the competence of
the union republics.

Article 29. Repealed.

CHAPTER III

Highest Agencies of State Power of the
Union of Soviet Socialist Republics

Article 30. The Supreme Soviet of the USSR shall be the highest agency of
state power of the USSR.

Article 31. The Supreme Soviet of the USSR shall exercise all rights vested
in the Union of Soviet Socialist Republics according to Article 14 of the Constitution, insofar as they do not, by virtue of the Constitution, come within the competence of agencies of the USSR which are accountable to the Supreme Soviet of
the USSR: the Presidium of the Supreme Soviet of the USSR, the Council of Ministers of the USSR, or Ministries of the USSR.

Article 32. The legislative power of the USSR shall be exercised exclusively
by the Supreme Soviet of the USSR.

Article 33. The Supreme Soviet of the USSR shall consist of two chambers:
the Soviet of the Union and the Soviet of Nationalities.

Article 34. The Soviet of the Union shall be elected by the citizens of the
USSR by electoral areas on the basis of one deputy for every 300,000 of population.

Article 35. The Soviet of Nationalities shall be elected by the citizens of the USSR by union and autonomous republics, autonomous regions, and national areas on the basis of 32 deputies from each Union Republic, 11 deputies from each Autonomous Republic, 5 deputies from each autonomous region, and one deputy from each national area.

Article 36. The Supreme Soviet of the USSR shall be elected for a term of four years.

Article 37. Both chambers of the Supreme Soviet of the USSR, the Soviet of the Union and the Soviet of Nationalities, shall have equal rights.

Article 38. The Soviet of the Union and the Soviet of Nationalities shall have equal powers of legislative initiative.

Article 39. A law shall be considered confirmed if it is adopted by both chambers of the Supreme Soviet by a simple majority of the votes in each chamber.

Article 40. Laws adopted by the Supreme Soviet of the USSR shall be published in the languages of the union republics over the signatures of the President and Secretary of the Presidium of the Supreme Soviet of the USSR.

Article 41. Sessions of the Soviet of the Union and the Soviet of Nationalities shall begin and terminate simultaneously.

Article 42. The Soviet of the Union shall elect a President of the Soviet of the Union and four Vice-Presidents.

Article 43. The Soviet of Nationalities shall elect a President of the Soviet of Nationalities and four Vice-Presidents.

Article 44. The Presidents of the Soviet of the Union and the Soviet of Nationalities shall direct the sessions of the respective chambers and shall be in charge of their internal procedure.

Article 45. Joint sessions of both chambers of the Supreme Soviet of the USSR shall be conducted alternately by the Presidents of the Soviet of the Union and the Soviet of Nationalities.

Article 46. Sessions of the Supreme Soviet of the USSR shall be convoked by the Presidium of the Supreme Soviet of the USSR twice a year.

Special sessions shall be convoked by the Presidium of the Supreme Soviet of the USSR at its discretion or upon the demand of one of the union republics.

Article 47.　In the event of disagreement between the Soviet of the Union and the Soviet of Nationalities, the question shall be referred for settlement to a conciliation commission formed by the chambers on a parity basis. If the conciliation commission does not arrive at a joint decision, or if its decision does not satisfy one of the chambers, the question shall be considered a second time in the chambers. If the two chambers fail to reach a joint decision, the Presidium of the Supreme Soviet of the USSR shall dissolve the Supreme Soviet of the USSR and order new elections.

Article 48.　The Supreme Soviet of the USSR, at a joint meeting of both chambers, shall elect a Presidium of the Supreme Soviet of the USSR, consisting of a President of the Presidium of the Supreme Soviet of the USSR, fifteen Vice-Presidents (one from each union republic), a Secretary of the Presidium, and twenty members of the Presidium of the Supreme Soviet of the USSR.

The Presidium of the Supreme Soviet of the USSR shall be accountable in all its activity to the Supreme Soviet of the USSR.

Article 49.　The Presidium of the Supreme Soviet of the USSR shall:

(a) convoke sessions of the Supreme Soviet of the USSR;

(b) issue edicts;

(c) give interpretation of the laws of the USSR in force;

(d) dissolve the Supreme Soviet of the USSR on the basis of Article 47 of the Constitution of the USSR and order new elections;

(e) conduct popular referenda on its own initiative or upon the demand of one of the union republics;

(f) annul decrees and regulations of the Council of Ministers of the USSR and of the Councils of Ministers of union republics in the event that they do not conform to law;

(g) in the interval between sessions of the Supreme Soviet of the USSR, remove from office and appoint individual Ministers of the USSR on the recommendation of the President of the Council of Ministers of the USSR with subsequent submission for confirmation by the Supreme Soviet of the USSR;

(h) institute orders and medals of the USSR and establish titles of honor of the USSR;

(i) award orders and medals of the USSR and confer titles of honor of the USSR;

(j) exercise the right of pardon;

(k) establish military titles, diplomatic ranks, and other special titles;

(l) appoint and remove the high command of the Armed Forces of the USSR;

(m) in the interval between sessions of the Supreme Soviet of the USSR, proclaim a state of war in the event of armed attack on the USSR or in the event of the necessity of fulfilling international treaty obligations on mutual defense against aggression;

(n) proclaim general or partial mobilization;

(o) ratify and denounce international treaties of the USSR;

(p) appoint and recall plenipotentiary representatives of the USSR in foreign states;

(q) receive credentials and letters of recall of diplomatic representatives of foreign states who are accredited to it;

(r) proclaim martial law in individual localities or throughout the USSR in the interests of the defense of the USSR or for the purpose of ensuring public order or state security.

Article 50.   The Soviet of the Union and the Soviet of Nationalities shall elect credentials commissions, which shall verify the authority of the deputies of each chamber.

On the recommendation of the credentials commissions, the chambers shall decide either to recognize the authority of or to annul the election of individual deputies.

Article 51.   The Supreme Soviet of the USSR, when it considers it necessary shall appoint investigating or inspection commissions on any matter.

All institutions and officials shall be obliged to fulfill demands of such commissions and to present to them necessary materials and documents.

Article 52.   A deputy of the Supreme Soviet of the USSR may not be brought to responsibility in court or arrested without the consent of the Supreme Soviet of the USSR, and in the interval between sessions of the Supreme Soviet of the USSR, without the consent of the Presidium of the Supreme Soviet of the USSR.

Article 53.   Upon the expiration of the authority of [a convocation of] the Supreme Soviet of the USSR or after its premature dissolution, the Presidium of the Supreme Soviet of the USSR shall retain its authority until a new Presidium of the

Supreme Soviet of the USSR is formed by the newly elected Supreme Soviet of the USSR.

Article 54. Upon the expiration of the authority of [a convocation of] the Supreme Soviet of the USSR or in the event of its premature dissolution, the Presidium of the Supreme Soviet of the USSR shall order new elections not more than two months from the day of expiration of the authority or dissolution of the [convocation of the] Supreme Soviet of the USSR.

Article 55. The newly elected Supreme Soviet of the USSR shall be convoked by the previous Presidium of the Supreme Soviet of the USSR not later than three months after the elections.

Article 56. The Supreme Soviet of the USSR, at a joint session of both chambers, shall form the Government of the USSR—the Council of Ministers of the USSR.

CHAPTER IV

Highest Agencies of State Power of
Union Republics

Article 57. The Supreme Soviet of a Union Republic shall be the highest agency of state power of the Union Republic.

Article 58. The Supreme Soviet of a Union Republic shall be elected by the citizens of the republic for a term of four years.

Norms of representation shall be established by the Constitutions of the union republics.

Article 59. The Supreme Soviet of a Union Republic shall be the sole legislative agency of the republic.

Article 60. The Supreme Soviet of a Union Republic shall:

(a) adopt a constitution of the republic and make amendments to it in accordance with Article 16 of the Constitution of the USSR;

(b) confirm Constitutions of the autonomous republics forming part of it [i.e., part of the union republic] and determine the boundaries of their territory;

(c) confirm the national-economic plan and the budget of the republic;

(d) have the right of amnesty and pardon of citizens convicted by judicial agencies of the Union Republic;

(e) establish the representation of the Union Republic in international relations;

(f) establish the manner of organizing republican military formations.

Article 61.   The Supreme Soviet of a Union Republic shall elect a Presidium of the Supreme Soviet of the Union Republic, consisting of a President of the Presidium of the Supreme Soviet of the Union Republic, Vice-Presidents, a Secretary of the Presidium, and members of the Presidium of the Supreme Soviet of the Union Republic.

The authority of the Presidium of the Supreme Soviet of a Union Republic shall be determined by the Constitution of the Union Republic.

Article 62.   For conducting its sessions the Supreme Soviet of a Union Republic shall elect a President of the Supreme Soviet of the Union Republic and Vice-Presidents.

Article 63.   The Supreme Soviet of a Union Republic shall form the Government of the Union Republic—the Council of Ministers of the Union Republic.

CHAPTER V

Agencies of State Administration of the
Union of Soviet Socialist Republics

Article 64.   The Council of Ministers of the USSR shall be the highest executive and administrative agency of state power of the Union of Soviet Socialist Republics.

Article 65.   The Council of Ministers of the USSR shall be responsible to the Supreme Soviet of the USSR and accountable to it, and in the interval between sessions of the Supreme Soviet [it shall be responsible] to the Presidium of the Supreme Soviet of the USSR, to which it shall be accountable.

Article 66.   The Council of Ministers of the USSR shall issue decrees and regulations on the basis of and in execution of the laws in force and shall verify their execution.

Article 67.   Decrees and regulations of the Council of Ministers of the USSR shall be binding throughout the territory of the USSR.

Article 68.   The Council of Ministers of the USSR shall:

(a) coordinate and give direction to the work of all-union and union-republican Ministries of the USSR, [to the work] of State Committees of the Council of Ministers of the USSR, and [to the work] of other institutions subordinate to it;

(b) take measures to carry out the national-economic plan and the state budget, and to strengthen the credit and monetary system;

(c) take measures for the securing of public order, for the defense of the interests of the state, and for the protection of the rights of citizens;

(d) exercise general direction in the sphere of relations with foreign states;

(e) fix the annual call-up of citizens for active military service and direct the general construction of the Armed Forces of the country;

(f) form State Committees of the USSR as well as, when necessary, special Committees and Chief Administrations attached to the Council of Ministers of the USSR for economic, cultural, or defense construction.

Article 69.   The Council of Ministers of the USSR shall have the right, in respect of those branches of administration and economy which lie within the competence of the USSR, to suspend decrees and regulations of the Councils of Ministers of Union republics, and to annul orders and instructions of Ministries of the USSR as well as acts of other institutions subordinate to it.

Article 70.   The Council of Ministers of the USSR shall be formed by the Supreme Soviet of the USSR, and shall consist of:

President of the Council of Ministers of the USSR;

First Vice-Presidents of the Council of Ministers of the USSR;

Vice-Presidents of the Council of Ministers of the USSR;

Ministers of the USSR;

President of the State Planning Committee of the Council of Ministers of the USSR;

President of the State Committee of the Council of Ministers of the USSR for Construction;

President of the State Committee of the Council of Ministers of the USSR for Material-technical Supply;

President of the Committee of People's Control of the USSR;

President of the State Committee of the Council of Ministers of the USSR for Questions of Labor and Wages;

President of the State Committee of the Council of Ministers of the USSR for Science and Technology;

President of the State Committee of the Council of Ministers of the USSR for Professional and Technical Education;

President of the State Committee for [Agricultural] Purchases of the Council of Ministers of the USSR;

President of the State Committee for Forestry of the Council of Ministers of the USSR;

President of the State Committee of the Council of Ministers of the USSR for Foreign Economic Relations;

President of the Committee of State Security attached to the Council of Ministers of the USSR;

President of the All-Union Combine "Soiuzsel'khoztekhnika" ["Union Agricultural Technology"] of the Council of Ministers of the USSR;

President of the Board of the State Bank of the USSR;

Chief of the Central Statistical Administration attached to the Council of Ministers of the USSR.

Presidents of the Council of Ministers of union republics shall be members ex officio of the Councilof Ministers of the USSR.

Article 71. The Government of the USSR or a Minister of the USSR to whom a question of a deputy of the Supreme Soviet of the USSR is addressed shall be obliged within not more than three days to give an oral or written reply in the appropriate chamber.

Article 72. Ministers of the USSR shall direct branches of state administration which come within the competence of the USSR.

Article 73. Ministers of the USSR shall issue, within the limits of the competence of their respective ministries, orders and instructions on the basis of and in execution of the laws in force, as well as of decrees and regulations of the Council of Ministers of the USSR, and shall verify their execution.

Article 74. Ministries of the USSR shall be either all-union or union-republican [ministries].

Article 75. All-Union Ministries shall direct the branches of state administration entrusted to them throughout the territory of the USSR either directly or through agencies appointed by them.

Article 76. Union-republican Ministries shall direct the branches of state administration entrusted to them, as a rule, through corresponding Ministries of the union republics, and shall administer directly only a definite and limited number of enterprises according to a list confirmed by the Presidium of the Supreme Soviet of the USSR.

Article 77. The [following] Ministries shall be all-union Ministries:
Aviation Industry;
Automotive Industry;
Foreign Trade;
Gas Industry;
Civil Aviation;
Machine-building;
Machine-building for the Light and Food Industries and for Household Implements;
Medical Industry;
Navy;
Defense Industry;
General Machine-building;
Instrument-making, Automation, and Control Systems;
Transport;
Radio Industry;
Medium Machine-building;
Machine-tool and Hand-tool Industry;
Machine-building for Construction, Roads, and Municipal Services;
Ship-building Industry;
Machine-building for Tractors and Farm Equipment;
Transport Construction;
Machine-building for Heavy Industry, Power and Transport;
Machine-building for the Chemical and Oil Industries;
Cellulose-Paper Industry;
Electronics Industry;
Electrical Engineering Industry.

Article 78.   The [following] Ministries shall be union-republican Ministries:
Higher and Specialized Secondary Education;
Geology;
Health;
Foreign Affairs;
Culture;
Light Industry;
Lumber and Woodworking Industry;
Soil and Water Conservation;
Installation and Special Construction;
Meat and Milk Industry;
Oil Extracting Industry;
Oil Refining and Petrochemical Industry;
Defense;
Protection of Public Order;
Food Industry;
Industrial Construction;
Construction Materials Industry;
Education;
Fisheries;
Communications;
Agricultural Construction;
Agriculture;
Construction;
Construction of Enterprises of Heavy Industry;
Trade;
Coal Industry;
Finance;
Chemical Industry;
Non-ferrous Metallurgy;
Ferrous Metallurgy;
Power and Electrification.

CHAPTER VI

Agencies of State Administration of
Union Republics

Article 79. The Council of Ministers of a Union Republic shall be the highest executive and administrative agency of state power of the Union Republic.

Article 80. The Council of Ministers of a Union Republic shall be responsible to the Supreme Soviet of the Union Republic and accountable to it, and in the interval between sessions of the Supreme Soviet of the Union Republic [it shall be responsible] to the Presidium of the Supreme Soviet of the Union Republic, to which it shall be accountable.

Article 81. The Council of Ministers of a Union Republic shall issue decrees and regulations on the basis of and in execution of the laws in force of the USSR and of the Union Republic, and of decrees and regulations of the Council of Ministers of the USSR, and shall verify their execution.

Article 82. The Council of Ministers of a Union Republic shall have the right to suspend decrees and regulations of Councils of Ministers of autonomous republics and to annul decisions and regulations of executive committees of Soviets of Working People's Deputies of territories, regions, and autonomous regions.

Article 83. The Council of Ministers of a Union Republic shall be formed by the Supreme Soviet of the Union Republic and shall consist of:

the President of the Council of Ministers of the Union Republic;

Vice-Presidents of the Council of Ministers;

Ministers;

Presidents of state committees and commissions and chiefs of other departments of the Council of Ministers formed by the Supreme Soviet of the Union Republic in accordance with the Constitution of the Union Republic.

Article 84. Ministers of a Union Republic shall direct branches of state administration which come within the competence of the Union Republic.

Article 85. Ministers of a Union Republic shall issue, within the limits of the competence of their respective ministries, orders and instructions on the basis of and in execution of the laws of the USSR and of the union republic, of

decrees and regulations of the Council of Ministers of the USSR and that of the Union Republic, and of orders and instructions of union-republican Ministries of the USSR.

Article 86. Ministries of a Union Republic shall be either union-republican or republican [ministries].

Article 87. Union-republican Ministries, being subordinate both to the Council of Ministers of the Union Republic and to the corresponding union-republican Ministry of the USSR, shall direct the branches of state administration entrusted to them.

Article 88. Republican Ministries, being directly subordinate to the Council of Ministers of the Union Republic, shall direct the branches of state administration entrusted to them.

CHAPTER VII

Highest Agencies of State Power of Autonomous Soviet Socialist Republics

Article 89. The Supreme Soviet of an ASSR [Autonomous Soviet Socialist Republic] shall be the highest agency of state power of the Autonomous Republic.

Article 90. The Supreme Soviet of an Autonomous Republic shall be elected by the citizens of the republic for a term of four years according to norms of representation established by the Constitution of the Autonomous Republic.

Article 91. The Supreme Soviet of an Autonomous Republic shall be the sole legislative agency of the ASSR.

Article 92. Each Autonomous Republic shall have its own constitution, which shall take into account the special features of the Autonomous Republic and which shall be drawn up in full conformity with the Constitution of the Union Republic.

Article 93. The Supreme Soviet of an Autonomous Republic shall elect a Presidium of the Supreme Soviet of the Autonomous Republic and shall form a Council of Ministers of the Autonomous Republic according to its Constitution.

CHAPTER VIII

Local Agencies of State Power

Article 94.   Soviets of Working People's Deputies shall be the agencies of State power in territories, regions, autonomous regions, areas, districts, cities, and rural localities (stanitsas, villages, hamlets, kishlaks, auls).

Article 95.   Soviets of Working People's Deputies of territories, regions, autonomous regions, areas, districts, cities, and rural localities (stanitsas, villages, hamlets, kishlaks, auls) shall be elected by the working people of the respective territory,   region, autonomous region, area, district, city, or rural locality for a term of two years.

Article 96.   Norms of representation for Soviets of Working People's Deputies shall be determined by the Constitutions of union republics.

Article 97.   Soviets of Working People's Deputies shall direct the activity of agencies of administration subordinate to them, shall secure the protection of state order, observance of the laws, and protection of the rights of citizens, shall direct local economic and cultural construction, [and] shall establish the local budget.

Article 98.   Soviets of Working People's Deputies shall adopt decisions and issue regulations within the limits of the rights vested in them by the laws of the USSR and of the Union Republic.

Article 99.   The executive and regulatory agencies of Soviets of Working People's Deputies of territories, regions, autonomous regions, areas, districts, cities, and rural localities shall be executive committees elected by them, consisting of a president, vice-presidents, a secretary, and members.

Article 100.   The executive and regulatory agencies of Soviets of Working People's Deputies in small settlements shall be, in accordance with the Constitutions of the union republics, a president, vice-president, and secretary elected by the Soviets of Working People's Deputies.

Article 101.   Executive agencies of Soviets of Working People's Deputies shall be directly accountable both to the Soviets of Working People's Deputies which elected them and to the executive agency of the superior Soviet of Working People's Deputies.

CHAPTER IX

The Courts and the Procuracy

Article 102. The administration of justice in the USSR shall be carried out by the Supreme Court of the USSR, supreme courts of union republics, territorial and regional courts, courts of autonomous republics and autonomous regions, area courts, special courts of the USSR, [and] people's courts.

Article 103. In all courts, cases shall be considered with the participation of people's assessors, except in instances specially provided by law.

Article 104. The Supreme Court of the USSR shall be the highest judicial agency. The Supreme Court of the USSR shall be charged with supervision over the judicial activity of judicial agencies of the USSR as well as of judicial agencies of union republics within the limits established by law.

Article 105. The Supreme Court of the USSR shall be elected by the Supreme Soviet of the USSR for a term of five years.

Presidents of Supreme Courts of union republics shall be members of the Supreme Court of the USSR ex officio.

Article 106. Supreme Courts of union republics shall be elected by the Supreme Soviets of union republics for a term of five years.

Article 107. Supreme Courts of autonomous republics shall be elected by the Supreme Soviets of autonomous republics for a term of five years.

Article 108. Territorial and regional courts, courts of autonomous regions, and area courts shall be elected by territorial, regional, or area Soviets of Working People's Deputies or by Soviets of Working People's Deputies of autonomous regions for a term of five years.

Article 109. People's judges of district (or city) people's courts shall be elected by the citizens of the district (or city) on the basis of universal, equal, and direct suffrage by secret ballot for a term of five years.

People's assessors of district (or city) people's courts shall be elected at general meetings of workers, employees, and peasants at the place of their work or residence, and of military personnel [at general meetings] in military units, for a term of two years.

Article 110. Judicial proceedings shall be conducted in the language of the Union or Autonomous Republic or autonomous region with persons not knowing that language being guaranteed full acquaintance with the materials of the case through an interpreter, as well as the right to speak in court in their native language.

Article 111. Examination of cases in all courts of the USSR shall be open, insofar as exceptions are not provided by law, with the accused being guaranteed the right to defense.

Article 112. Judges shall be independent and subordinate only to law.

Article 113. Supreme supervision over strict execution of the laws by all Ministries and institutions subordinate to them and also by individual officials, as well as by citizens of the USSR, shall be vested in the Procurator General of the USSR.

Article 114. The Procurator General of the USSR shall be appointed by the Supreme Soviet of the USSR for a term of seven years.

Article 115. Republican, territorial, and regional procurators, as well as procurators of autonomous republics and autonomous regions, shall be appointed by the Procurator General of the USSR for a term of five years.

Article 116. Area, district, and city procurators shall be appointed by procurators of union republics, with confirmation by the Procurator General of the USSR, for a term of five years.

Article 117. Agencies of the procuracy shall exercise their functions independently of any local agencies whatsoever, being subordinate only to the Procurator General of the USSR.

CHAPTER X

Fundamental Rights and Duties of Citizens

Article 118. Citizens of the USSR shall have the right to labor, that is, the
right to a guaranteed job with payment for their labor in accordance with its
quantity and quality.

The right to labor shall be guaranteed by the socialist organization of the national economy, the steady growth of the productive forces of Soviet society, the
elimination of the possibility of economic crises, and the liquidation of unemployment.

Article 119. Citizens of the USSR shall have the right to rest and leisure.

The right to rest and leisure shall be guaranteed by the establishment of a
seven-hour working day for workers and employees, the reduction of the working
day to six hours for certain professions with arduous working conditions, and to
four hours in shops with especially arduous working conditions; by the establishment of annual vacations with full pay for workers and employees; and by provision of an extensive network of sanatoria, rest homes, and clubs for the service
of the working people.

Article 120. Citizens of the USSR shall have the right to economic security
in old age, as well as in case of sickness or loss of working capacity.

This right shall be guaranteed by extensive development of social insurance
for workers and employees at state expense, by free medical service for the
working people, and by provision of an extensive network of health resorts for
the use of the working people.

Article 121. Citizens of the USSR shall have the right to education.

This right shall be guaranteed by universal, compulsory eight-year education,
by extensive development of secondary general polytechnical education, professional-technical education, secondary specialized, and higher education based on
the bond of instruction with life, with production, by comprehensive development
of evening and correspondence education, by freedom from [tuition] charges for
all types of education, by the system of state stipends, by instruction in [primary

and secondary] schools in the native language, and by the organization at plants and on state and collective farms of free production, technical, and agricultural instruction for the working people.

Article 122. Women in the USSR shall be accorded equal rights with men in all spheres of economic, state, cultural, and social-political life.

The possibility of exercising these rights of women shall be guaranteed by providing women with an equal right with men to labor, payment for labor, rest and leisure, social insurance, and education, by state protection of the interests of mother and child, by state aid to mothers with many children and to unmarried mothers, by providing vacations for women during pregnancy with preservation of support, and by an extensive network of maternity homes, day nurseries, and kindergartens.

Article 123. Equality of rights of citizens of the USSR, regardless of their nationality or race, in all spheres of economic, state, cultural, and social-political life shall be an indefeasible law.

Any kind of direct or indirect restriction of rights or, conversely, establishment of direct or indirect privileges of citizens on account of their race or nationality, and also any advocacy of racial or national exclusiveness or of hatred or contempt, shall be punished by law.

Article 124. In order to guarantee to citizens freedom of conscience, the church in the USSR shall be separated from the state, and the school from the church. Freedom of religious worship and freedom of anti-religious propaganda shall be recognized for all citizens.

Article 125. In conformity with the interests of the working people and in order to strengthen the socialist system, citizens of the USSR shall be guaranteed by law:

(a) freedom of speech;

(b) freedom of the press;

(c) freedom of assembly and meetings;

(d) freedom of street processions and demonstrations.

These rights of citizens shall be guaranteed by providing the working people and their organizations with printing presses, stocks of paper, public buildings, streets, communications facilities, and other material conditions necessary for their exercise.

Article 126.   In conformity with the interests of the working people and in order to develop organizational initiative and political activism among the masses of the people, citizens of the USSR shall be guaranteed the right to unite in social organizations—trade unions, cooperative associations, youth organizations, sports and defense organizations, cultural, technical, and scholarly societies; and the most active and conscious citizens in the ranks of the working class, the toiling peasantry, and the laboring intelligentsia shall be voluntarily united in the Communist Party of the Soviet Union, which shall be the vanguard of the working people in their struggle to build communist society and the leading core of all organizations of the working people, both social and state.

Article 127.   Inviolability of the person shall be guaranteed to citizens of the USSR. No one may be subjected to arrest except by decree of a court or with the sanction of a procurator.

Article 128.   Inviolability of citizens' dwellings and secrecy of correspondence shall be protected by law.

Article 129.   The USSR shall afford the right of asylum to foreign citizens persecuted for defending the interests of the working people, for their scholarly activities, or for their struggle for national liberation.

Article 130.   Every citizen of the USSR shall be obliged to observe the Constitution of the Union of Soviet Socialist Republics, to carry out the laws, to maintain labor discipline, to have an honest attitude toward social duty, and to respect the rules of socialist community life.

Article 131.   Every citizen of the USSR shall be obliged to safeguard and strengthen social, socialist ownership as the sacred and inviolable foundation of the Soviet system, as the source of the wealth and might of the motherland, and as the source of the prosperous and cultured life of all the working people.

Persons who commit offenses against social, socialist ownership shall be enemies of the people.

Article 132.   Universal military obligation shall be law.

Military service in the Armed Forces of the USSR shall be the honorable obligation of citizens of the USSR.

Article 133.   Defense of the fatherland shall be the sacred duty of every citizen of the USSR. Treason to the motherland—violation of the oath of allegiance, desertion to the enemy, infliction of harm on the military might of the state, espionage—shall be punished with all the severity of the law as the gravest male-faction.

CHAPTER XI

The Electoral System

Article 134. Elections of deputies to all Soviets of Working People's Deputies — the Supreme Soviet of the USSR, Supreme Soviets of union republics, territorial and regional Soviets of Working People's Deputies, Supreme Soviets of autonomous republics, Soviets of Working People's Deputies of autonomous regions, and area, district, city, and rural (stanitsa, village, hamlet, kishlak, aul) Soviets of Work-ing People's Deputies—shall be carried out by the voters on the basis of univer-sal, equal, and direct suffrage by secret ballot.

Article 135. Elections of deputies shall be universal: all citizens of the USSR who have attained the age of 18 years regardless of race, nationality, sex, religious confession, educational qualifications, domicile, social origin, property status, or past activities, shall have the right to participate in elections of deputies, with the exception of persons who have been declared insane in the procedure establish-ed by law.

Any citizen of the USSR who has attained the age of 23 years may be elected as deputy to the Supreme Soviet of the USSR regardless of race, nationality, sex, religious confession, educational qualifications, domicile, social origin, property status, or past activities.

Article 136. Elections of deputies shall be equal: each citizen shall have one vote; all citizens shall participate in elections on an equal basis.

Article 137. Women shall enjoy the right to elect and to be elected on equal terms with men.

Article 138. Citizens serving in the Armed Forces of the USSR shall enjoy the right to elect and to be elected on equal terms with all [other] citizens.

Article 139. Elections of deputies shall be direct: elections to all Soviets of

Working People's Deputies, from rural and city Soviets of Working People's Deputies up to the Supreme Soviet of the USSR, shall be carried out directly by the citizens, by direct elections.

Article 140. Voting at elections of deputies shall be secret.

Article 141. Candidates in elections shall be nominated by electoral areas.
The right to nominate candidates shall be guaranteed to social organizations and societies of the working people—communist party organizations, trade unions, cooperatives, youth organizations, cultural societies.

Article 142. Every deputy shall be obliged to render an account before the voters for his own work and for the work of the Soviet of Working People's Deputies, and he may be recalled at any time by decision of a majority of the voters in the procedure established by law.

CHAPTER XII

Arms, Flag, Capital

Article 143. The state arms of the Union of Soviet Socialist Republics shall consist of a sickle and hammer against a globe depicted in sunrays and in a frame of ears of grain, with the inscription in the languages of the union republics: "Proletarians of All Countries, Unite!" At the top of the arms shall be a five-pointed star.

Article 144. The state flag of the Union of Soviet Socialist Republics shall consist of red cloth with a drawing of a gold sickle and hammer in the upper corner near the flagstaff and above them a red five-pointed star bordered in gold. The proportion of the width to the length shall be 1 : 2.

Article 145. The capital of the Union of Soviet Socialist Republics shall be the city of Moscow.

CHAPTER XIII

Procedure for Amending the Constitution

Article 146. The Constitution of the USSR shall be amended only by a decision of the Supreme Soviet of the USSR adopted by a majority of not less than 2/3 of the votes in each of its chambers.

2. CONSTITUTION OF THE RSFSR

Introductory Note

The RSFSR Constitution was adopted by the Fifth All-Russian Congress of Soviets on July 10, 1918. At that time the RSFSR was the only Soviet republic.

The Constitution was amended significantly following enactment of the first USSR Constitution in 1924 and again after adoption of the 1936 all-union constitution. Like the USSR Constitution, the Constitution of the RSFSR undergoes frequent amendment to account for changes in economic organization and in administrative-territorial subdivisions.

The principal significance of the RSFSR Constitution, as well as of the constitutions of the other fourteen union republics and the twenty autonomous republics, lies in their detailed provisions concerning their respective governmental structures. The chapters on the social structure, rights and duties of citizens, and the electoral system repeat almost verbatim the corresponding provisions of the Constitution of the USSR.

CONSTITUTION (BASIC LAW) OF THE RUSSIAN
SOVIET FEDERATED SOCIALIST REPUBLIC

(confirmed by the Seventeenth All-Russian Congress of
Soviets, January 21, 1937, as amended to October 1, 1968)

CHAPTER I

The Social Structure

Article 1. The Russian Soviet Federated Socialist Republic shall be a socialist state of workers and peasants.

Article 2. Soviets of Working People's Deputies, which grew and became
strong as a result of the overthrow of the power of the landlords and capitalists
and the victory of the dictatorship of the proletariat, shall constitute the political foundation of the RSFSR.

Article 3. All power in the RSFSR shall belong to the working people of the
city and country as represented by the Soviets of Working People's Deputies.

Article 4. The socialist system of economy and socialist ownership of the
instruments and means of production established as a result of the liquidation
of the capitalist system of economy, the abolition of private ownership of the
instruments and means of production, and the annihilation of the exploitation of
man by man, shall constitute the economic foundation of the RSFSR.

Article 5. Socialist ownership in the RSFSR shall have either the form of
state ownership (the wealth of the whole people) or the form of cooperative and
collective-farm ownership (ownership on the part of individual collective farms,
ownership on the part of cooperative units).

Article 6. The land, its minerals, waters, forests, mills, factories, mines,
quarries, rail, water, and air transport, banks, means of communication, large

state-organized agricultural enterprises (state farms, machine-tractor stations, etc.), as well as municipal enterprises and the bulk of the housing in the cities and at industrial sites, shall constitute state ownership, that is, the wealth of the whole people.

Article 7. Social enterprises in collective farms and cooperative organizations, with their livestock and implements, goods produced by collective farms and cooperative organizations, and also their common buildings, shall constitute social, socialist ownership on the part of collective farms and cooperative organizations.

Each collective-farm household, in addition to its basic income from the social collective-farm economy, shall have for personal use a small plot of household land and in personal ownership a subsidiary husbandry on the household plot, a dwelling house, livestock, poultry, and minor agricultural implements, in accordance with the charter of the agricultural artel.

Article 8. The land occupied by collective farms shall be secured to them for their use free of charge and for an unlimited time, that is, in perpetuity.

Article 9. Alongside the socialist system of economy, constituting the predominant form of economy in the RSFSR, the law shall permit the small-scale private economy of individual peasants and handicraftsmen based on personal labor and precluding the exploitation of the labor of others.

Article 10. The right of personal ownership on the part of citizens in the income and savings from their labor, in a dwelling house and subsidiary household economy, in household articles, and in articles of personal use and convenience, as well as the right to inherit [objects of] personal ownership of citizens, shall be protected by law.

Article 11. The economic life of the RSFSR shall be determined and directed by the state national-economic plan in the interests of increasing social wealth, of steadily raising the material and cultural level of the working people, of fortifying the independence of the socialist state, and of increasing its defense capability.

Article 12. Labor in the RSFSR shall be an obligation and a matter of honor for every able-bodied citizen in accordance with the principle: "He who does not work, neither shall he eat."

31

In the RSFSR the principle of socialism shall be carried out: "From each according to his ability, to each according to his labor."

CHAPTER II

The State Structure

Article 13. With a view to carrying out mutual assistance along economic and political lines as well as defense lines, the Russian Soviet Federated Socialist Republic has voluntarily united with [the following] Soviet Socialist Republics, with equal rights—Ukrainian SSR, Belorussian SSR, Uzbek SSR, Kazakh SSR, Georgian SSR, Azerbaijan SSR, Lithuanian SSR, Moldavian SSR, Latvian SSR, Kirghiz SSR, Tajik SSR, Armenian SSR, Turkmen SSR, Estonian SSR—into a union state, the Union of Soviet Socialist Republics.

Proceeding therefrom, the RSFSR shall secure to the USSR, as represented by its highest agencies of state power and agencies of state administration, the rights defined by Article 14 of the Constitution of the USSR.

Outside the limits of Article 14 of the Constitution of the USSR, the RSFSR shall exercise state power independently, fully preserving its sovereign rights.

Article 14. The Russian Soviet Federated Socialist Republic shall consist of [the following] territories: Altai, Krasnodar, Krasnoyarsk, Primorye, Stavropol', Khabarovsk; of [the following] regions: Amur, Arkhangel'sk, Astrakhan, Belgorod, Briansk, Vladimir, Volgograd, Vologda, Voronezh, Gor'kii, Ivanovo, Irkutsk, Kaliningrad, Kalinin, Kaluga, Kamchatka, Kemerovo, Kirov, Kostroma, Kuibyshev, Kurgan, Kursk, Leningrad, Lipetsk, Magadan, Moscow, Murmansk, Novgorod, Novosibirsk, Omsk, Orenburg, Orlov, Penza, Perm', Pskov, Rostov, Riazan', Saratov, Sakhalin, Sverdlovsk, Smolensk, Tambov, Tomsk, Tula, Tiumen', Ulianovsk, Cheliabinsk, Chitinsk, Yaroslavl'; of [the following] autonomous soviet socialist republics: Bashkirian, Buriat, Daghestan, Kabardian-Balkarian, Kalmyk, Karelian, Komi, Mari, Mordovian, North Ossetian, Tartar, Tuva, Udmurt, Chechen-Ingush, Chuvash, Yakut; of [the following] autonomous regions: Adygei, Gorno-Altai, Jewish, Karachai-Cherkess, Khakass.

Article 15. The Russian Soviet Federated Socialist Republic reserves for itself the right to secede from the Union of Soviet Socialist Republics.

Article 16.   The territory of the RSFSR may not be changed without the consent of the RSFSR.

Article 16-a.   The Russian Soviet Federated Socialist Republic shall have the right to enter into direct relations with foreign states, to conclude agreements with them, and to exchange diplomatic and consular representatives.

Article 16-b.   The Russian Soviet Federated Socialist Republic shall have its own republican military formations.

Article 17.   The laws of the USSR shall be binding in the territory of the RSFSR.

Article 18.   Every citizen of the RSFSR shall be a citizen of the USSR.
Citizens of all other union republics shall enjoy in the territory of the RSFSR the same rights as citizens of the RSFSR.

Article 19.   The competence of the Russian Soviet Federated Socialist Republic, as represented by its highest agencies of state power and agencies of state administration, shall embrace:

(a) adoption of a Constitution of the RSFSR and supervision over its observance;

(b) confirmation of Constitutions of autonomous soviet socialist republics;

(c) presentation for confirmation by the Supreme Soviet of the USSR of the formation of new autonomous republics and autonomous regions within the RSFSR;

(d) confirmation of the boundaries and district divisions of autonomous soviet socialist republics and autonomous regions;

(e) establishment of territorial and regional divisions of the RSFSR, and of the boundaries and district divisions of territories and regions;

(f) legislation of the RSFSR;

(g) protection of state order and of the rights of citizens;

(h) confirmation of the national-economic plan of the RSFSR; confirmation of the state budget of the RSFSR and of the report on its execution;

(i) direction of national-economic accounting;

(j) establishment of state and local taxes, duties, and non-tax revenues, in accordance with the legislation of the USSR;

(k) direction of the implementation of the budgets of autonomous republics and of the local budgets of territories and regions;

(l) direction of insurance and savings banks;

(m) administration of banks and industrial, agricultural, and trade enterprises and organizations of republican rank, as well as direction of industry and construction of union-republican and local rank;

(n) supervision and overseeing of the condition and administration of enterprises of union rank;

(o) establishment of the system of use of land, minerals, forests, and waters;

(p) direction of housing and municipal services, of housing construction, and of the organization of public services and amenities in cities and in other populated areas; highway construction; direction of transport and communications;

(q) labor legislation;

(r) legislation on marriage and the family;

(s) direction of health;

(t) direction of social security;

(u) direction of primary, secondary, and higher education;

(v) direction of cultural-educational and scholarly organizations and institutions of the RSFSR and administration of cultural-educational and scholarly organizations and institutions of all-republican importance;

(w) direction and organization of physical culture and sports;

(x) legislation on court organization and court procedure; civil and criminal codes;

(y) granting of the rights of citizenship of the RSFSR;

(z) amnesty and pardon of citizens convicted by judicial agencies of the RSFSR;

(aa) establishment of representation of the RSFSR in international relations;

(bb) establishment of a procedure for organizing military formations of the RSFSR.

Article 20. Each Autonomous Republic shall have its own constitution, which shall take into account the special features of the Autonomous Republic and which shall be drawn up in full conformity with the Constitution of the RSFSR and the Constitution of the USSR.

Article 21. The laws of the RSFSR shall be binding in the territory of an Autonomous Republic. In the event that a law of an Autonomous Republic diverges from a law of the RSFSR, the law of the RSFSR shall prevail.

CHAPTER III

Highest Agencies of State Power of the
Russian Soviet Federated Socialist Republic

Article 22. The Supreme Soviet of the RSFSR shall be the highest agency of state power of the RSFSR.

Article 23. The Supreme Soviet of the RSFSR shall exercise all rights vested in the RSFSR according to Articles 13 and 19 of the Constitution of the RSFSR, insofar as they do not, by virtue of the Constitution, come within the competence of agencies of the RSFSR which are accountable to the Supreme Soviet of the RSFSR— the Presidium of the Supreme Soviet of the RSFSR, the Council of Ministers of the RSFSR, Ministries of the RSFSR.

Article 24. The Supreme Soviet of the RSFSR shall be the sole legislative agency of the RSFSR.

Article 25. The Supreme Soviet of the RSFSR shall be elected by the citizens of the RSFSR by electoral areas for a term of four years on the basis of one deputy for every 150,000 of population.

Article 26. A law shall be considered confirmed if it is adopted by the Supreme Soviet of the RSFSR by a simple majority of the votes.

Article 27. Laws adopted by the Supreme Soviet of the RSFSR shall be published over the signatures of the President and Secretary of the Presidium of the Supreme Soviet of the RSFSR.

Article 28. The Supreme Soviet of the RSFSR shall elect a President of the Supreme Soviet of the RSFSR and eight Vice-Presidents.

Article 29. The President of the Supreme Soviet of the RSFSR shall direct the meetings of the Supreme Soviet of the RSFSR and shall be in charge of its internal procedure.

Article 30. Sessions of the Supreme Soviet of the RSFSR shall be convoked by the Presidium of the Supreme Soviet of the RSFSR twice a year.

Special sessions shall be convoked by the Presidium of the Supreme Soviet of the RSFSR at its discretion or upon the demand of one third of the deputies of the Supreme Soviet.

Article 31.   The Supreme Soviet of the RSFSR shall elect a Presidium of the Supreme Soviet of the RSFSR, consisting of a President of the Presidium of the Supreme Soviet of the RSFSR, seventeen Vice-Presidents (including one Vice-President from each autonomous republic), a Secretary of the Presidium, and fourteen members of the Presidium of the Supreme Soviet of the RSFSR.

Article 32.   The Presidium of the Supreme Soviet of the RSFSR shall be accountable to the Supreme Soviet of the RSFSR in all its activity.

Article 33.   The Presidium of the Supreme Soviet of the RSFSR shall:
(a) convoke sessions of the Supreme Soviet of the RSFSR;
(b) issue edicts;
(c) give interpretation of the laws of the RSFSR;
(d) conduct popular referenda;
(e) annul decrees and regulations of the Council of Ministers of the RSFSR and the Councils of Ministers of autonomous republics, as well as decisions and regulations of territorial and regional Soviets of Working People's Deputies and Soviets of Working People's Deputies of autonomous regions, in the event that they do not conform to law;
(f) in the interval between sessions of the Supreme Soviet of the RSFSR, remove from office and appoint individual Ministers of the RSFSR on the recommendation of the President of the Council of Ministers of the RSFSR, with subsequent submission for confirmation by the Supreme Soviet of the RSFSR;
(g) establish titles of honor of the RSFSR;
(h) confer titles of honor of the RSFSR;
(i) exercise the right of pardon of citizens convicted by judicial agencies of the RSFSR;
(j) appoint and recall diplomatic representatives of the RSFSR in foreign states;
(k) receive credentials and letters of recall of diplomatic representatives of foreign states who are accredited to it.

Article 34.   The Supreme Soviet of the RSFSR shall elect a credentials commission, which shall verify the authority of the deputies of the Supreme Soviet of the RSFSR.

On the recommendation of the credentials commission, the Supreme Soviet of the RSFSR shall decide either to recognize the authority of or to annul the election of individual deputies.

Article 35. The Supreme Soviet of the RSFSR, when it considers it necessary, shall appoint investigating or inspection commissions on any matter.

All institutions and officials shall be obliged to fulfill requests of such commissions and to present to them necessary materials and documents.

Article 36. A deputy of the Supreme Soviet of the RSFSR may not be brought to responsibility in court or arrested without the consent of the Supreme Soviet of the RSFSR or, in the interval between sessions of the Supreme Soviet of the RSFSR, without the consent of the Presidium of the Supreme Soviet of the RSFSR.

Article 37. Upon the expiration of the authority of the Supreme Soviet of the RSFSR, the Presidium of the Supreme Soviet of the RSFSR shall order new elections not more than two months from the day of expiration of the authority of the Supreme Soviet of the RSFSR.

Article 38. Upon the expiration of the authority of the Supreme Soviet of the RSFSR, the Presidium of the Supreme Soviet of the RSFSR shall retain its authority until a new Presidium of the Supreme Soviet of the RSFSR is formed by the newly elected Supreme Soviet of the RSFSR.

Article 39. The newly elected Supreme Soviet of the RSFSR shall be convoked by the previous Presidium of the Supreme Soviet of the RSFSR not later than three months after the elections.

Article 40. The Supreme Soviet of the RSFSR shall form the Government of the RSFSR—the Council of Ministers of the RSFSR.

CHAPTER IV

Agencies of State Administration of the
Russian Soviet Federated Socialist Republic

Article 41. The Council of Ministers of the RSFSR shall be the highest executive and administrative agency of state power of the RSFSR.

Article 42. The Council of Ministers of the RSFSR shall be responsible to the Supreme Soviet of the RSFSR and accountable to it, and in the interval between sessions of the Supreme Soviet of the RSFSR [it shall be responsible] to the Presidium of the Supreme Soviet of the RSFSR, to which it shall be accountable.

Article 43. The Council of Ministers of the RSFSR shall issue decrees and regulations on the basis of and in execution of the laws of the USSR and the RSFSR and the decrees and regulations of the Council of Ministers of the USSR and shall verify their execution.

Article 44. Decrees and regulations of the Council of Ministers of the RSFSR shall be binding throughout the territory of the RSFSR.

Article 45. The Council of Ministers of the RSFSR shall:

(a) coordinate and give direction to the work of Ministries of the RSFSR and other institutions subordinate to it, coordinate and verify the work of agents of all-union Ministries;

(b) take measures to carry out the national-economic plan;

(c) take measures to carry out the state and local budgets of the RSFSR;

(d) take measures for the securing of public order, for the defense of the interests of the state, and for the protection of the rights of citizens;

(e) give direction to and verify the work of Councils of Ministers of autonomous republics, direct and verify the work of executive committees of territorial and regional Soviets of Working People's Deputies;

(f) form, when necessary, special Committees and Chief Administrations attached to the Council of Ministers of the RSFSR for economic or cultural construction;

(g) exercise direction in the sphere of relations of the RSFSR with foreign states on the basis of the general procedure established by the USSR for relations of union republics with foreign states;

(h) direct the organization of military formations of the RSFSR.

Article 46. The Council of Ministers of the RSFSR shall have the right to annul decisions and regulations of executive committees of territorial and regional Soviets of Working People's Deputies and of executive committees of Soviets of Working People's Deputies of autonomous regions, as well as to suspend decrees and regulations of Councils of Ministers of autonomous republics and decisions and regulations of territorial and regional Soviets of Working People's Deputies and of Soviets of Working People's Deputies of autonomous regions.

The Council of Ministers of the RSFSR shall have the right to annul orders and instructions of Ministers of the RSFSR.

Article 47. The Council of Ministers of the RSFSR shall be formed by the Supreme Soviet of the RSFSR and shall consist of:

the President of the Council of Ministers of the RSFSR;

First Vice-Presidents of the Council of Ministers of the RSFSR;

Vice-Presidents of the Council of Ministers of the RSFSR;

Ministers of the RSFSR;

the President of the State Planning Commission of the RSFSR;

the President of the State Committee of the Council of Ministers of the RSFSR for Construction;

the President of the State Committee of the Council of Ministers of the RSFSR for Utilization of Labor Resources;

the President of the State Committee of the Council of Ministers of the RSFSR for Professional and Technical Education;

the President of the All-Russian Combine "Rossel'khoztekhnika" ["Russian Agricultural Technology"] of the Council of Ministers of the RSFSR;

the Chief of the Central Statistical Administration attached to the Council of Ministers of the RSFSR.

Article 48. The Government of the RSFSR or a Minister of the RSFSR to whom a question of a deputy of the Supreme Soviet of the RSFSR is addressed shall be obliged within not more than three days to give an oral or written reply in the Supreme Soviet of the RSFSR.

Article 49. Ministers of the RSFSR shall direct branches of state administration which come within the competence of the RSFSR.

Article 50. Ministers of the RSFSR shall issue, within the limits of the competence of their respective ministries, orders and instructions on the basis of and in execution of laws of the USSR and of the RSFSR, decrees and regulations of the Council of Ministers of the USSR and the Council of Ministers of the RSFSR, and orders and instructions of union-republican Ministries of the USSR, and shall verify their execution.

Article 51. Ministries of the RSFSR shall be either union-republican or republican [ministries].

Article 52. Union-republican Ministries of the RSFSR, being subordinate
both to the Council of Ministers of the RSFSR and to the corresponding union-
republican Ministries of the USSR, shall direct branches of state administration
of the RSFSR entrusted to them, with the exception of only a limited number of
enterprises according to a list confirmed by the Presidium of the Supreme Soviet
of the USSR.

Article 53. Republican Ministries of the RSFSR, being directly subordinate
to the Council of Ministers of the RSFSR, shall direct branches of state administration entrusted to them.

Article 54. The [following] Ministries of the RSFSR shall be union-republican Ministries of the RSFSR:

Higher and Specialized Secondary Education;

Geology;

Health;

Foreign Affairs;

Culture;

Light Industry;

Forestry;

Soil and Water Conservation;

Meat and Dairy Industry;

Defense;

Food Industry;

Construction Materials Industry;

Education;

Fisheries;

Rural Construction;

Agriculture;

Trade;

Finance.

Article 55. The [following] Ministries of the RSFSR shall be republican Ministries of the RSFSR:

Automotive Transport and Highways;

Household Services;

Municipal Services;

Local Industry;

River Fleet;

Social Security;

Construction;

Fuel Industry;

Grain Produce and the Mixed Feed Industry.

CHAPTER V

Highest Agencies of State Power of Autonomous Soviet Socialist Republics

Article 56. The Supreme Soviet of an ASSR [Autonomous Soviet Socialist Republic] shall be the highest agency of state power of the Autonomous Republic.

Article 57. The Supreme Soviet of an Autonomous Republic shall be elected by the citizens of the republic for a term of four years according to norms of representation established by the Constitution of the Autonomous Republic.

Article 58. The Supreme Soviet of an Autonomous Republic shall be the sole legislative agency of the ASSR.

Article 59. The Supreme Soviet of an Autonomous Republic shall:

(a) adopt a Constitution of the Autonomous Republic and submit it for confirmation by the Supreme Soviet of the RSFSR.

(b) establish the district divisions of the Autonomous Republic and the borders of districts and cities and submit them for confirmation by the Supreme Soviet of the RSFSR;

(c) confirm the national-economic plan and the budget of the Autonomous Republic;

(d) confer titles of honor of the Autonomous Republic.

Article 60. The Supreme Soviet of an Autonomous Republic shall elect a Presidium of the Supreme Soviet of the ASSR consisting of a President of the Presidium of the Supreme Soviet of the ASSR, Vice-Presidents, a Secretary of the Presidium, and members of the Presidium of the Supreme Soviet of the ASSR.

Article 61. The Presidium of the Supreme Soviet of an Autonomous Republic shall be accountable to the Supreme Soviet of the ASSR.

Article 62. The authority of the Presidium of the Supreme Soviet of an Autonomous Republic shall be determined by the Constitution of the ASSR.

Article 63. For conducting its sessions the Supreme Soviet of an Autonomous Republic shall elect a President and Vice-Presidents of the Supreme Soviet of the ASSR.

Article 64. The Supreme Soviet of an Autonomous Republic shall form the Government of the Autonomous Republic—the Council of Ministers of the ASSR.

CHAPTER VI

Agencies of State Administration of Autonomous Soviet Socialist Republics

Article 65. The Council of Ministers of an ASSR shall be the highest executive and regulatory agency of state power of the ASSR.

Article 66. The Council of Ministers of an Autonomous Republic shall be responsible to the Supreme Soviet of the ASSR and accountable to it, and in the interval between sessions of the Supreme Soviet of the Autonomous Republic [it shall be responsible] to the Presidium of the Supreme Soviet of the Autonomous Republic, to which it shall be accountable.

Article 67. The Council of Ministers of an Autonomous Republic shall issue decrees and regulations on the basis of and in execution of the laws of the USSR, RSFSR, and Autonomous Republic, and of decrees and regulations of the Councils of Ministers of the USSR and RSFSR, and shall verify their execution.

Article 68. The Council of Ministers of an Autonomous Republic shall have the right to annul orders and instructions of Ministries of the ASSR, decisions and regulations of executive committees of area, city, and district Soviets of Working People's Deputies in the territory of the ASSR, as well as to suspend decisions and regulations of area, city, and district Soviets of Working People's Deputies.

Article 69. The Council of Ministers of an Autonomous Republic shall be formed by the Supreme Soviet of the Autonomous Republic and shall consist of:

the President of the Council of Ministers of the Autonomous Republic;

Vice-Presidents of the Council of Ministers;

the Ministers of:

> Household Services;
>
> Health;
>
> Municipal Services;
>
> Culture;
>
> Protection of Public Order;
>
> Education;
>
> Agriculture;
>
> Social Security;
>
> Trade;
>
> Finance;

President of the State Planning Commission;

President of the Committee of People's Control of the Autonomous Republic;

President of the Committee of State Security attached to the Council of Ministers of the Autonomous Republic;

Chiefs of Administrations:

> for Construction and Architecture;
>
> for Utilization of Labor Resources;
>
> of Supply and Sales;
>
> of Construction and Repair of Roadways;

and in addition, in accordance with the special features of the economy of the republic and with confirmation by the Supreme Soviet of the RSFSR;

Ministers or Chiefs of Administrations of:

> Forestry;
>
> Soil and Water Conservation;
>
> Local Industry;
>
> Food Industry;
>
> Construction Materials Industry;
>
> Fuel Industry.

Article 70. Ministers of an Autonomous Republic shall direct the branches of state administration which come within the competence of the Autonomous Republic according to the Constitution of the RSFSR and the Constitution of the ASSR.

Article 71. Ministers of an Autonomous Republic shall issue orders and instructions within the limits of the competence of their respective Ministries on the basis of and in execution of the laws of the USSR, RSFSR, and ASSR, decrees and regulations of the Councils of Ministers of the USSR, RSFSR and ASSR, and orders and instructions of Ministers of the RSFSR.

Article 72. Ministries of an Autonomous Republic, being subordinate both to the Council of Ministers of the ASSR and to the corresponding Ministries of the RSFSR, shall direct branches of state administration entrusted to them.

CHAPTER VII

Agencies of State Power of
Autonomous Regions

Article 73. The Soviet of Working People's Deputies of an autonomous region shall be the agency of state power of the autonomous region.

Article 74. The Soviet of Working People's Deputies of an autonomous region shall be elected by the citizens of the autonomous region for a term of two years according to norms of representation determined by the Constitution of the RSFSR.

Article 75. The executive and regulatory agency of the Soviet of Working People's Deputies of an autonomous region shall be the executive committee elected by it.

Article 76. The Soviet of Working People's Deputies of each autonomous region shall present for confirmation by the Supreme Soviet of the RSFSR a "Statute on the Autonomous Region," which shall take into account the special nationality features of the autonomous region.

CHAPTER VIII

Local Agencies of State Power

Article 77. Soviets of Working People's Deputies shall be the agencies of state power in territories, regions, autonomous regions, national areas, administrative areas, districts, cities, settlements, and rural localities (stanitsas, villages, hamlets, auls).

Article 78. Territorial and regional Soviets of Working People's Deputies, Soviets of Working People's Deputies of national and administrative areas, district, city, district in large cities, settlement, and rural (stanitsa, village, hamlet, aul) Soviets of Working People's Deputies shall be elected by the working people of the respective territory, region, national area, administrative area, district, city, settlement, or rural locality for a term of two years.

Article 79. Soviets of Working People's Deputies (of a territory, region, area, district, city, settlement, or rural locality) shall direct cultural-political and economic construction in their territory, draw up the local budget, direct the work of subordinate administrative agencies, secure the protection of state order, aid in increasing the defense capability of the country, and ensure observance of the laws and protection of the rights of citizens.

Article 80. Soviets of Working People's Deputies shall adopt decisions and issue regulations within the limits of the rights granted to them by the laws of the USSR, RSFSR, and Autonomous Republic.

Article 81. The executive and regulatory agencies of territorial and regional Soviets of Working People's Deputies, of the Soviets of Working People's Deputies of national and administrative areas, and of district, city, settlement, and rural Soviets of Working People's Deputies shall be executive committees elected by them, consisting of a president, vice-presidents, a secretary, and members.

Article 82. The executive and regulatory agency of rural Soviets of Working People's Deputies (of stanitsas, hamlets, and auls) in small rural settlements shall be a president, vice-president, and secretary elected by them.

Article 83. Executive committees of Soviets of Working People's Deputies (of a territory, region, area, district, city, settlement, or rural locality) shall exercise direction over cultural-political and economic construction in their territory on the basis of decisions of the corresponding Soviets of Working People's Deputies and superior state agencies.

Article 84. Sessions of territorial and regional Soviets of Working People's Deputies shall be convoked by their executive committees at least four times a year.

Article 85. Sessions of district Soviets of Working People's Deputies and Soviets of Working People's Deputies of administrative areas shall be convoked by their executive committees at least six times a year.

Article 86. Sessions of city, city district, and rural Soviets of Working People's Deputies shall be convoked by their executive agencies at least six times a year, and sessions of city Soviets of Working People's Deputies in cities divided into districts at least four times a year.

Article 87. Territorial and regional Soviets of Working People's Deputies, Soviets of Working People's Deputies of national and administrative areas, and district and city Soviets of Working People's Deputies shall elect for the period of their session a president and a secretary to conduct the meetings of the session.

Article 88. The president of a rural Soviet shall convoke the rural Soviet and conduct its meetings.

Article 89. Executive agencies of Soviets of Working People's Deputies shall be directly accountable both to the Soviet of Working People's Deputies which elected them and to the executive agency of the superior Soviet of Working People's Deputies.

Article 90. Superior executive committees of Soviets of Working People's Deputies shall have the right to annul decisions and regulations of inferior executive committees and to suspend decisions and regulations of inferior Soviets of Working People's Deputies.

Article 91. Superior Soviets of Working People's Deputies shall have the right to annul decisions and regulations of inferior Soviets of Working People's Deputies and their executive committees.

Article 92. Territorial and regional Soviets of Working People's Deputies shall form the following sections and administrations within their executive committees:

sections of—

> health;
> public education;
> general;
> organizational-instructional;

construction and architecture;

social security;

finance;

administrations of—

household , services;

municipal services;

culture;

local industry;

meat and milk industry;

preservation of public order;

food industry;

construction materials industry;

agriculture;

construction and repair of roadways;

fuel industry;

trade;

a planning commission;

and in addition, territorial and regional Soviets of Working People's Deputies, in accordance with the special features of the economy of the territory or region and with confirmation by the Council of Ministers of the RSFSR, may also form other departments or administrations within their executive committees.

Article 93. In accordance with the conditions of a territory or region, all-union Ministries shall form their own administrations attached to territorial or regional Soviets of Working People's Deputies on the basis of laws of the USSR and of the RSFSR.

Article 94. Sections and administrations of executive committees of territorial and regional Soviets of Working People's Deputies shall be subordinate   in their activity both to the territorial or regional Soviet of Working People's Deputies and its executive committee and to the corresponding RSFSR Ministry.

Article 95. Soviets of Working People's Deputies of administrative areas and their executive committees shall form sections and conduct their work   on the basis of laws and edicts of the supreme agencies of the RSFSR and decisions of territorial and regional Soviets of Working People's Deputies.

Article 96. District Soviets of Working People's Deputies shall form the following sections within their executive committees:

health;

culture;

militia;

public education;

general;

social security;

construction and repair of roadways;

finance;

a planning commission;

and in addition, in accordance with the special features of the economy of the district and with confirmation by the territorial or regional Soviet of Working People's Deputies, district Soviets of Working People's Deputies shall form sections or administrations of:

municipal services;

local industry;

trade.

Article 97. Repealed.

Article 98. Sections of executive committees of district Soviets of Working People's Deputies shall be subordinate in their activity both to the district Soviet of Working People's Deputies and its executive committee and to the corresponding section of the executive committee of the territorial or regional Soviet of Working People's Deputies.

Article 99. City Soviets of Working People's Deputies shall form the following sections within their executive committees:

health;

culture;

public education;

general;

social security;

trade;

finance;

an administration of municipal services;

an administration or section (or division) of the militia;

a planning commission;

and in addition, in accordance with the special features of the industry of the city and its urban and suburban economy:

local industry.

Article 100. Sections of executive committees of city Soviets of Working People's Deputies shall be subordinate in their activity both to the city Soviet of Working People's Deputies and its executive committee and to the corresponding section of the executive committee of the district Soviet of Working People's Deputies or directly to the corresponding section of the executive committee of the territorial or regional Soviet of Working People's Deputies.

Article 101. Sections of executive committees of the city Soviets of Working People's Deputies of Moscow and Leningrad shall be subordinate in their activity both to the Soviet of Working People's Deputies of Moscow or Leningrad and its executive committee and directly to the corresponding RSFSR Ministry.

Article 102. Soviets of Working People's Deputies of national areas and their executive committees shall exercise in the territory of the area the rights and duties placed upon them by the "Statute on National Areas," as well as by decisions of the corresponding territorial or regional Soviet of Working People's Deputies.

A "Statute on National Areas" shall be established by the Supreme Soviet of the RSFSR.

CHAPTER IX

Budget of the Russian Soviet Federated Socialist Republic

Article 103. The state budget of the RSFSR shall be compiled by the Council of Ministers of the RSFSR and shall be submitted by them for confirmation by the Supreme Soviet of the RSFSR.

The state budget of the RSFSR confirmed by the Supreme Soviet of the RSFSR shall be published for the information of all.

Article 104. The Supreme Soviet of the RSFSR shall elect a budget commission which shall report to the Supreme Soviet its conclusion concerning the state budget of the RSFSR.

Article 105. The report on the execution of the state budget of the RSFSR shall be confirmed by the Supreme Soviet of the RSFSR and shall be made known by being published.

Article 106. In the budgets of autonomous republics and in local territorial and regional budgets, as well as in the budgets of autonomous regions, national and administrative areas, and of district, city, and rural Soviets, there shall be included the revenue from the local economy and deductions from state revenue received in its territory, as well as receipts from local taxes and duties in amounts established by legislation of the USSR and of the RSFSR.

CHAPTER X

The Courts and the Procuracy

Article 107. The administration of justice in the RSFSR shall be carried out by the Supreme Court of the RSFSR, Supreme Courts of autonomous republics, territorial and regional courts, courts of autonomous regions, courts of national areas, courts of administrative areas, special USSR courts established by decree of the Supreme Soviet of the USSR, and people's courts.

Article 108. In all courts, cases shall be considered with the participation of people's assessors, except in instances specially provided by law.

Article 109. The Supreme Court of the RSFSR shall be the highest judicial agency of the RSFSR. The Supreme Court of the RSFSR shall be charged with supervision over the judicial activities of all judicial agencies of the RSFSR, [including those of] autonomous republics and regions.

Article 110. The Supreme Court of the RSFSR shall be elected by the Supreme Soviet of the RSFSR for a term of five years.

Article 111. Supreme Courts of autonomous republics shall be elected by the Supreme Soviets of autonomous republics for a term of five years.

Article 112.   Territorial and regional courts, courts of autonomous regions, and courts of national and administrative areas shall be elected by territorial or regional Soviets of Working People's Deputies, by Soviets of Working People's Deputies of autonomous regions, or by Soviets of Working People's Deputies of national or administrative areas for a term of five years.

Article 113.   People's judges of district (or city) people's courts shall be elected by the citizens of the district (or city) on the basis of universal, equal, and direct suffrage by secret ballot for a term of five years.

People's assessors of district (or city) people's courts shall be elected at general meetings of workers, employees, and peasants [voting] by place of employment or residence and [at general meetings] of military personnel [voting] by military units for a term of two years.

Article 114.   Judicial proceedings in the RSFSR shall be conducted in the Russian language or in the language of the autonomous republic, autonomous region, or national area with persons not knowing that language being guaranteed full acquaintance with the materials of the case through an interpreter, as well as the right to speak in court in their native language.

Article 115.   Examination of cases in all courts of the RSFSR shall be open, insofar as exceptions are not provided by law, with the accused being guaranteed the right to defense.

Article 116.   Judges shall be independent and subordinate only to law.

Article 117.   Supreme supervision over precise execution of the laws in the territory of the RSFSR by all ministries and institutions subordinate to them and also by individual officials, as well as by citizens, shall be carried out both directly by the Procurator General of the USSR and through the Procurator of the RSFSR.

Article 118.   The Procurator of the RSFSR shall be appointed by the Procurator General of the USSR for a term of five years.

Article 119.   Territorial and regional procurators, as well as procurators of autonomous republics and autonomous regions, shall be appointed by the Procurator General of the USSR for a term of five years.

Article 120.   Procurators of national and administrative areas and district and city procurators shall be appointed by the Procurator of the RSFSR with confirmation by the Procurator General of the USSR for a term of five years.

Article 121. Agencies of the procuracy shall exercise their functions independently of any local agencies whatsoever, being subordinate only to the Procurator General of the USSR.

CHAPTER XI

Fundamental Rights and Duties of Citizens

Article 122. Citizens of the RSFSR shall have the right to labor, that is, the right to a guaranteed job with payment for their labor in accordance with its quantity and quality.

The right to labor shall be guaranteed by the socialist organization of the national economy, the steady growth of the productive forces of Soviet society, the elimination of the possibility of economic crises, and the liquidation of unemployment.

Article 123. Citizens of the RSFSR shall have the right to rest and leisure.

The right to rest and leisure shall be guaranteed by the establishment of a seven-hour working day for workers and employees, the reduction of the working day to six hours for certain professions with arduous working conditions, and to four hours in shops with especially arduous working conditions; by the establishment of annual vacations with full pay for workers and employees; and by provision of an extensive network of sanatoria, rest homes, and clubs for the service of the working people.

Article 124. Citizens of the RSFSR shall have the right to economic security in old age, as well as in case of sickness or loss of working capacity.

This right shall be guaranteed by extensive development of social insurance for workers and employees at state expense, by free medical service for the working people, and by provision of an extensive network of health resorts for the use of the working people.

Article 125. Citizens of the RSFSR shall have the right to education.

This right shall be guaranteed by universal, compulsory eight-year education, by extensive development of secondary general polytechnical education, professional-technical education, secondary specialized, and higher education based on the bond of instruction with life, with production, by comprehensive development of evening and correspondence education, by freedom from [tuition] charges for all types of education, by the system of state stipends, by instruction in [primary and secondary] schools in the native language, and by the organization at plants, and on state and collective farms of free production, technical, and agricultural instruction for the working people.

Article 126. Women in the RSFSR shall be accorded equal rights with men in all spheres of economic, state, cultural, and social-political life.

The possibility of exercising these rights of women shall be guaranteed by providing women with an equal right with men to labor, payment for labor, rest and leisure, social insurance, and education, by state protection of the interests of mother and child, by state aid to mothers with many children and to unmarried mothers, by providing vacations for women during pregnancy with preservation of support, and by an extensive network of maternity homes, day nurseries, and kindergartens.

Article 127. Equality of rights of citizens of the RSFSR, regardless of their nationality or race, in all spheres of economic, state, cultural, and social-political life shall be an indefeasible law.

Any kind of direct or indirect restriction of rights or, conversely, establishment of direct or indirect privileges of citizens on account of their race or nationality, and also any advocacy of racial or national exclusiveness or of hatred or contempt, shall be punished by law.

Article 128. In order to guarantee to citizens freedom of conscience, the church in the RSFSR shall be separated from the state, and the school from the church. Freedom of religious worship and freedom of anti-religious propaganda shall be recognized for all citizens.

Article 129. In conformity with the interests of the working people and in order to strengthen the socialist system, citizens of the RSFSR shall be guaranteed by law:

(a) freedom of speech;

(b) freedom of the press;

(c) freedom of assembly and meetings;

(d) freedom of street processions and demonstrations.

These rights of citizens shall be guaranteed by providing the working people and their organizations with printing presses, stocks of paper, public buildings, streets, communications facilities, and other material conditions necessary for their exercise.

Article 130. In conformity with the interests of the working people and in order to develop organizational initiative and political activism among the masses of the people, citizens of the RSFSR shall be guaranteed the right to unite in social organizations—trade unions, cooperative associations, youth organizations, sports and defense organizations, cultural, technical, and scholarly societies; and the most active and conscious citizens in the ranks of the working class, the toiling peasantry, and the laboring intelligentsia shall be voluntarily united in the Communist Party of the Soviet Union, which shall be the vanguard of the working people in their struggle to build communist society and the leading core of all organizations of the working people, both social and state.

Article 131. Inviolability of the person shall be guaranteed to citizens of the RSFSR. No one may be subjected to arrest except by decree of a court or with the sanction of a procurator.

Article 132. Inviolability of citizens' dwellings and secrecy of correspondence shall be protected by law.

Article 133. The RSFSR shall afford the right to asylum to foreign citizens persecuted for defending the interests of the working people, for their scholarly activities, or for their struggle for national liberation.

Article 134. Every citizen of the RSFSR shall be obliged to observe the Constitution of the Russian Soviet Federated Socialist Republic, to carry out the laws, to maintain labor discipline, to have an honest attitude toward social duty, and to respect the rules of socialist community life.

Article 135. Every citizen of the RSFSR shall be obliged to safeguard and strengthen social, socialist ownership as the sacred and inviolable foundation of the Soviet system, as the source of the wealth and might of the motherland, and as the source of the prosperous and cultured life of all the working people.

Persons who commit offenses against social, socialist ownership shall be enemies of the people.

Article 136. Universal military obligation shall be law.

Military service in the Armed Forces of the USSR shall be the honorable obligation of citizens of the RSFSR.

Article 137. Defense of the fatherland shall be the sacred duty of every citizen of the RSFSR. Treason to the motherland—violation of the oath of allegiance, desertion to the enemy, infliction of harm on the military might of the state, espionage—shall be punished with all the severity of the law as the gravest malefaction.

CHAPTER XII

The Electoral System

Article 138. Elections of deputies to all Soviets of Working People's Deputies—the Supreme Soviet of the RSFSR, territorial and regional Soviets of Working People's Deputies, Supreme Soviets of autonomous republics, Soviets of Working People's Deputies of autonomous regions, Soviets of Working People 's Deputies of national and administrative areas, district, city, and rural (stanitsa, village, hamlet, aul) Soviets of Working People's Deputies—shall be carried out by the voters on the basis of universal, equal, and direct suffrage by secret ballot.

Article 139. Elections of deputies shall be universal: all citizens of the RSFSR who have attained the age of 18 years regardless of race, nationality, sex, religious confession, educational qualifications, domicile, social origin, property status, or past activities, shall have the right to participate in elections of deputies and to be elected, with the exception of persons who have been declared insane in the procedure established by law.

Any citizen of the RSFSR who has attained the age of 21 years may be elected as deputy to the Supreme Soviet of the RSFSR or as deputy to the Supreme Soviet of an ASSR regardless of race, nationality, sex, religious confession, educational qualifications, domicile, social origin, property status, or past activities.

Article 140. Elections of deputies shall be equal: each citizen shall have one vote; all citizens shall participate in elections on an equal basis.

Article 141. Women shall enjoy the right to elect and to be elected on equal terms with men.

Article 142. Citizens serving in the Armed Forces of the USSR shall enjoy the right to elect and to be elected on equal terms with all [other] citizens.

Article 143. Elections of deputies shall be direct: elections to all Soviets of Working People's Deputies, from rural and city Soviets of Working People's Deputies up to the Supreme Soviet of the RSFSR, shall be carried out directly by the citizens, by direct elections.

Article 144. Voting at elections of deputies shall be secret.

Article 145. Elections to territorial, regional, area, district, city, rural, and settlement Soviets of Working People's Deputies of the RSFSR shall be conducted by electoral areas according to norms established by the "Statute on Elections to Territorial, Regional, Areas, District, City, Rural, and Settlement Soviets of Working People's Deputies of the RSFSR."

Article 146. Candidates in elections shall be nominated by electoral areas.

The right to nominate candidates shall be guaranteed to social organizations and societies of the working people— communist party organizations, trade unions, cooperatives, youth organizations, cultural societies.

Article 147. Every deputy shall be obliged to render an account before the voters for his own work and for the work of the Soviet of Working People's Deputies and may be recalled at any time by decision of a majority of the voters in the procedure established by law.

CHAPTER XIII

Arms, Flag, Capital

Article 148. The state arms of the Russian Soviet Federated Socialist Republic shall consist of a drawing of a gold sickle and hammer placed criss-crossed with handles downward on a red background in sunrays and in a frame of ears of grain, with the inscription: "RSFSR" and "Proletarian of All Countries, Unite!"

Article 149. The state flag of the Russian Soviet Federated Socialist Republic shall consist of red cloth with a light blue stripe at the flagstaff along the whole width of the flag. The light blue stripe shall be one eighth the length of the flag. In the upper lefthand corner of the red cloth shall be depicted a gold sickle and hammer and above them a red five-pointed star, framed in a gold der. The proportion of the flag's width to its length shall be 1 : 2.

Article 150. The capital of the Russian Soviet Federated Socialist Republic shall be the city of Moscow.

CHAPTER XIV

Procedure for Amending the Constitution

Article 151. The Constitution of the RSFSR shall be amended only by a decision of the Supreme Soviet of the RSFSR adopted by a majority of not less than two thirds of the votes of the Supreme Soviet.

3. RULES OF THE COMMUNIST PARTY OF THE SOVIET UNION

Introductory Note

The activities of the Communist Party of the Soviet Union are governed by two documents, the Program and the Rules. The Program of the Communist Party was adopted by the Twenty-Second Party Congress in 1961 and was preceded by only two other Party programs, those adopted by the Russian Communist Party in 1903 and in 1919. The Party Program is a policy document which describes Party aims for a given historical period. In its 1961 version the Program sets forth in general terms the tasks of the party in constructing a communist society.

The Rules of the Communist Party, on the other hand, regulate organizational matters and the rights and duties of Party members. Unlike the Party Program, the Rules have been amended at almost every Party Congress. The Twenty-Second Party Congress of 1961 introduced major changes in the direction of greater intra-party democracy, calling for periodic change of leadership in higher Party agencies, including the Central Committee (Article 25), removal of a member of the Central Committee on a two-thirds vote of the Committee (Article 26), and collectivity of leadership rather than rule by a single individual as the highest principle of Party leadership (Article 28).

RULES OF THE COMMUNIST PARTY OF THE SOVIET UNION

(adopted by the 22nd Congress of the Communist Party
of the Soviet Union, October 31, 1961, amended by the 23rd
Congress of the Communist Party of the Soviet Union, April 8, 1966)

The Communist Party of the Soviet Union is the militant tested vanguard of the Soviet people, uniting on a voluntary basis the advanced, most conscious part of the working class, collective-farm peasantry, and intelligentsia of the USSR.

Founded by V. I. Lenin as the advanced contingent of the working class, the Communist Party has followed a glorious path of struggle and has led the working class and the toiling peasantry to the victory of the Great October Socialist Revolution and to the establishment of the dictatorship of the proletariat in the USSR. Under the direction of the Communist Party, exploiting classes in the Soviet Union have been liquidated, and the moral and political unity of Soviet society has been formed and strengthened. Socialism has triumphed fully and finally. The Communist Party, the party of the working class, has now become the party of the entire Soviet people.

The party exists for the people and serves the people. It is the highest form of social-political organization, the guiding and directing force of Soviet society. The party directs the great creative activity of the Soviet people and lends an organized, planned, scientific character to their struggle for the achievement of the final goal—the victory of communism.

The CPSU constructs its work on the foundation of unconditional observance of the Leninist norms of party life, the principle of collectivity of leadership, the full development of intra-party democracy, the industry and initiative of communists, and criticism and self-criticism.

The inviolable law of life of the CPSU is ideological and organizational unity, solidarity of its ranks, and the high conscious discipline of all communists. Any manifestation of factionalism or groupism is incompatible with Marxist-Leninist party spirit and with being in the party. The party frees itself of persons who violate the Program or Rules of the CPSU or who by their conduct compromise the exalted title of communist.

In all its activity the CPSU is guided by Marxist-Leninist doctrine and by the Program based thereon, which defines the basic tasks of the party for the period of the construction of communist society.

Creatively developing Marxism-Leninism, the CPSU struggles decisively against any manifestations of revisionism and dogmatism, which are profoundly alien to revolutionary theory.

The Communist Party of the Soviet Union is an essential component of the international communist and worker movement. It stands firmly on the tested Marxist-Leninist principles of proletarian internationalism and actively fosters the strengthening of the unity of the entire international communist and worker movement and of the fraternal ties with the great army of communists of all countries.

I.

Party Members,
Their Duties and Rights

1. Any citizen of the Soviet Union may be a member of the CPSU who acknowledges the Program and Rules of the party, takes an active part in the construction of communism, works in one of the party organizations, carries out party decisions, and pays membership dues.

2. A party member shall be obliged:

(a) to struggle for the creation of the material and technical base of communism, to serve as an example of the communist attitude toward labor, to raise labor productivity, to be a skirmisher in all that is new and progressive, to support and propagate advanced methods, to master techniques, to improve his qualifications, to safeguard and increase social, socialist ownership, [which is] the foundation of the might and the flowering of the Soviet Motherland;

(b) firmly and steadfastly to put party decisions into action, to explain party policy to the masses, to aid in strengthening and broadening the party's ties with the people, to be considerate and attentive toward individuals, to respond promptly to the needs and requirements of the working people;

(c) to take an active part in the political life of the country, in the administration of state affairs, and in economic and cultural construction; to set an example in fulfilling his social duty; to help in developing and strengthening communist social relations;

(d) to master Marxist-Leninist theory, to raise his conceptual level, to aid in forming and educating the man of communist society; to struggle decisively against any manifestations of bourgeois ideology, against the remnants of private property psychology, religious prejudices, and other remnants of the past, to observe the principles of communist morality, to place social above personal interests;

(e) to be an active conductor of the ideas of socialist internationalism and Soviet patriotism to the masses of the working people, to struggle against remnants of nationalism and chauvinism, to foster by word and deed the strengthening of friendship among the peoples of the USSR and [the strengthening] of the fraternal ties of the Soviet people with peoples of countries of the socialist camp and with proletarians and the working people of all countries;

(f) to strengthen by all possible means the conceptual and organizational unity of the party, to safeguard the party from penetration into its ranks by people unworthy of the exalted title of communist, to be truthful and honest before the party and the people, to display vigilance, to guard party and state secrets;

(g) to develop criticism and self-criticism, boldly to expose shortcomings and to achieve their elimination, to combat ostentation, conceit, complacency, and localist tendencies, to give a decisive rebuff to all attempts to suppress criticism, to speak out against any acts which cause harm to the party or state, and to inform party agencies about them, up to the Central Committee of the CPSU;

(h) undeviatingly to implement the party line in the selection of cadres according to their political and professional qualifications; to be uncompromising whenever Leninist principles of selection and education of cadres are violated;

(i) to observe party and state discipline, which is binding on all party members alike; the party has one discipline, one law for all communists regardless of their past services or the posts they occupy;

(j) to foster by all possible means the strengthening of the defensive might of the USSR, to wage an unflagging struggle for peace and friendship among peoples.

3. A party member shall have the right:

(a) to elect and be elected to party agencies;

(b) freely to discuss questions of party policy and practice at party meetings, conferences, congresses, at sessions of party committees, and in the party press, to submit proposals, openly to express and defend his opinion prior to the adoption of a decision by the organization;

(c) to criticize any communist at party meetings, conferences, congresses, and committee plenums, regardless of the post he occupies; persons guilty of suppression of criticism or of persecution of criticism must be brought to strict party responsibility, up to expulsion from the ranks of the CPSU;

(d) to participate personally in party meetings or in sessions of bureaus or committees when his activity or conduct is being discussed;

(e) to address questions, petitions, or proposals to any party body, up to the Central Committee of the CPSU, and to demand a substantive reply.

4. Admission to membership in the party shall be handled exclusively on an individual basis. Conscious, active workers, peasants, and representatives of the intelligentsia, who are dedicated to the cause of communism, shall be admitted as party members. New members shall be admitted from among candidates who have gone through the established probation period.

Persons who have attained the age of 18 years may be admitted into the party. Young people up to the age of 23 years inclusive may enter the party only through the Komsomol.

The procedure for admitting new members into the party from among candidates shall be as follows:

(a) applicants for party membership must submit recommendations from three members of the CPSU who have been party members for not less than five years and who have known the applicant professionally and socially for not less than one year.

Note 1. Applicants from the Komsomol shall submit a recommendation from the district or city Komsomol committee, which shall be equivalent to the recommendation of one party member.

Note 2. Members and candidate members of the Central Committee of the CPSU shall refrain from giving recommendations.

(b) the question of admitting a new member shall be discussed and decided by a general meeting of the primary party organization; its decision shall be considered adopted if not less than two thirds of the party members present at the meeting voted for it and shall enter into force after confirmation by the district committee or, in cities not divided into districts, by the city party committee.

When the question of admitting a new member into the party is being discussed, the presence of the persons giving recommendations shall not be obligatory;

(c) citizens of the USSR who were formerly members of communist or worker parties of other countries shall be admitted into the Communist Party of the Soviet Union on the basis of rules established by the Central Committee of the CPSU.

Persons who were formerly members of other parties shall be admitted into the CPSU in the usual manner but with obligatory confirmation by the regional or territorial party committee or by the central committee of the union-republican party organization.

5. Persons giving recommendations shall bear responsibility before party organizations for the objectivity of their characterization of the political, professional, and moral qualifications of persons being recommended.

6. Party seniority of new party members shall be counted from the day of the decision of the general meeting of the primary party organization to admit the given candidate as a party member.

7. The procedure for registering party members and candidate members and for transfer from one organization to another shall be determined by the appropriate instructions of the Central Committee of the CPSU.

8. If a party member or candidate member has not paid membership dues without valid reasons for a period of three months, the matter shall be discussed in the primary party organization. If it appears that such party member or candidate member has in fact lost contact with the party organization, then he shall be considered as having left the party; the primary party organization shall adopt a decision to this effect and submit it for confirmation by the district or city party committee.

9. For nonfulfillment of duties under the Rules or for other offenses, a party member or candidate member shall be brought to responsibility and may be subjected to the following penalties: admonition, reprimand (or severe reprimand), reprimand (or severe reprimand) with a notation in his registration card. The highest measure of party punishment shall be expulsion from the party.

For minor offenses, measures of party education and pressure in the form of comradely criticism or a party censure, warning, or reproof must be applied.

In deciding the question of expulsion from the party, maximum attention must be ensured, and the grounds for accusations preferred against a communist must be thoroughly investigated.

10. The question of expelling a communist from the party shall be decided by a general meeting of the primary party organization. A decision of a primary party organization to expel a member shall be considered adopted if not less than two thirds of the party members present at the meeting voted for it, and shall enter into force after confirmation by the district or city party committee.

Until confirmation by the district or city party committee of a decision expelling [a member] from the CPSU, a communist shall retain his party card or candidate's card and shall have the right to attend closed party meetings.

A person expelled from the party shall retain the right to submit an appeal within two months to higher party agencies, up to the Central Committee of the CPSU.

11. The question of bringing to party responsibility members or candidate members of the central committee of a union-republican party organization or of a territorial, regional, area, city, or district party committee, as well as members of inspection commissions, shall be considered by primary party organizations.

Decisions of party organizations imposing penalties on members or candidate members of those party committees or on members of inspection commissions shall be adopted in the usual procedure.

Proposals of party organizations to expel [a member] from the CPSU shall be communicated to the party committee of which the communist in question is a member. Decisions to expel from the party members or candidate members of the central committee of a union-republican party organization or of a territorial, regional, area, city, or district party committee, or members of inspection commissions, shall be adopted at a plenum of the respective committee by a majority of two thirds of the votes of its members.

The question of expelling from the party a member or candidate member of the Central Committee of the CPSU or a member of the Central Inspection Commission shall be decided by a party congress or, during intervals between congresses, by a Plenum of the Central Committee by a majority of two thirds of the members of the Central Committee.

12. If a party member commits a criminally punishable offense, he shall be expelled from the Party and brought to responsibility in accordance with the Law.

13. Appeals by persons who have been expelled from the party or who have received penalties, as well as [appeals] from decisions of party organizations expelling [a member] from the party, shall be considered by the appropriate party agencies within one month from the day of their receipt.

II.

Candidates for Party Membership

14. Applicants for party membership shall go through a probation period as candidates, necessary in order to become more familiar with the Program and Rules of the CPSU and to prepare for entrance into the party. The party organization must help the candidate prepare for entrance into the CPSU and must check his personal qualifications.

The probation period for candidates shall be one year.

15. The procedure for admitting persons as candidates (admission on an individual basis, submission of recommendations, decision of the primary organization to admit and its confirmation) shall be the same as for admission of party members.

16. Upon the expiration of the probation period, the primary party organization shall consider and decide the question of admitting the candidate to party membership. If during the probation period the candidate did not prove himself and on the basis of personal qualifications cannot be admitted to CPSU membership, then the party organization shall render a decision refusing him admission as a party member, and after confirmation of such a decision by the district or city party committee, he shall be considered as having left [the status of] candidacy for membership in the CPSU.

17. Candidates for party membership shall participate in all activities of the party organization and shall enjoy the right to a consultative vote at party meetings. Candidates for party membership may not be elected to governing party agencies or as delegates to party conferences or congresses.

18. Candidates for membership in the CPSU shall pay party dues in the same amounts as party members.

III.

Organizational Structure of the Party. Intra-Party Democracy

19. The governing principle of the organizational structure of the party shall be democratic centralism, which signifies:

(a) election of all governing agencies in the party from the lowest to the highest;

(b) periodic accounting of party agencies before their own party organizations and before superior agencies;

(c) strict party discipline and subordination of the minority to the majority;

(d) the unconditional binding force of decisions of higher agencies upon lower agencies.

20. The party shall be organized on a territorial and occupational basis: primary organizations shall be created at places of work of communists and shall be combined into district, city, etc., organizations on a territorial basis. An organization serving a given territory shall be higher than all party organizations serving parts of that territory.

21. All party organizations shall be autonomous in deciding local questions, provided that such decisions do not contradict party policy.

22. The highest governing agency of a party organization shall be: the general meeting (for primary organizations), the conference (for district, city, area, regional, and territorial organizations), the congress (for union-republican party organizations and for the Communist Party of the Soviet Union).

23. The general meeting, conference, or congress shall elect a bureau or committee, which shall be its executive agency and which shall direct all the everyday work of the party organization.

24. Elections of party agencies shall be conducted by closed (i.e., secret) ballot. At elections all party members shall have an unlimited right to challenge candidates and to criticize them. Voting must be conducted separately for each candidate. A candidate shall be considered elected if more than half of the participants of the meeting, conference, or congress voted for him.

In elections of all party agencies—from primary organizations up to the Central Committee of the CPSU—the principle of systematic renewal of their composition and of continuity of leadership shall be observed.

25. A member or candidate member of the Central Committee of the CPSU must in all his activity justify the great trust placed in him by the party. If a member or candidate member of the Central Committee of the CPSU fails to uphold his honor and dignity, he may not remain in the Central Committee. The question of removing a member or candidate member from the Central Committee of the CPSU shall be decided at a Plenum of the Central Commttteee by closed (i.e., secret) ballot. A decision shall be considered adopted if not less than two thirds of all the members of the Central Committee of the CPSU vote for it.

The question of removing a member or candidate member of the central committee of a union-republican party organization or of a territorial, regional, area, city, or district party committee from that party agency shall be decided at a plenum of the respective committee. A decision shall be considered adopted if as the result of a closed (i.e., secret) ballot not less than two thirds of the votes of the members of the given committee are cast in its favor.

If a member of the Central Inspection Commission does not justify the great trust placed in him by the party, he must be removed from the Commission. This question shall be decided at a meeting of the Central Inspection Commission. A decision shall be considered adopted if as the result of a closed (i.e., secret) ballot not less than two thirds of the votes of the members of the Central Inspection Commission are cast in favor of removing a member of the Central Inspection Commission from that agency.

The question of removing members of inspection commissions of republican, territorial, regional, area, city, or district party organizations from those commissions shall be decided at meetings of the respective commissions in the procedure established for members and candidate members of party committees.

26. Free and business-like discussion of questions of party policy in individual party organizations or in the party as a whole shall be the inalienable right of a party member and an important principle of intra-party democracy. Only on the basis of intra-party democracy is it possible to cultivate criticism and self-criticism and to strengthen party discipline, which must be conscious and not mechanical.

Discussions of controversial or insufficiently elucidated issues may be held within the framework of individual organizations or of the party as a whole.

A party-wide discussion shall be necessary:

(a) if such a necessity is recognized by several party organizations at the regional or republican level;

(b) if within the Central Committee there is not a sufficiently strong majority on major questions of party policy;

(c) if the Central Committee of the CPSU considers it necessary to consult the entire party on a question of policy.

A broad discussion, especially a discussion of all-union proportions on questions of party policy, must be so conducted as to ensure free disclosure of party members' views and to exclude the possibility of attempts at forming factional groups damaging to party unity or of attempts at splitting the party.

27. The highest principle of party leadership shall be collectivity of leadership, which is an essential condition for the normal functioning of party organizations, for proper education of cadres, and for the development of activism and initiative among communists. Cult of personality and violations of intra-party democracy connected with it cannot be tolerated in the party; they are incompatible with the Leninist principles of party life.

Collectivity of leadership shall not exempt individuals from personal responsibility for work entrusted to them.

28. Central committees of union-republican party organizations and territorial, regional, area, city, and district party committees shall in the interval between congresses or conferences, systematically inform their party organizations about their work.

29. Meetings of the activists of district, city, area, regional, and territorial party organizations and of union-republican party organizations shall be convoked in order to discuss major party decisions and to work out measures for their execution, as well as to consider questions concerning local life.

IV.

Highest Agencies of the Party

30. The supreme agency of the Communist Party of the Soviet Union shall be a party congress. Ordinary congresses shall be convoked by the Central

Committee at least once every four years. The convocation of a party congress and its agenda shall be announced at least one-and-one-half months before the congress. Extraordinary congresses shall be convoked by the Central Committee of the party on its own initiative or upon the demand of not less than one third of the party members represented at the last party congress. Extraordinary congresses shall be convoked within two months [thereafter]. A congress shall be considered properly constituted if there are represented at it not less than one half of all members of the party.

Norms of representation for a party congress shall be established by the Central Committee.

31. If the Central Committee of the party fails to convoke an extraordinary congress within the time indicated in section 30, the organizations which demanded convocation of the extraordinary congress shall have the right to form an organizational committee which shall have the rights of the Central Committee of the party with regard to convoking an extraordinary congress.

32. A congress shall:

(a) hear and confirm reports of the Central Committee, the Central Inspection Commission, and other central organizations;

(b) review, amend, and confirm the Program and the Rules of the party;

(c) determine the party line on questions of domestic and foreign policy, consider and decide major questions of communist construction;

(d) elect the Central Committee and the Central Inspection Commission.

33. The number of members to be elected to the Central Committee and to the Central Inspection Commission shall be established by a congress. If vacancies have occurred in the Central Committee, they shall be filled from among the candidate members of the Central Committee of the CPSU elected by a congress.

34. The Central Committee of the Communist Party of the Soviet Union shall, during intervals between congresses, direct all activities of the party, [including those] of local party agencies, shall select and place leading cadres, shall give direction to the work of central state and social organizations of the working people through party groups in them, shall set up various party agencies, institutions, and enterprises and direct their activity, shall appoint the editorial boards of central newspapers and journals working under its control, [and] shall allocate the funds of the party budget and supervise its execution.

The Central Committee shall represent the CPSU in relations with other parties.

35. The Central Committee of the CPSU shall regularly inform party organizations about its work.

36. The Central Inspection Commission of the CPSU shall inspect the affairs of central party agencies to see that they are handled expeditiously and correctly, and [shall inspect] central party agencies and shall audit the finances and undertakings of the Central Committee of the CPSU.

37. The Central Committee of the CPSU shall hold not less than one plenary meeting every six months. Candidate members of the Central Committee shall attend meetings of Central Committee plenums with the right of a consultative vote.

38. The Central Committee of the Communist Party of the Soviet Union shall elect: for direction of the work of the party between Central Committee Plenums, a Politburo; for direction of everyday work, chiefly in selecting cadres and in organizing the verification of the execution [of party decisions], a Secretariat. The Central Committee shall elect a General Secretary of the Central Committee of the CPSU.

39. The Central Committee of the Communist Party of the Soviet Union shall organize a Party Control Committee attached to the Central Committee.

The Party Control Committee attached to the Central Committee of the CPSU shall:

(a) verify observance of party discipline by members and candidate members of the CPSU, bring to responsibility communists guilty of violating the Program or Rules of the party, or party or state discipline, as well as persons violating party morality;

(b) consider appeals from decisions of central committees of union-republican party organizations and territorial and regional party committees expelling [a member] from the party or imposing party penalties.

40. In the interval between party congresses, the Central Committee of the CPSU may if necessary convoke an All-Union Party Conference to discuss questions of party policy which have arisen. The procedure for conducting an All-Union Party Conference shall be determined by the Central Committee of the CPSU.

V.

Republican, Territorial, Regional Area, City, and District Party Organizations

41. Republican, territorial, regional, area, city, and district party organizations and their committees shall be governed in their acitivity by the Program and Rules of the CPSU; they shall, within the republic, territory, region, area, city, or district, conduct all work necessary to carry our party policy and shall organize execution of directives of the Central Committee of the CPSU.

42. The fundamental duties of republican, territorial, regional, area, city, and district party organizations and of their governing agencies shall be:

(a) political and organizational work among the masses and mobilization of them for achieving the tasks of communist construction, for the development by all possible means of industrial and agricultural production, and for fulfullment and overfulfillment of state plans; concern for the steady improvement of the material well-being and cultural level of the working people;

(b) organization of ideological work, propaganda of Marxism-Leninism, improvement of communist consciousness among the working people, direction of the local press, radio, and television, supervision over the activity of cultural and educational institutions;

(c) direction of Soviets, trade unions, the komsomol, cooperatives, and other social organizations through party groups in them, ever broader enlistment of the working people in the work of these organizations, and development of the initiative and activism of the masses as a necessary condition for the gradual transition from socialist state rule to communist social self-administration.

Party organizations shall not replace soviet, trade union, cooperative, or other social organizations of the working people and must not allow confusion of functions between party and other agencies or unnecessary parallelism in their work;

(d) selection and placement of leading cadres and education of them in the spirit of communist ideals, honesty and truthfulness, and a high degree of re-

71

sponsibility before the party and the people for the work entrusted to them;

(e) large-scale enlistment of communists in the conduct of party work as non-staff personnel on the basis of social activity;

(f) organization of various party institutions and enterprises within their republic, territory, region, area, city, or district [and] direction of their activity; allocation of party funds within their organization; [giving] information to its superior party organization on a systematic basis and accountability to it in its work.

Governing Agencies of Republican, Territorial and Regional Party Organizations

43. The highest agency of a regional, territorial, or republican party organization shall be the regional or territorial party conference or the congress of the union-republican party organization and, during intervals between them, the regional or territorial committee or the central committee of the union-republican party organization.

44. Ordinary regional and territorial conferences shall be convoked by the regional or territorial committee once every two years. Ordinary congresses of a union-republican party organization shall be convoked by the central committee of the party organization at least once every four years. Extraordinary conferences and congresses shall be convoked by decision of the regional or territorial committee or of the central committee of the union-republican party organization or upon the demand of one third of the members of the organizations which make up the regional, territorial, or republican party organization.

Norms of representation for the regional or territorial conference or for the congress of a union-republican party organization shall be established by the respective party committee.

Regional and territorial conferences and congresses of a union-republican party organization shall hear reports of the regional or territorial committee or of the central committee of the union-republican party organization and of the inspection commission; they shall discuss at their discretion other questions of party, economic, or cultural construction; they shall elect the regional or territorial committee or the central committee of the union-republican party organization, the inspection commission, and delegates to the congress of the CPSU.

In the interval between congresses of union-republican party organizations, central committees of such party organizations may if necessary convoke republican party conferences in order to discuss major questions of the activity of party organizations. The procedure for conducting republican party conferences shall be determined by the central committees of union-republican party organizations.

45. Regional and territorial committees and central committees of union-republican party organizations shall elect a bureau, including committee secretaries. Secretaries must have party standing of not less than five years. Chairmen of party commissions, heads of committee sections, and editors of party newspapers and journals shall also be confirmed at committee plenums.

Secretariats may be created in regional or territorial party committees or in central committees of union-republican party organizations to consider everyday matters and to verify execution [of party decisions].

46. The plenum of a regional or territorial committee or of the central committee of a union-republican party organization shall be convoked at least once every four months.

47. Regional and territorial committees and central committees of union-republican party organizations shall direct area, city, and district party organizations, shall verify their activity, and shall systematically hear reports of area, city, and district party committees.

Party organizations of autonomous republics, as well as of autonomous and other regions which form part of territories or union republics, shall work under the direction of territorial committees and of the central committees of union-republican party organizations.

Governing Agencies of Area, City, and District (Rural and City) Party Organizations

48. The highest agency of an area, city, or district party organization shall be the area, city, or district party conference or the general meeting of communists convoked by the area, city, or district committee at least once every two years, and also extraordinary conferences and meetings convoked by decision of

the committee or upon the demand of one third of the total number of party members of the respective party organization.

The area, city, or district conference (or meeting) shall hear reports of the committee and of the inspection commission, shall discuss at its discretion other questions of party, economic, and cultural construction, and shall elect the area, city, or district committee, the inspection commission, and delegates to the regional or territorial conference or to the congress of the union-republican party organization.

Norms of representation for the area, city, or district conference shall be established by the appropriate party committee.

49. An area, city, or district committee shall elect a bureau, including committee secretaries, and shall also confirm heads of committee sections and newspaper editors. Secretaries of area, city, and district committees must have party standing of not less than three years. Committee secretaries shall be confirmed by the regional or territorial committee or by the central committee of the union-republican party organization.

50. Area, city, and district committees shall organize and confirm primary party organizations, shall direct their activity, shall systematically hear reports on the work of party organizations, and shall keep a register of communists.

51. The plenum of an area, city, or district committee shall be convoked at least once every three months.

52. Area, city, and district committees shall have non-staff instructors, shall create permanent or temporary commissions on various questions of party work, and shall use other forms of enlisting communists in the activity of the party committee on a social basis.

VI.

Primary Party Organizations

53. The basic unit of the party shall be primary organizations.

Primary party organizations shall be created at the place of work of party members—in plants, factories, state farms, and other enterprises, in collective farms, units of the Soviet Army, institutions, educational establishments, etc., where there are not fewer than three party members. In addition, territorial primary party organizations may be created at the place of residence of communists in rural localities and housing administrations.

54. At enterprises and in collective farms and institutions with more than 50 party members and candidates, party organizations may be created within the general primary party organization in shops, sectors, farms, brigades, sections, etc., with the permission of the district, city, or area committee.

Within shop, sector, etc., organizations, as well as within primary party organizations numbering fewer than 50 members and candidates, party groups may be created in brigades or other production units.

55. The highest agency of a primary party organization shall be a party meeting which shall be conducted at least once each month. In party organizations which have shop organizations, a general party meeting shall be conducted at least once every two months.

In large party organizations numbering over 300 communists, a general party meeting shall be convoked whenever necessary at times established by the party committee or upon the demand of several shop party organizations.

56. For handling everyday work, a primary or shop party organization shall elect a bureau for one year in numbers established by a party meeting. In primary and shop party organizations containing fewer than 15 party members, a bureau shall not be elected but rather a secretary of the party organization and his deputy.

Secretaries of primary and shop party organizations must have party standing of not less than one year.

In primary party organizations containing fewer than 150 party members, official positions which release party workers [from their regular employment] shall, as a rule, not be established.

57. Party committees may be created at large enterprises and in institutions numbering over 300 party members and candidates, and also in necessary instances in organizations numbering over 100 communists, in view of special features of production or size of territory, with permission of the regional or territorial committee or of the central committee of the union-republican party organization, with shop party organizations of such enterprises and institutions being granted the rights of a primary party organization.

In party organizations of collective and state farms, party committees may be created if there are 50 communists.

A party committee shall be elected for a term of one year, [and] its numbers shall be determined by a general party meeting or conference.

58. Party committees of primary organizations numbering over 1000 Communists may, with permission of the central committee of the union-republican party organization, be granted the rights of a district party committee in matters of the admission [of new members] into the CPSU, the keeping of a registry of party members and candidates, and the consideration of personal cases of communists. Within these organizations party committees may be created in necessary instances in shops, with party organizations in production sectors being granted the rights of a primary party organization.

Party committees which have been granted the rights of a district party committee shall be elected for a term of two years.

59. A primary party organization shall be governed in its activity by the Program and Rules of the CPSU. It shall conduct its work directly among the working people, shall rally them around the Communist Party of the Soviet Union, and shall organize the masses to give life to party policy and to struggle for the building of communism.

A primary party organization shall:

(a) admit new members into the CPSU;

(b) educate communists in the spirit of devotion to the party cause, steadfastness in their ideals, and communist morality;

(c) organize the study by communists of Marxist-Leninist theory in close conjunction with the practice of communist construction, and oppose any attempts at revisionist distortions of Marxism-Leninism or at dogmatic interpretation;

(d) concern itself with raising the vanguard role of communists in labor and in the social-political and economic life of the enterprise, collective farm, institution, educational establishment, etc.;

(e) act as the organizer of the working people in resolving the regular tasks of communist construction and be in charge of socialist competition for fulfilling state plans and the obligations of the working people; mobilize the masses for uncovering and making better use of the internal reserves of enterprises and collective farms and for large-scale introduction into production of the achievements of science and technology and the experience of the more advanced workers; see to the strengthening of labor discipline, the steady growth of labor productivity, and the improvement of the quality of production; concern itself with preserving and increasing the social wealth at enterprises and on state and collective farms;

(f) conduct mass agitation and propaganda work, educate the masses in the spirit of communism, and help the working people develop the skills of administration of state and social affairs;

(g) on the basis of broad development of criticism and self-criticism wage a struggle against manifestations of bureaucratism, localist tendencies, and violations of state discipline, thwart attempts at deceiving the state, and take measures against laxity, negligence, and waste at enterprises, on collective farms, and in institutions;

(h) render assistance to the area, city, or district committee in all its activity and report to it about its work.

A party organization must see to it that every communist observes in his own life and cultivates among the working people the moral principles laid down in the Program of the CPSU and in the moral code of the builder of communism:

— devotion to the cause of communism and love for the socialist Motherland and for the countries of socialism;

— conscientious labor for the good of society: he who does not work, neither shall he eat;

— concern by everyone for preserving and increasing the social wealth;

— high consciousness of public duty and impatience with violations of social interests;

— collectivism and comradely mutual assistance: one for all, and all for one;

— humane relations and mutual respect among people: man is to man a friend, comrade, and brother;

— honesty and truthfulness, moral purity, simplicity and modesty in social and personal life;

— mutual respect in the family, concern for the education of children;

— irreconcilability with injustice, parasitism, dishonesty, careerism, greed;

— friendship and brotherhood among all the peoples of the USSR, impatience with national and racial animosity;

— irreconcilability with enemies of communism, of the cause of peace, and of the freedom of peoples;

— fraternal solidarity with the working people of all countries [and] with all peoples.

60. Primary party organizations of production and trade enterprises, of state and collective farms, as well as of architectural organizations, construction bureaus, and research institutes directly involved in production, shall enjoy the right of control over the activity of the administration [of such agencies].

Party organizations of ministries, of state committees, and of other central and local soviet and economic institutions and departments, which do not enjoy the functions of control over the activity of the administration, must exert an active influence on the improvement of the work of the apparatus, must educate the personnel in the spirit of high responsibility for the cause entrusted to them, must take measures to strengthen state discipline [and] to improve services to the population, must wage a decisive struggle against bureaucratism and red tape, and must promptly inform the appropriate party agencies of shortcomings in the work of institutions as well as of individuals, regardless of the posts they occupy.

VII.

The Party and the Komsomol

61. The All-Union Leninist Communist Union of Youth shall be an independently acting social organization of youth, an active helper and reserve of the party. The Komsomol shall help the party educate youth in the spirit of communism, draw it into the practical work of constructing a new society, prepare a generation of versatile people who will live, work, and administer social affairs under communism.

62. Komsomol organizations shall enjoy the right of broad initiative in discussing and placing before appropriate party organizations questions concerning the work of an enterprise, collective farm, or instituion. They must be in practice active conductors of party directives in all spheres of communist construction, especially where there are no primary party organizations.

63. The VLKSM shall work under the direction of the Communist Party of the Soviet Union. The work of local VLKSM organizations shall be directed and controlled by the appropriate republican, territorial, regional, area, city, or district party organizations.

In their work of communist education of youth, agencies and primary party organizations shall rely on komsomol organizations [and] shall support and spread the useful beginnings they have made.

64. Members of the VLKSM who are admitted into the CPSU shall leave the komsomol from the moment they enter the party, unless they occupy executive posts in komsomol organizations.

VIII.

Party Organizations in the Soviet Army

65. Party organizations in the Soviet Army shall be governed in their activity by the Program and Rules of the CPSU and shall work on the basis of instructions confirmed by the Central Committee.

Party organizations in the Soviet Army shall ensure that party policy is carried out in the Armed Forces, shall rally their personnel around the Communist Party, shall educate soldiers in the spirit of the ideas of Marxism-Leninism [and] of selfless devotion to the socialist Motherland, shall actively foster the strengthening of the unity of the army and the people, shall concern itself with the strengthening of military discipline, shall mobilize personnel to fulfill the tasks of military and political training, to master new techniques and weapons, and irreproachably to execute their military duty [and] the orders and regulations of the command.

66. Direction of party work in the Armed Forces shall be effectuated by the Central Committee of the CPSU through the Chief Political Administration of the Soviet Army and Navy, functioning with the rights of a section of the Central Committee of the CPSU.

Party standing of five years shall be obligatory for chiefs of political administrations of military districts and fleets [and] chiefs of political sections of armies; party standing of three years [shall be obligatory] for chiefs of political sections of [lesser] military units.

67. Party organizations and political agencies of the Soviet Army shall maintain close ties with local party committees [and] shall systematically inform

them about political work in military units. Secretaries of military party organizations and directors of political agencies shall participate in the work of local party committees.

IX.

Party Groups in Non-Party Organizations

68. Party groups shall be organized at congresses, conferences, [and] assemblies convoked by soviet, trade union, cooperative, or other mass organizations of the working people, as well as in the elected agencies of such organizations, if there are not fewer than three party members. The task of such groups shall be to increase by all possible means the influence of the party and to carry out its policies among non-party people, to strengthen party and state discipline, to combat bureaucratism, [and] to verify execution of party and soviet directives.

69. Party groups shall be subordinate to their respective party agencies — to the Central Committee of the Communist Party of the Soviet Union, to the central committee of the union-republican party organization, to the territorial, regional, area, city, district party committee.

In all matters party groups shall be obliged to govern themselves strictly and steadfastly by decision of governing party agencies.

X.

Party Funds

70. Funds of the party and of its organizations shall consist of membership dues, income from party undertakings, and other revenue.

71. Monthly membership dues for party members and candidates shall be established in the following amounts:

Those having monthly wages		
up to 50 rubles	shall pay	10 kopeks
from 51 to 100 rubles	" "	0.5 per cent
from 101 to 150 rubles	" "	1.0 per cent

from 151 to 200 rubles	shall pay	1.5 per cent
from 201 to 250 rubles	" "	2.0 per cent
from 251 to 300 rubles	" "	2.5 per cent
over 300 rubles	" "	3.0 per cent

of the monthly wage.

72. An entrance fee of two per cent of monthly wages shall be paid on admission as a candidate member of the party.

4. GENERAL STATUTE ON USSR MINISTRIES

Introductory Note

The General Statute on USSR Ministries, adopted by the USSR Council of Ministers in July 1967, supersedes the 1923 General Statute on USSR People's Commissariats (as the ministries were then called).

The new statute makes few changes in the organizational structure of the ministries, retaining the division of all ministries into all-union and union-republican ministries. The principal significance of the new statute lies in its regulation of the functions of those ministries (of which there are nearly fifty) which are in charge of branches of Soviet industry and commerce. Previously no piece of legislation had defined the rights and duties of ministries in carrying out these economic functions.

GENERAL STATUTE ON USSR MINISTRIES

(confirmed by a decree of the Council of Ministers of the USSR, July 10, 1967)

Principal Tasks and Basic Questions of the Organization of the Work of a USSR Ministry

1. A USSR ministry shall be a central agency of state administration exercising direction over a particular branch of the national economy.

A USSR ministry shall bear responsibility before the party, state, and people for the condition and further development of the branch, for scientific and technical progress and the technological level of production, for the quality of goods produced, and for the fullest possible satisfaction of the needs of the country in all types of goods [produced by] the branch.

2. The principal tasks of a USSR ministry shall be:

to secure the development by all possible means of the branch entrusted to it as a component part of the national economy of the country, high tempos of development of production and of growth of labor productivity on the basis of scientific and technical progress with the aim of satisfying as fully as possible the needs of the national economy and of the defense of the country in all types of goods;

to fulfill the assignments of the state plan and to ensure strict observance of state discipline;

to ensure production of high-quality goods with minimum expenditures of social labor, to raise production efficiency, to improve utilization of basic assets and of labor, material, and financial resources;

to carry out a unified technology policy in the branch, to introduce the latest achievements of science and technology and progressive experience, and to ensure high technical and economic production indicators;

to utilize capital investment rationally and raise its effectiveness, to reduce

costs and accelerate construction work, to put new production capacities and basic assets to use promptly, and also to master production capacities rapidly;

to introduce scientific organization of labor and administration, to provide
enterprises, organizations, and institutions in the ministry's system with qualified cadres, to create conditions for the best possible utilization of the knowledge
and experience of personnel, to promote young specialists who have shown pro-
mise to executive work;

to improve the housing, recreational, and everyday living conditions of workers and employees, to create safe working conditions in production.

3. A USSR ministry shall carry out the planned direction of [its] branch on a
scientific basis, taking into account the requirements of an integrated development of the national economy of the USSR, union republics, and economic regions
of the country.

4. A USSR ministry shall ensure a correct combination of economic and administrative methods of direction, the fullest utilization of such economic levers
as profit, price, bonus, and credit, introduction of efficient systems of administration using electronic and computer technology, [and] improvement of the
structure and of the organizational forms of administration.

5. A USSR ministry shall ensure effectuation of the Leninist principles of
selection, promotion, and placement of leading economic, engineering, and scientific cadres, shall concentrate its attention on verification and control over execution by leading cadres of directives and decisions of the Party and Government,
shall conduct work with the participation of social organizations to educate cadres in the spirit of a communist attitude toward labor [and] strict observance of
state interests and discipline, shall ensure a correct combination of material and
moral incentives for raising social production and for increasing responsibility
on the part of each working person for the work entrusted to him and for the overall results of the work of the collective.

6. In accordance with the Constitution of the USSR, a USSR ministry shall be
an all-union or a union-republican [ministry] and shall be formed by the Supreme
Soviet of the USSR.

An all-union ministry shall direct the branch entrusted to it throughout the
territory of the USSR directly or through agencies created by it.

A union-republican ministry of the USSR shall direct the branch entrusted to
it, as a rule, through union-republican ministries of the same name and shall

manage enterprises, organizations, and institutions of union rank directly or through agencies created by it.

7. A USSR ministry, union-republican ministries of the same name, and enterprises, organizations, and institutions subordinate to them shall comprise the unified system of that ministry.

Union-republican ministries of union republics shall be subordinate to the Council of Ministers of the corresponding union republic and to the union-republican USSR ministry of the same name. Statutes on union-republican ministries of union republics and the structure and number of personnel of the central apparatus of these ministries shall be confirmed by the Council of Ministers of the union republic in agreement with the union-republican USSR ministry of the same name.

8. A USSR ministry shall decide all questions pertaining to the branch within the limits of the rights granted it and may entrust resolution of individual questions which come within its competence to union-republican ministries of the same name, as well as to enterprises, organizations, or institutions of union rank.

A USSR ministry shall be obliged strictly to observe the rights of union-republican ministries of the same name, as well as the rights provided by the Statute on the Socialist State Production Enterprise and other provisions of the legislation in force for enterprises, organizations, and institutions in the ministry's system, and to foster by all possible means the development of their economic independence and initiative.

A USSR ministry in its activity shall maintain contacts and collaborate with other ministries and departments in working out and resolving inter-branch questions.

9. A USSR ministry which is in charge of the production of goods manufactured by enterprises of several ministries shall participate in planning the output of such goods by enterprises which do not come within its system and shall work out problems connected with improving the technological level of such products.

10. A USSR ministry shall ensure protection of socialist state ownership in enterprises, organizations, and institutions in the ministry's system and an attitude of care toward it.

11. A USSR ministry shall ensure the development of democratic principles in administration, shall create conditions for the manifestation of initiative and for active participation of the working people and their social organizations in

work to improve production and to eliminate shortcomings in the activity of the ministry and enterprises, organizations, and institutions subordinate to it.

Questions pertaining to the labor and everyday life of workers and employees shall be decided by the ministry, taking into account proposals of soviet and trade union agencies and, in cases provided by legislation in force, jointly or by agreement with such agencies.

12. A USSR ministry shall be governed in its activity by the laws of the USSR, by edicts of the Presidium of the Supreme Soviet of the USSR, by decrees and regulations of the Government of the USSR, and by other normative acts, by the present General Statute, as well as by the Statute on the given ministry confirmed by the Council of Ministers of the USSR and shall ensure correct application of prevailing legislation at enterprises and in organizations and institutions of the ministry's system.

A USSR ministry shall write up summaries of its experience in applying legislation in the branch entrusted to it, [and] shall work out proposals for improving [such legislation] and shall submit them for consideration by the Council of Ministers of the USSR.

13 A USSR ministry shall organize its work on the basis of a combination of collegiality and one-man management in the discussion and decision of all questions relating to direction of the branch, establishing the precise responsibility of officials for the condition of affairs in the sector of work entrusted to them and for the fulfillment of particular assignments.

14. A USSR ministry shall be headed by a minister appointed, in accordance with the Constitution of the USSR, by the Supreme Soviet of the USSR or, in the interval between sessions, by the Presidium of the Supreme Soviet of the USSR with subsequent submission for confirmation by the Supreme Soviet of the USSR.

A USSR minister shall have deputies, [who shall be] appointed by the Council of Ministers of the USSR. Allocation of duties among the deputy ministers shall be made by the minister.

15. In a USSR ministry there shall be formed a collegium, composed of the minister (as president) and the deputy ministers ex officio, as well as of other leading personnel of the ministry.

Members of the collegium of the ministry shall be confirmed by the Council of Ministers of the USSR.

16. A USSR minister shall bear personal reponsibility for fulfilling the tasks and duties with which the ministry is charged [and] shall establish the degree of

responsibility of deputy ministers, heads of chief administrations, and directors of other subdivisions of the ministry for the activity of enterprises, organizations, and institutions in the ministry's system.

17. A USSR minister, within the limits of competence of the ministry, shall issue orders and instructions on the basis of, and in execution of, the laws in force as well as of the decrees and regulations of the Council of Ministers of the USSR, and shall issue directives binding on union-republican ministries of the same name and on enterprises, organizations, and institutions in the ministry's system, and shall verify their execution.

USSR ministers shall issue joint orders or instructions in necessary instances.

18. The collegium of a USSR ministry, at its regularly held meetings, shall consider basic questions pertaining to the development of the branch and other questions of the ministry's activity, shall discuss questions concerning the practical direction of enterprises, organizations, and institutions, [and concerning] verification of the execution [of decisions, and] selection and utilization of cadres [and shall discuss] drafts of major edicts and instructions, shall hear reports of ministers of union-republican ministries of the same name, reports of chief administrations, of administrations and sections of the ministry, and of enterprises, organizations, and institutions in the ministry's system.

Decisions of the collegium shall be put into effect, as a rule, by orders of the minister. In the event of disagreements between the minister and the collegium, the minister shall put into effect his own decision, reporting to the Council of Ministers of the USSR about the disagreements which have arisen, and the members of the collegium, in their turn, may communicate their opinion to the Council of Ministers of the USSR.

19. To consider proposals regarding the basic directions of the development of science and technology, to determine a scientifically-based unified technology policy for the branch, [and] to work out recommendations for the utilization and introduction into production of the latest achievements of domestic and foreign science, technology, and progressive experience, there shall be created in a USSR ministry a scientific and technological (or scientific) council composed of prominent scholars, highly qualified specialists, [and] production innovators, as well as representatives of scientific and technological societies and other organizations.

The composition of the scientific and technological (or scientific) council and a statute on it shall be confirmed by the minister.

20. A USSR ministry shall create, reorganize, and liquidate enterprises, organizations, and institutions of union rank within the limits of the labor plan (or budget appropriations) established for it.

Decisions to create, reorganize, or liquidate enterprises, organizations, or institutions shall be adopted by a union-republican USSR ministry after preliminary consideration of such questions in necessary instances with the Councils of Ministers of the corresponding union republics.

A USSR ministry shall confirm charters of enterprises and statutes (or charters) on organizations and institutions of union rank.

21. A USSR ministry shall form an arbitrazh to consider economic disputes between enterprises, organizations, and institutions in the ministry's system. The arbitrazh of the ministry shall be granted the right to issue orders for compulsory execution of decisions rendered by it. A statute on the arbitrazh shall be confirmed by the minister.

22. The structure and number of personnel of the central apparatus of a USSR ministry shall be confirmed by the Council of Ministers of the USSR.

The table of organization of the central apparatus of the ministry, as well as statutes on chief administrations and on administrations and sections of the ministry, shall be confirmed by the minister. Statutes on chief administrations and on administrations and sections shall define their authority within the limits of the competence of the ministry.

Chief administrations and administrations and sections of the ministry may be transferred to [the system of] economic accountability by the minister.

23. A USSR ministry shall, in the established procedure, convoke meetings of its activists, with participation of social organizations, at which reports on measures to fulfill decisions of the Party and Government [and] major problems of the development of the branch shall be heard and discussed, and also questions connected with improving the activity of the ministry and of its subordinate enterprises, organizations, and institutions shall be discussed on the basis of the expansion of criticism and self-criticism.

24. A USSR ministry shall organize prompt and attentive consideration of letters (and statements and complaints) of the working people, reaching the correct decision of the questions posed in such letters, and shall also take measures to eliminate shortcomings in the activity of enterprises, organizations, and institutions in the ministry's system, which are communicated in letters of the working people.

STATUTE ON USSR MINISTRIES

Functions of a USSR Ministry

In the field of planning a USSR ministry shall:

25. Study the needs of the national economy for products of the branch, and carry out the planning of the development of the branch, ministry-wide and by territory, in accordance with the tasks of development of the entire national economy of the country [and] the economy of the union republics and economic regions, taking into account specialization and cooperation in production.

Work out projects for the development and location of industry in the branch, forward them to the Councils of Ministers of the union republics, and consider proposals received from them regarding such projects.

26. Ensure rational utilization and replacement of natural resources, taking into consideration, in exploiting them, the interests of other branches and of the national economy as a whole; take necessary measures to protect the air, soil, and waters from pollution by industrial and economic waste, sewage, radioactive substances, and production by-products, [and] to preserve the plant and animal world.

27. On the basis of control figures for the development of the national economy of the USSR, determine control figures for perspective and annual plans and send them to union-republican ministries of the same name [and] to enterprises, organizations, and institutions of union rank.

On the basis of control figures for the development of the national economy of the USSR and of draft plans presented by union-republican ministries of the same name [and] by enterprises, organizations, and institutions of union rank, [and] taking into account proposals of Councils of Ministers of union republics, work out drafts of perspective and annual plans, ministry-wide and by territory, and present them to the Council of Ministers of the USSR and to Gosplan of the USSR.

With the participation of union-republican ministries of the same name and enterprises, organizations, and institutions of union rank, consider and confirm for them, perspective and annual plans in accordance with the established indicators [and] corresponding to the assignments of the national-economic plan, ensuring coordination of all parts and indicators of such plans.

A USSR ministry shall communicate to the Councils of Ministers of union republics control figures, draft plans, and confirmed plans for union-republican ministries of the same name [and] for enterprises, organizations, and institutions of union rank (except indicators for production of defense products).

28. Work out and put into effect measures connected with the sale by enterprises in the ministry's system of products produced by them.

Determine production volumes for enterprises in the ministry's system with respect to types of products not provided in the national-economic plan, taking into account proposals of interested agencies.

Take measures to develop rational economic ties for enterprises, organizations, and institutions in the ministry's system.

29. Organize the work of the compiling of drafts of perspective and annual plans by enterprises, organizations, and institutions in the ministry's system, work out methodological directives on preparation of drafts of such plans, and confirm forms for the technical-industrial-financial plans of enterprises.

30. Ensure fulfillment of established plans by all enterprises, organizations, and institutions in the ministry's system.

31. Work out and confirm, in the established procedure, technical and economic standards, norms of expenditure and of reserves of raw materials, fuel, [and] other materials, and norms of expenditure of electrical energy for production and use needs; establish a list of standards and norms to be confirmed by union-republican ministries of the same name and by enterprises, organizations, and institutions in the ministry's system; ensure introduction of the confirmed standards and norms.

32. Confirm or present for confirmation, in accordance with legislation in force, prices and tariffs for products and services of enterprises and organizations in the ministry's system; exercise supervision over correct application of prices and tariffs by enterprises, organizations, and institutions in the ministry's system.

33. Organize primary accounting in enterprises, organizations, and institutions in the ministry's system, [and] confirm for them forms for primary accounting; receive, in the established procedure, statistical and bookkeeping reports; carry out measures to centralize accounting work and to introduce progressive accounting methods.

In the field of science and technology a USSR ministry shall:

34. Conduct systematic work to evaluate the technological and economic level of the branch's production and the products which it puts out, determine the ways of the most efficient utilization of scientific and technological achievements, and

ensure a high technological level of development of the branch on the basis of the achievements of domestic and foreign science and technology.

35. Ensure the working out of scientific and technological problems in the branch from the research stage to the introduction into production of the results obtained, and also carry out work connected with the solution of integrated inter-branch scientific and technological questions.

36. Direct the activity of scientific research institutions and of construction-drafting organizations in the ministry's system and carry out measures to improve the planning and organization of scientific research and experimental construction work and to raise their efficiency.

37. Provide scientific research institutions and construction-drafting organizations with necessary production-experimentation facilities corresponding to contemporary technological standards.

38. Ensure the working out and introduction into production of new types of products corresponding to contemporary achievements in science and technology and to the needs of the national economy, and also the working out and introduction into production of high-efficiency technological processes and methods of organization of production, [and] carry out measures for integrated mechanization and automation of production and for utilization of more economical materials and raw materials.

In agreement with the appropriate ministries and departments of the USSR, decide questions concerning the removing of obsolete products from production.

Study the experience of expolitation and utilization of products turned out, [and] devise and take measures to eliminate construction and production defects uncovered in products [and] to increase the dependability and lengthen the period of service of items.

39. Work out and present for confirmation drafts of state standards; ensure introduction of state standards and contemporary means and methods of measuring and testing the quality of goods, and also [ensure] supervision over observance of standards and over the condition of measuring and testing equipment.

For individual types of goods for which there are no state standards, confirm normative technological documentation for the branch.

40. Organize scientific and technological information services, ensure the preparation and issuance in the established procedure of scientific and technological literature for the branch.

41. Direct the development of invention and rationalization; work out perspec-

tive and current topical plans for invention and rationalization; ensure introduction of inventions and rationalization proposals. A ministry shall conduct work in the development of invention and rationalization jointly with the Central Committee of the trade union and the Central Council of the All-Union Society of Inventors and Rationalizers.

42. Ensure extensive study and utilization of domestic and foreign patent data in working out new and improving existing techniques and technology and [ensure] the patentability of machinery, instruments, equipment, and other products, as well as of technological processes; ensure that enterprises and scientific research and other organizations present, in the established procedure, applications for issuance of USSR author's certificates and, when expedient, for patenting inventions abroad.

43. Work out and present, in the established procedure, proposals for the purchase abroad of licenses for the most technologically and economically progressive machinery, equipment, materials, and technological processes; ensure the speediest mastery of production of products under licenses which have been purchased.

In the field of capital construction a USSR ministry shall:

44. Carry out capital construction in the ministry's system, ensure the efficient utilization of capital investment, rational location of new construction, preferential development of the more progressive production sectors of the branch, priority channeling of capital investment for technological re-equipping of existing enterprises, improvement of inter-branch and intra-branch proportions, concentration of capital investment in construction projects nearing completion, and reduction of uncompleted construction.

Capital construction shall, as a rule, be conducted by means of sub-contracts.

45. Work out and confirm, in the established procedure, technological and economic standards and indicators, optimal capacities for enterprises in the branch which are being newly constructed, re-constructed, or enlarged, and norms for the drafting of technological improvements.

Ensure the working out and confirmation of technological and economic criteria and assignments for planning the construction of new enterprises, buildings, and structures in the branch and [for planning] the reconstruction and enlargement of existing ones.

46. Work out and confirm, in the established procedure, lists of construction projects, as well as lists of projected exploratory operations for construction in future years.

Ensure the prompt working out, confirmation, and issuance to construction projects of the necessary documentation for plans and budgets.

Exercise supervision over the quality of the documentation for plans and budgets and over observance of the budget cost which has been confirmed for the construction, as well as technical supervision over the quality of construction and installation work and of equipment delivered for buildings under construction; organize supervision by the designers over construction.

47. Ensure the financing of construction projects and the supplying of them with equipment, materials, and items whose delivery is the obligation of the party placing the order.

Exercise supervision over the placing of orders for equipment for capital construction by subordinate enterprises and organizations, in accordance with the funds and appropriations allotted for its acquisition.

Work out measures to mobilize internal resources in construction and exercise supervision over their fulfillment.

48. Ensure that production capacities and basic assets be put into use promptly and also that production capacities be mastered rapidly.

Appoint, within the limits of its competence, state commissions for the acceptance for exploitation of enterprises, buildings, and structures whose construction has been completed, confirm documents of acceptance, and take decisions to close the overall budget-finance accounts.

49. Organize capital repair of basic assets, ensuring modernization and improvement of the technological level and productivity of equipment, as well as improvement of the technological and operational condition of buildings and structures; carry out measures to raise the quality of repair work and to reduce its cost.

In the field of material-technical supply a USSR ministry shall:

50. Determine the needs of enterprises, organizations, and institutions in the ministry's system for raw materials, fuel, equipment, and other material resources, dispose of the material resources allocated to the ministry, and bear responsibility for material-technical supply of such enterprises, organizations, and institutions.

51. Distribute the funds allocated to the ministry for raw materials, fuel, equipment, and other material resources among union-republican ministries of the same name and among enterprises, organizations, and institutions of union rank, and also re-distribute the aforementioned funds, in necessary instances, taking into

account fulfillment and over-fulfillment of the production program and the plan of capital construction.

52. Work out and confirm plans for intra-branch cooperative deliveries of goods, taking into account the ensuring of delivery of products to users in other branches.

53. Exercise supervision over the use of funds in raw materials, fuel, equipment, and other material resources, as well as over prompt conclusion of contracts for the delivery of products and over the fulfillment of contractual obligations by enterprises, organizations, and institutions in the ministry's system.

54. Ensure proper storage and utilization of raw materials, fuel, equipment, and other material resources by enterprises, organizations, and institutions of the ministry's system, and take measures for the disposition of superfluous and unused material resources.

55. Work out and carry out measures for economical expenditure of materials, raw materials, and fuel, for reduction of production losses, for utilization of production by-products and secondary raw materials, and other measures directed to the efficient utilization of material resources.

In the field of finance and credit a USSR ministry shall:

56. Carry out measures to strengthen [the system of] economic accountability, to raise the profitability and maximize the accumulations of enterprises and organizations in the ministry's system, [and] to utilize efficiently basic assets, circulating assets, and bank credits.

Finance, in the established procedure, enterprises, organizations, and institutions of union rank and direct their financial activity.

Exercise supervision over utilization of financial resources in the ministry's system.

57. Ensure fulfillment of financial plans by union-republican ministries of the same name and by enterprises and organizations of union rank, preservation of its own circulating assets, prompt settlement of accounts with workers and employees, with the budget, with suppliers, with contractors, and with the banks, as well as transfer by enterprises and organizations of their own assets designated for financing capital construction and capital repair and for other aims envisaged by the financial plan.

58. Form, in the established procedure, a fund for mastering new techniques, a fund for bonuses for creation and introduction of new techniques, and other centralized funds, as well as reserves for giving financial aid to enterprises and organizations of union rank.

59. Organize, jointly with banking institutions, the introduction of the most economic and progressive forms of settlement of accounts in order to facilitate acceleration of payments, liquidity of circulating assets, and the strengthening of payments discipline; participate in organizaing and conducting offsets of mutual indebtedness by enterprises, organizations, and institutions in the ministry's system.

60. Open in banks general accounts for redistributing among enterprises and organizations of union rank their own circulating assets, profit, sums for formation of the fund for mastering new technology, and other assets, as well as separate accounts for assets in the reserve for financial aid to enterprises and organizations and assets in the reserve for amortization deductions for capital repair.

61. Consider the overall reports and balance sheets of union-republican ministries of the same name, confirm reports and balance sheets of chief administrations, of administrations and sections of the ministry, [and] of enterprises, organizations, and institutions of union rank; compile overall reports and balance sheets for the various types of the ministry's activity.

62. Organize supervisory and inspection work in the ministry's system; ensure, in accordance with the legislation in force on departmental supervision, the regular holding of inspections, the comprehensive analysis of the state of economic acitvity, the verification of preservation of monetary assets and material values, [and] the observance of economy measures; exercise supervision over the correct handling and reliability of accounting and reporting in the ministry's system, as well as over measures taken to protect state property and to compensate for material damage which has been caused.

In the field of cadres, labor, and wages a USSR ministry shall:

63. Provide enterprises, organizations, and institutions in the ministry's system with qualified cadres of personnel, organize the training of cadres and the raising of their qualifications; study the cadres in the ministry's sytem, ensure a combination of old experienced cadres and young capable personnel, create conditions for promoting to executive work politically mature specialists who know their work well and enjoy respect and confidence in the collective; take measures directed to the creation of permanent cadres in the ministry's system.

64. Work out the basic directions of the improvement of the scientific organization of labor in the branch, and direct the work of introducing the scientific organization of labor and administration in enterprises, organizations, and insti-

tutions in the ministry's sytem; ensure the taking of measures for further improvement of working conditions and for making them more healthy, and for strict observance of safety rules and the requirements of production sanitation.

65. Work out and introduce, in the established procedure, in enterprises, organizations, and institutions in the ministry's system, uniform and model norms of production (or of service), standards for number of personnel, [and] wage-qualifications manuals.

Jointly with the Central Committee of the trade union, organize the work of reviewing norms of production (and service) in enterprises and organizations in the ministry's system and carry out other measures to improve the normatization of labor.

66. Confirm model organizational frameworks and model staffs for enterprises, organizations, and institutions in the ministry's system.

67. Ensure correct application of existing conditions for the payment of labor and the giving of bonuses as well as a correct correlation between the growth of labor productivity and growth of wages; exercise supervision over the expenditure of wage funds and incentive funds.

68. Establish and modify salaries for personnel of the ministry's central apparatus, observing salary schedules and not exceeding the limits of the wage fund calculated on the basis of average salaries.

69. Work out and confirm, in agreement with the Central Committee of the trade union, or present for confirmation, branch norms on labor protection and rules on the techniques of safety and of production sanitation.

70. Jointly with the Central Committee of the trade union, determine the basic directions of collective contracts, taking into account the concrete tasks for development of the branch, direct the conclusion of collective contracts, and exercise supervision over their fulfillment.

71. Ensure, with the assistance of the Central Committee of the trade union, improvement of housing, recreational, and everyday living conditions for the personnel of enterprises, organizations, and institutions in the ministry's system, as well as the carrying out of health measures.

72. Jointly with the Central Committee of the trade union, organize socialist competition, confirm conditions for all-union competition in the ministry's system, institute, in the established procedure, circulating Red Banners with money bonuses, foster the development of the movement for communist labor [and] for a

high degree of professionalism in production.

Jointly with the Central Committee of the trade union, total the results of socialist competition and award the circulating Red Banners and money bonuses to the winning collectives, confer titles on enterprise and organization collectives of communist labor, organize the study, the summarizing, and the dissemination of progressive labor methods and progressive experience.

In the field of economic, scientific and technological, and cultural ties with foreign countries a USSR ministry shall:

73. Carry on economic, scientific and technological, and cultural ties with foreign countries in the established procedure and ensure fulfillment of obligations of the USSR pertaining to the branch which arise out of treaties and agreements concluded with foreign states.

74. Work out measures for long-range development of economic and scientific and technological collaboration in the field of the particular branch of the economy between the USSR and socialist countries on the principles of mutual advantage and comradely mutual assistance.

Prepare proposals for coordination of plans for developing the branch with plans for developing corresponding branches in the member countries of the Council of Economic Mutual Assistance and other interested socialist states, as well as proposals for development of economically efficient and stable inter-state specialization and cooperation in the branch.

75. Ensure fulfillment of assignments for production of export goods corresponding to the demands of foreign markets, take measures to expand the production for export of goods whose sale yields a high return in foreign exchange, take part in working out and carrying out measures related to problems of export of products of the branch, as well as to problems of the import of goods the demand for which it is economically expedient to satisfy through purchase abroad.

76. The present General Statute, insofar as it pertains to the mutual relations of a USSR ministry with union-republican ministries of the same name, relates as well to union-republican chief administrations, administrations, and combines of the same name and to other union-republican agencies of the republics which form part of the system of the USSR ministry.

77. A USSR ministry shall have a seal bearing a depiction of the State Arms of the USSR and its own name.

5. STATUTE ON ELECTIONS TO THE
SUPREME SOVIET

Introductory Note

The Statute on Elections to the Supreme Soviet of the USSR, enacted January 9, 1950, superseded the only previous such statute, issued in 1937 by the USSR Central Executive Committee in preparation for the first elections to the Supreme Soviet, which had been created by the USSR Constitution of 1936. The 1950 law raised the minimum age for deputies from eighteen to twenty-three years (in conformity with a constitutional amendment) and changed the size of electoral areas and sectors. Since 1950 the only important amendment has been the elimination of deprivation of voting rights as a criminal penalty (again as result of a constitutional amendment).

Prior to 1936, soviets (the word means "council") existed only at the rural district and city level. These soviets were elected directly by the people. Deputies to soviets in turn elected congresses of soviets at higher levels. These congresses of soviets, together with local soviets in the cities, jointly elected the USSR Congress of Soviets, the highest legislative agency in the country.

The USSR Constitution of 1936 replaced the congresses of soviets with supreme soviets at the USSR, republican and autonomous republic levels and with soviets at the regional level. All these new soviets, like the older city and rural soviets, are elected by popular vote.

Elections to union-republican supreme soviets, to autonomous republic supreme soviets, and to lower soviets are modeled on those to the USSR Supreme Soviet, but are conducted on the basis of separate electoral statutes. The Statute on Elections to Territorial, Regional, Area, District, City, Rural, and Settlement Soviets of Working People's Deputies of the RSFSR, for example, varies from the Statute on Elections to the Supreme Soviet of the USSR in the time periods established for registering candidates and for posting lists of voters and lists of electoral areas prior to elections and in the size of electoral areas and

98

electoral commissions; in addition, the minimum age for deputies to RSFSR territorial, regional, area, district, city, rural, and settlement soviets is eighteen,
while the corresponding minimum is twenty-three years for deputies to the USSR
Supreme Soviet. Since all soviets at the republican level and below are unicam-
eral, electoral statutes provide for single electoral areas rather than the two
separate electoral areas required for elections to the two chambers of the USSR
Supreme Soviet.

STATUTE ON ELECTIONS TO THE
SUPREME SOVIET OF THE USSR

(confirmed by an edict of the Presidium of the Supreme Soviet
of the USSR, January 9, 1950, with amendments and additions made
by edicts of the Presidium of the Supreme Soviet of the USSR of
December 27, 1961, and March 19, 1966)

CHAPTER I

The Electoral System

Article 1. On the basis of Article 134 of the Constitution of the USSR, elections of deputies to the Supreme Soviet of the USSR shall be carried out by the voters on the basis of universal, equal, and direct suffrage by secret ballot.

Article 2. On the basis of Article 135 of the Constitution of the USSR, elections of deputies shall be universal: all citizens of the USSR who have reached the age of 18 years, regardless of race, nationality, sex, religious confession, educational qualifications, domicile, social origin, property status, or past activities, shall have the right to participate in elections of deputies to the Supreme Soviet of the USSR, with the exception of persons who have been adjudged insane in the procedure established by law.

Article 3. Any citizen of the USSR who has reached the age of 23 years may be elected as deputy to the Supreme Soviet of the USSR regardless of race, nationality, sex, religious confession, educational qualifications, domicile, social origin, property status, or past activities.

Article 4. On the basis of Article 136 of the Constitution of the USSR, elections of deputies shall be equal: each citizen shall have one vote; all citizens shall participate in elections to the Supreme Soviet of the USSR on an equal basis.

Article 5. On the basis of Article 137 of the Constitution of the USSR, women shall participate in elections and may be elected to the Supreme Soviet of the USSR on equal terms with men.

Article 6. On the basis of Article 138 of the Constitution of the USSR, citizens serving in the Armed Forces of the USSR shall enjoy the right to elect and to be elected to the Supreme Soviet of the USSR on equal terms with all [other] citizens.

Article 7. On the basis of Article 139 of the Constitution of the USSR, elections of deputies shall be direct: the election of deputies to the Supreme Soviet of the USSR shall be carried out directly by the citizens, by direct elections.

Article 8. On the basis of Article 140 of the Constitution of the USSR, voting at elections of deputies to the Supreme Soviet of the USSR shall be secret.

Article 9. Persons residing in the territory of the USSR who are not citizens of the USSR but are citizens or subjects of foreign states shall not have the right to take part in elections or to be elected to the Supreme Soviet of the USSR.

Article 10. On the basis of Article 141 of the Constitution of the USSR, candidates in elections to the Supreme Soviet of the USSR shall be nominated by electoral areas.

Article 11. Expenses connected with holding elections to the Supreme Soviet of the USSR shall be borne by the state.

CHAPTER II

Lists of Voters

Article 12. All citizens who have the right to vote and who reside (permanently or temporarily) in the territory of a given Soviet at the time the lists are compiled and who have attained the age of 18 years by election day shall be included in the lists of voters.

Article 13. No voter may be entered in more than one list of voters.

Article 14. Persons adjudged insane in the procedure established by law shall not be entered in the lists of voters.

Article 15. Lists of voters shall be compiled in cities by executive committees of city Soviets of Working People's Deputies, in cities divided into districts by executive committees of district Soviets, in settlements by executive committees of settlement Soviets, and in rural localities by executive committees of rural (stanitsa, village, hamlet, kishlak, aul) Soviets of Working People's Deputies.

Article 16. Lists of voters who are in military units or troop formations shall be compiled over the signature of the commanding officer. All other military personnel shall be included in lists of voters at their place of residence by the appropriate executive committees of Soviets of Working People's Deputies.

Article 17. Lists of voters shall be compiled by each electoral sector according to a form confirmed by the Presidium of the Supreme Soviet of the USSR, in alphabetical order, indicating last name, first name, patronymic, age, and place of residence of the voter, and shall be signed by the president and secretary of the executive committee of the Soviet of Working People's Deputies.

Article 18. Thirty days before the elections the executive committee of a Soviet of Working People's Deputies shall post the lists of voters for public inspection or shall provide voters an opportunity to familiarize themselves with such lists in the building of the Soviet or electoral sector.

Article 19. The original of lists of voters shall be kept either in the executive committee of the Soviet of Working People's Deputies or in the military unit or troop formation.

Article 20. If a voter changes his place of residence between the time of publication of the list of voters and the day of the elections, the appropriate executive committee of the Soviet of Working People's Deputies shall issue him a "Certification of the Right to Vote" according to a form established by the Presidium of the Supreme Soviet of the USSR and shall make the notation in the list of voters: "departed;" at the new place of residence (permanent or temporary), the voter shall be included in the list of voters upon presentation of the "Certification of the Right to Vote" as well as a certificate of identity.

Article 21. Petitions concerning irregularities in the list of voters (non-inclusion in the list, exclusion from the list, distortion of a last name, first name, or patronymic, incorrect inclusion in the list) shall be submitted to the executive committee of the Soviet of Working People's Deputies which published the lists, which shall be obliged not later than 3 days thereafter to consider every petition concerning irregularities in the list of voters.

Article 22. In considering a petition concerning irregularities in the list of voters, an executive committee of a Soviet of Working People's Deputies shall be obliged either to enter the necessary corrections in the list of voters or to issue to the petitioner a written declaration of its grounds for rejecting his petition.

Article 23. In the event he disagrees with the decision of an executive com-mittee of a Soviet of Working People's Deputies concerning a question of an ir-regularity in the list of voters, the petitioner may submit a complaint to the People's Court, which shall be obliged not later than 3 days thereafter to consid-er the complaint in an open court session, calling in the petitioner and a repre-sentative of the executive committee of the Soviet, and to communicate its deci-sion promptly both to the petitioner and to the executive committee of the Soviet. The decision of the People's Court shall be final.

CHAPTER III

Electoral Areas for Elections to the Soviet
of the Union and the Soviet of Nationalities

Article 24. On the basis of Article 34 of the Constitution of the USSR, the So-viet of the Union shall be elected by the citizens of the USSR by electoral areas formed according to the norm: 300 thousand population per area. One deputy shall be elected from each electoral area for elections to the Soviet of the Union.

Article 25. On the basis of Article 35 of the Constitution of the USSR, the So-viet of Nationalities shall be elected by the citizens of the USSR by union and autonomous republics, autonomous regions, and national areas.

Electoral areas for elections to the Soviet of Nationalities shall be formed according to the norm: 32 areas in each union republic, 11 areas in each autono-mous republic, 5 areas in each autonomous region, and one electoral area in each national area. One deputy shall be elected from each electoral area for el-ections to the Soviet of Nationalities.

Article 26. Formation of electoral areas for elections to the Soviet of the Union and the Soviet of Nationalities shall be carried out by the Presidium of the Supreme Soviet of the USSR.

A list of electoral areas for elections to the Soviet of the Union and the Soviet of Nationalities shall be published by the Presidium of the Supreme Soviet of the USSR not later than two months before election day.

CHAPTER IV

Electoral Sectors

Article 27. For the receipt of ballots and the counting of votes, the territory of cities and districts forming part of electoral areas shall be divided into electoral sectors, which shall be the same for elections to the Soviet of the Union and the Soviet of Nationalities.

Article 28. Electoral sectors shall be formed in cities by executive committees of city Soviets of Working People's Deputies, in cities   divided   into districts by executive committees of district Soviets of Working People's Deputies, and in rural localities by executive committees of district Soviets of Working People's Deputies.

Electoral sectors shall be formed not later than 45 days before the elections.

Article 29. Electoral sectors shall be formed on the basis of one electoral sector for a population of 500 to 3000 people.

Article 30. In rural settlements or in groups of rural settlements containing less than 500 but not under 100 people, separate electoral sectors may be formed.

Article 31. In distant northern and eastern districts where small settlements predominate, as well as in mountain districts, electoral sectors may be formed with a population of less than 100 people, but not under 50 people.

Article 32. Military units and troop formations shall constitute separate electoral sectors numbering not less than 50 and not more than 3000 voters, which shall form part of the electoral area at the place where the unit or troop formation is located.

Article 33. On vessels with not less than 25 voters which are under sail on election day, separate electoral sectors may be formed which shall form part of the electoral area at the place where the vessel is registered.

Article 34. At hospitals, maternity homes, sanitoria, and homes for invalids with not less than 50 voters, separate electoral sectors shall be formed.

In hospitals with several wings, electoral sectors may be formed for separate wings if each of them contains not less than 50 voters.

Article 35. For receipt of ballots from voters having a "Certification of the Right to Vote" who are in transit on election day, electoral sectors shall be formed in long-distance passenger trains, as well as at large railroad stations and in airports.

CHAPTER V

Electoral Commissions

Article 36. The Central Electoral Commission for elections to the Supreme Soviet of the USSR shall be composed of representatives from professional organizations of workers and employees, cooperative organizations, communist party organizations, youth organizations, and from cultural, technical, and scholarly societies and other social organizations and societies of the working people registered in the procedure established by law, as well as [representatives] from meetings of workers and employees at enterprises and institutions, military personnel in military units, meetings of peasants in collective farms and rural localities, and state farm workers and employees in state farms.

Article 37. The Central Electoral Commission shall include a president, vice-president, secretary, and 24 members and shall be established by the Presidium of the Supreme Soviet of the USSR not later than 50 days before the elections.

Article 38. The Central Electoral Commission shall:

(a) oversee in the course of the elections strict execution of the "Statute on Elections to the Supreme Soviet of the USSR" throughout the territory of the USSR;

(b) consider complaints against improper actions of electoral commissions and render final decisions on [such] complaints;

(c) establish sample voting boxes, a form and color for ballots, a form for the protocol of the Area Electoral Commission for registration of candidates, a form for protocols for counting of votes, a form for certifications of election, and sample seals for electoral commissions;

(d) register elected deputies in the Supreme Soviet of the USSR;

(e) turn the record of election proceedings over to the credentials commissions of the Soviet of the Union and of the Soviet of Nationalities.

Article 39. In each union and autonomous republic, autonomous region, and national area, there shall be formed Electoral Commissions of the union or autonomous republic, autonomous region, or national area for elections to the Soviet of Nationalities.

Article 40. Electoral Commissions for elections to the Soviet of Nationalities shall be composed of representatives from professional organizations of workers and employees, cooperative organizations, communist party organizations, youth organizations, and from cultural, technical, and scholarly societies and other social organizations and societies of the working people registered in the procedure established by law, as well as [representatives] from meetings of workers and employees at enterprises and institutions, military personnel in military units, meetings of peasants in collective farms and rural localities, and state farm workers and employees in state farms.

Article 41. Electoral Commissions of a union or autonomous republic, autonomous region, or national area for elections to the Soviet of Nationalities shall include a president, vice-president, secretary, and 10 to 16 members and shall be confirmed by Presidiums of the Supreme Soviets of union or autonomous republics or by executives committees of Soviets of Working People's Deputies of autonomous regions or national areas not later than 50 days before the elections.

Article 42. The Electoral Commission of a union or autonomous republic, autonomous region, or national area for elections to the Soviet of Nationalities shall:

(a) oversee in the course of the elections to the Soviet of Nationalities strict execution of the "Statute on Elections to the Supreme Soviet of the USSR" in the territory of the republic, autonomous region, or national area;

(b) consider complaints against improper actions of electoral commissions for elections to the Soviet of Nationalities.

Article 43. In each area for elections to the Soviet of the Union there shall be formed an Area Electoral Commission for elections to the Soviet of the Union.

Article 44. Area Electoral Commissions for elections to the Soviet of the Union shall be composed of representatives from professional organizations of workers and employees, cooperative organizations, communist party organizations, youth organizations, and from cultural, technical, and scholarly societies and other social organizations and societies of the working people registered in the procedure established by law, as well as [representatives] from meetings of workers and employees at enterprises and institutions, military personnel in military units, meetings of peasants in collective farms and rural localities, and state farm workers and employees in state farms.

Article 45. Area Electoral Commissions for elections to the Soviet of the Union shall include a president, vice-president, secretary, and 8 members and shall be confirmed in republics with division into territories or regions by executive committees of territorial or regional Soviets of Working People's Deputies, and in republics without division into regions or territories by Presidiums of Supreme Soviets of republics not later than 50 days before the elections.

Article 46. An Area Electoral Commission for elections to the Soviet of the Union shall:

(a) oversee in the course of the elections to the Soviet of the Union strict execution of the "Statute on Elections to the Supreme Soviet of the USSR" in the territory of its electoral area;

(b) consider complaints against improper actions of Sector Electoral Commissions and render decisions on [such] complaints;

(c) oversee timely formation of electoral sectors by the appropriate executive committees of Soviets of Working People's Deputies;

(d) oversee timely compilation and public notification of lists of voters;

(e) register candidates for deputy who have been nominated in accordance with the requirements of the Constitution of the USSR and the "Statute on Elections to the Supreme Soviet of the USSR;"

(f) supply Sector Electoral Commissions with ballots for elections to the Soviet of the Union conforming to the established form;

(g) count the votes and determine the results of elections for the area;

(h) issue a certification of election to a deputy who has been elected;

(i) present the record of election proceedings to the Central Electoral Commission.

Article 47. In each area for elections to the Soviet of Nationalities there shall be formed an Area Electoral Commission for elections to the Soviet of Nationalities.

Article 48. Area Electoral Commissions for elections to the Soviet of Nationalities shall be composed of representatives from professional organizations of workers and employees, cooperative organizations, communist party organizations, youth organizations, and from cultural, technical, and scholarly societies and other social organizations and societies of the working people registered in the procedure established by law, as well as [representatives] from meetings of workers and employees at enterprises and institutions, military personnel in military units, meetings of peasants in collective farms and rural localities, and state farm workers and employees in state farms.

Article 49. Area Electoral Commissions for elections to the Soviet of Nationalities shall include a president, vice-president, secretary, and 8 members
and shall be confirmed by Presidiums of Supreme Soviets of union and autonomous republics and by executive committees of Soviets of Working People's Deputies of autonomous regions and national areas not later than 50 days before the
elections.

Article 50. An Area Electoral Commission for elections to the Soviet of the
Nationalities shall:

(a) oversee in the course of the elections to the Soviet of Nationalities strict
execution of the "Statute on Elections to the Supreme Soviet of the USSR" in the
territory of its electoral area;

(b) consider complaints against improper actions of Sector Electoral Commissions and render decisions on [such] complaints;

(c) oversee timely formation of electoral sectors by the appropriate executive
committees of Soviets of Working People's Deputies;

(d) oversee timely compilation and public notification of lists of voters;

(e) register candidates for deputy who have been nominated in accordance
with the requirements of the Constitution of the USSR and the "Statute on Elections to the Supreme Soviet of the USSR;"

(f) supply Sector Electoral Commissions with ballots for elections to the Soviet of Nationalities conforming to the established form:

(g) count the votes and determine the results of elections for the area;

(h) issue a certification of election to a deputy who has been elected;

(i) present the record of election proceedings either to the Electoral Commission of the union or autonomous republic for elections to the Soviet of Nationalities or to the Electoral Commission of the autonomous region or national area
for elections to the Soviet of Nationalities, as appropriate.

Article 51. In every electoral sector there shall be formed a Sector Electoral
Commission which shall be the same for elections to the Soviet of the Union and
the Soviet of Nationalities.

Sector Electoral Commissions shall be composed of representatives from
professional organizations of workers and employees, cooperative organizations,
communist party organizations, youth organizations, and from cultural, technical,
and scholarly societies and other social organizations and societies of the work-

ing people registered in the procedure established by law, as well as [represent-atives] from meetings of workers and employees at enterprises and institutions, military personnel in military units, meetings of peasants in collective farms and rural localities, and state farm workers and employees in state farms.

Article 52. Sector Electoral Commissions shall include a president, vice-president, secretary, and 4 to 8 members and, in electoral sectors containing a population of less than 300 people, a president, secretary, and 1 to 3 members, and shall be confirmed in cities by executive committees of city Soviets of Work-ing People's Deputies, in cities wi th division into districts by executive commit-tees of district Soviets, and in rural areas by executive committees of district Soviets not later than 40 days before the elections.

The president or secretary of a Sector Electoral Commission shall be freed from his usual work 30 days before election day with pay at his usual place of work.

Article 53. A Sector Electoral Commission shall:

(a) accept petitions concerning irregularities in the list of voters and submit them for consideration by the executive committee of the Soviet which published the list;

(b) receive ballots for the electoral sector;

(c) count the votes for each candidate for deputy;

(d) transfer the record of election proceedings either to the Area Electoral Commission for elections to the Soviet of the Union or to the Area Electoral Commission for elections to the Soviet of Nationalities, as appropriate.

Article 54. Sessions of the Central Electoral Commission, of Electoral Com-missions for elections to the Soviet of Nationalities of union and autonomous re-publics, autonomous regions, and national areas, of Area Electoral Commissions for elections to the Soviet of the Union, and of Area Electoral Commissions for elections to the Soviet of Nationalities, as well as of Sector Electoral Commis-sions, shall be considered valid if more than half the total membership of the commissions participates in them.

Article 55. All questions in electoral commissions shall be decided by a simple majority of the votes; if the votes are evenly divided, the vote of the pre-sident shall be decisive.

Article 56. The Central Electoral Commission, Electoral Commissions of union and autonomous republics, autonomous regions, and national areas for elections to the Soviet of Nationalities, Area Electoral Commissions for elections to the Soviet of the Union, Area Electoral Commissions for elections to the Soviet of Nationalities, and Sector Electoral Commissions shall have their own seals according to a model established by the Central Electoral Commission.

CHAPTER VI

Procedure for Nominating Candidates for
Deputy of the Supreme Soviet of the USSR

Article 57. On the basis of Article 141 of the Constitution of the USSR, candidates for deputy shall be nominated by electoral areas.

The right of nominating candidates for deputy of the Supreme Soviet of the USSR shall be guaranteed to social organizations and societies of the working people — communist party organizations, trade unions, cooperative organizations, youth organizations, and cultural societies.

Article 58. The right of nominating candidates for deputy of the Supreme Soviet of the USSR shall be exercised both by the central agencies of social organizations and societies of the working people and by their republican, territorial, regional, and district agencies, as well as by general meetings of workers and employees at enterprises and institutions and of military personnel in military units, and by general meetings of peasants in collective farms and rural localities and of state farm workers and employees in state farms.

Article 59. A candidate for deputy of the Supreme Soviet of the USSR may be voted for in only one area.

Article 60. Candidates for deputy may not be members of Area Electoral Commissions for elections to the Soviet of the Union or to the Soviet of Nationalities or of the Sector Electoral Commissions of that area where they have been nominated as candidates for deputy.

Article 61. A social organization or society of the working people which has nominated a candidate for deputy of the Supreme Soviet of the USSR shall be obliged to present the following documents to the Area Electoral Commission for registration of the candidate:

(a) a protocol of the meeting or session at which the candidate for deputy was nominated, signed by the members of the Presidium and indicating their place of residence; the protocol must indicate the name of the organization which nominated the candidate, the place, time, and number of participants of the meeting or session, the last name, first name, and patronymic of the candidate for deputy, his age, place of residence, party membership or non-membership,and occupation;

(b) a declaration of the candidate for deputy of his agreement to be voted for in the given electoral area from the organization which nominated him.

Article 62. Not later than 30 days before the elections, all social organizations or societies of the working people which have nominated candidates for deputy of the Supreme Soviet of the USSR shall be obliged to register the candidates for deputy either in the Area Electoral Commission for elections to the Soviet of the Union or in the Area Electoral Commission for elections to the Soviet of Nationalities, as appropriate.

Article 63. Area Electoral Commissions for elections to the Soviet of the Union and for elections to the Soviet of Nationalities shall be obliged to register all candidates for deputy of the Supreme Soviet of the USSR nominated by social organizations and societies of the working people in accordance with the requirements of the Constitution of the USSR and the "Statute on Elections to the Supreme Soviet of the USSR."

Article 64. The last name, first name, patronymic, age, occupation, and party membership or non-membership of every registered candidate for deputy of the Supreme Soviet of the USSR, and the name of the social organization which nominated the candidate, shall be published either by the Area Electoral Commission for elections to the Soviet of the Union or by the Area Electoral Commission for elections to the Soviet of Nationalities, as appropriate, not later than 25 days before the elections.

Article 65. All registered candidates for deputy of the Supreme Soviet of the USSR must be included on the ballot.

Article 66. The refusal of an Area Electoral Commission for elections to the Soviet of the Union to register a candidate for deputy may be appealed within two days to the Central Electoral Commission, whose decision shall be final.

Article 67. The refusal of an Area Electoral Commission for elections to the Soviet of Nationalities to register a candidate may be appealed within two days to the Electoral Commission of the union or autonomous republic, autonomous region, or national area, and the decision of the latter [may be appealed] to the Central Electoral Commission. The decision of the Central Electoral Commission shall be final.

Article 68. An Area Electoral Commission for elections to the Soviet of the Union and an Area Electoral Commission for elections to the Soviet of Nationalities shall be obliged, not later than 15 days before the elections to the Supreme Soviet of the USSR, to print and send out ballots to all Sector Electoral Commissions.

Article 69. Ballots shall be printed according to a form established by the Central Electoral Commission in the languages of the population of the relevant electoral area and in an amount sufficient for all the voters.

Article 70. Every organization which has nominated a candidate registered in an Area Electoral Commission, as well as every citizen of the USSR, shall be guaranteed the right of unrestricted campaigning [literally, agitation] for such candidate at meetings, in the press, and by other methods, according to Article 125 of the Constitution of the USSR.

CHAPTER VII

Procedure for Voting

Article 71. Elections to the Supreme Soviet of the USSR shall be conducted in the course of a single day, which shall be the same for the entire USSR.

Article 72. A day for elections to the Supreme Soviet of the USSR shall be established by the Presidium of the Supreme Soviet of the USSR not later than two months before the time for elections. Elections shall be held on a non-work day.

Article 73. Every day for the last 20 days before the elections Sector Electoral Commissions shall publish or widely circulate to the voters by some other means the day of the elections and the place of the elections.

Article 74. The casting of votes by the voters shall be conducted on election day from 6 o'clock in the morning until 10 o'clock in the evening local time.

Article 75. At 6 o'clock in the morning on election day the president of the

Sector Electoral Commission shall, in the presence of its members, check the ballot boxes and verify that there is a list of voters compiled according to the established form, after which he shall close and stamp the boxes with the seal of the commission and shall invite the voters to begin casting votes.

Article 76. At the polling place special rooms shall be set aside or individual booths equipped for the voters to fill out ballots. The presence in such rooms or booths of any person whatsoever, including members of the electoral commission, except for the persons voting, shall be forbidden while voters are filling out ballots.

Article 77. Each voter shall vote personally, appearing for this purpose at the polling place. Votes shall be cast by the voters by dropping ballots into a ballot box.

Article 78. A voter appearing at a polling place shall present to the secretary of the Sector Electoral Commission, or to a member of the Sector Electoral Commission authorized for such purpose, either a passport or a collective-farm booklet or a trade union card or other certificate of identity and, after his name is verified on the list of voters and a notation is made in the list of voters, shall receive ballots conforming to an established model.

Article 79. A voter in a place set aside for filling out ballots shall leave on each ballot the last name of the candidate for whom he is voting, crossing out the last names of the rest; then the voter shall proceed to a ballot box and shall drop the ballots into it.

Article 80. Voters who are unable because of illiteracy or any physical defect to fill out the ballots themselves shall have the right to invite any other voter into the room where ballots are filled out for the purpose of filling out the ballots.

Article 81. Electioneering [literally, electoral agitation] at a polling place during the casting of votes shall not be allowed.

Article 82. Persons appearing at a polling place with a "Certification of the Right to Vote" according to Article 20 of the present "Statute on Elections to the Supreme Soviet of the USSR" shall be entered by the Sector Electoral Commission on the list of voters, which shall be signed by the president and secretary of the Sector Electoral Commission.

Article 83. The president of the Sector Electoral Commission shall bear responsibility for order at a polling place, and his regulations shall be binding on all present.

113

Article 84. On election day at 10 o'clock in the evening the president of a Sector Electoral Commission shall declare the casting of votes to be concluded, and the commission shall begin opening the ballot boxes.

CHAPTER VIII

Determination of the Results of Elections

Article 85. Specially authorized representatives of social organizations and societies of the working people, as well as representatives of the press, shall have the right to be present in the place where a Sector Electoral Commission counts the votes during the counting of the votes.

Article 86. A Sector Electoral Commission, having opened the boxes, shall check by the list of voters the number of ballots cast against the number of persons who received ballots and shall enter the results of [such] a check in the protocol.

Article 87. The president of the Sector Electoral Commission shall announce the results of the voting for each ballot in the presence of all the members of the Sector Electoral Commission.

Article 88. Ballots on which the voter left [the name of] more than one candidate, as well as ballots not conforming to the established model, shall be deemed invalid.

Article 89. If doubt arises about the validity of a ballot, the question shall be decided by the Sector Electoral Commission by a vote, and a notation thereof shall be made in the protocol.

Article 90. The counting of votes cast for each candidate for deputy and the recording of the results of the voting shall be done separately for elections to the Soviet of the Union and for elections to the Soviet of Nationalities.

Article 91. The Sector Electoral Commission shall draw up according to an established form a protocol of the voting in three copies, and Sector Electoral Commissions located in the territory of autonomous republics, autonomous regions, and national areas [shall draw up a protocol] in four copies, signed by the members of the Sector Electoral Commission, including without fail the president and secretary.

Article 92. The protocol of the voting of a Sector Electoral Commission must indicate:

(a) the time of the commencement and conclusion of the casting of votes;

(b) the total number of voters who are on the list of voters;

(c) the number of voters who received ballots;

(d) the number of voters who took part in the voting, separately for elections to the Soviet of the Union and for elections to the Soviet of Nationalities;

(e) the number of ballots deemed invalid, separately for elections to the Soviet of the Union and for elections to the Soviet of Nationalities;

(f) the number of ballots on which the last names of all the candidates were crossed out, separately for elections to the Soviet of the Union and for elections to the Soviet of Nationalities;

(g) the results of the counting of the votes for each candidate;

(h) a brief exposition of petitions and complaints submitted to the Sector Electoral Commission, and decisions adopted by the Sector Electoral Commission.

Article 93. After the counting of the votes has been completed and the protocol drawn up, the president of the Sector Electoral Commission shall announce the results of the voting at a session of the commission.

Article 94. One copy of the protocol of the voting drawn up by the Sector Electoral Commission shall be forwarded within 24 hours by special courier to the Area Electoral Commission for elections to the Soviet of the Union; the second copy of the protocol of the voting drawn up by the Sector Electoral Commission shall be sent within 24 hours by special courier to the Area Electoral Commission for elections to the Soviet of Nationalities.

Article 95. All ballots (the valid separately from those deemed invalid), those for the Soviet of the Union separately from those for the Soviet of Nationalites, must be stamped with the seal of the Sector Electoral Commission and, together with the last copy of the protocol of the voting and the seal, turned over by the president of the Sector Electoral Commission for safekeeping [as follows]: in cities, to executive committees of city Soviets of Working People's Deputies, and in cities with division into districts, to executive committees of district Soviets; in rural areas, to executive committees of district Soviets of Working People's Deputies.

Article 96. Executive committees of Soviets of Working People's Deputies shall be charged with the duty of keeping ballots until [otherwise] instructed by the Presidium of the Supreme Soviet of the USSR.

Article 97. Specially authorized representatives of social organizations and societies of the working people, as well as representatives of the press, shall have the right to be present during the counting of the votes in the place where the Area Electoral Commission counts the votes.

Article 98. An Area Electoral Commission shall count the votes on the basis of the protocols presented by the Sector Electoral Commissions and shall establish the number of votes cast for each candidate for deputy.

Article 99. An Area Electoral Commission for elections to the Soviet of the Union and an Area Electoral Commission for elections to the Soviet of Nationalities from a union republic shall draw up a protocol of the voting in two copies, and an Area Electoral Commission for elections to the Soviet of Nationalities from an autonomous republic, autonomous region, or national area shall draw up a protocol of the voting in three copies, signed by the members of the Area Electoral Commission, including without fail the president and secretary.

Article 100. The protocol of the voting of an Area Electoral Commission must indicate:

(a) the number of Sector Electoral Commissions for the area;

(b) the number of Sector Electoral Commissions which presented protocols of voting;

(c) the total number of voters for the area;

(d) the number of voters who received ballots;

(e) the number of voters who took part in the voting;

(f) the number of ballots deemed invalid;

(g) the number of ballots on which the last names of all the candidates were crossed out;

(h) the number of votes cast for each candidate for deputy;

(i) a brief exposition of petitions and complaints submitted to the Area Electoral Commission, and decisions adopted by the Area Electoral Commission.

Article 101. After the protocol has been signed, the president of an Area Electoral Commission at a meeting of the commission shall announce the results of the elections.

Article 102. A candidate for deputy of the Supreme Soviet of the USSR who has received an absolute majority of the votes, i.e., more than one half of all the votes cast for the area and deemed valid, shall be considered elected.

Article 103. The president of an Area Electoral Commission shall issue to a candidate who has been elected as a deputy a certification of his election as a deputy of the Supreme Soviet of the USSR.

Article 104. Not later than 24 hours after the counting of the votes has been completed the president of an Area Electoral Commission for elections to the Soviet of the Union, as well as the president of an Area Electoral Commission for elections to the Soviet of Nationalities, shall be obliged to send the first copy of the protocol in typewritten form by special courier to the Central Electoral Commission and the second copy of the protocol to the Electoral Commission of the union republic, autonomous republic, autonomous region, or national area for elections to the Soviet of Nationalities.

Article 105. If none of the candidates received an absolute majority of the votes, the appropriate Area Electoral Commission shall make a special notation to that effect in the protocol and shall inform the Central Electoral Commission and the Electoral Commission of the union or autonomous republic, autonomous region, or national area for elections to the Soviet of Nationalities and shall at the same time announce a run-off between the two candidates who received the greatest number of votes and shall also name a day for the run-off not later than two weeks after the conclusion of the first round of the elections.

Article 106. If the number of votes cast for the area is less than half the number of voters having the right to vote for that area, all Area Electoral Commission for elections to the Soviet of the Union or for elections to the Soviet of Nationalities shall make a notation to that effect in the protocol and shall without delay inform the Central Electoral Commission and the Electoral Commission of the union or autonomous republic, autonomous region, or national area for elections to the Soviet of Nationalities. In such event the Central Electoral Commission shall order new elections not later than two weeks after the first elections.

Article 107. A run-off between candidates for deputy as well as new elections in lieu of those deemed invalid shall be conducted according to the lists of voters compiled for the first elections and in full conformity with the present "Statute on Elections to the Supreme Soviet of the USSR."

Article 108. In the event of the departure of a deputy from membership in the Supreme Soviet of the USSR, the Presidium of the Supreme Soviet of the USSR, not later than two months after the departure of the deputy from membership in the Supreme Soviet of the USSR, shall order elections of a new deputy in the appropriate electoral area.

Article 109.   Anyone who through force, deception, threats, or bribery shall obstruct a citizen of the USSR in the free exercise of his right to elect and to be elected to the Supreme Soviet of the USSR shall bear the criminal responsibility established by law.

Article 110.   An official or member of an election commission who has forged electoral documents, knowingly miscounted votes, or violated the secrecy of voting shall bear the criminal responsibility established by law.

6. STATUTE ON PERMANENT COMMISSIONS OF THE SUPREME SOVIET

Introductory Note

The 1967 Statute on Permanent Commissions of the Soviet of the Union and of the Soviet of Nationalities of the Supreme Soviet of the USSR is the first general statute ever enacted to regulate the permanent commissions which function in each of the two chambers of the USSR Supreme Soviet. Previously, there had been individual statutes for certain of the permanent commissions, while others operated without statutes.

The 1967 statute brings about no fundamental change in the operations of the commissions, but was enacted in response to the significant increase in the number of commissions which took place in 1966. Previously the only permanent commissions had been the commissions of legislative proposals, budget commissions, foreign affairs commissions, credentials commissions, and (in the Soviet of Nationalities only) the economic commission. In 1966 there were added permanent commissions for industry, transport, and communications, for construction and the construction materials industry, for agriculture, for health and social insurance, for education, science, and culture, and for trade and household services. These newly-formed commissions are referred to as "branch commissions" in the Statute (Article 13). As part of this reform, the budget commissions were re-named the planning- budget commissions, and the economic commission of the Soviet of Nationalities was abolished.

Permanent commissions function not only in the all-union Supreme Soviet, but also in the supreme soviets of union and autonomous republics as well as in soviets at lower levels. (See Document 9.) Branch commissions were in fact formed in supreme soviets of union and autonomous republics during the late 1950's and early 1960's, well before they were instituted in the USSR Supreme Soviet.

STATUTE ON PERMANENT COMMISSIONS OF THE SOVIET OF THE UNION AND OF THE SOVIET OF NATIONALITIES OF THE SUPREME SOVIET OF THE USSR

(confirmed by a law of the Supreme Soviet of the USSR, October 12, 1967)

I. Fundamental Principles of the Organization and Activity of Permanent Commissions and the Procedure for their Formation

Article 1.   Permanent commissions of the Soviet of the Union and of the Soviet of Nationalities shall be auxiliary agencies of the chambers, formed for preliminary consideration and preparation of questions within the competence of the Supreme Soviet of the USSR, as well as for active assistance in carrying out decisions of the Supreme Soviet of the USSR.

Article 2.   The basic tasks of permanent commissions of the Soviet of the Union and of the Soviet of Nationalities shall be:

to work out proposals for consideration by the corresponding chamber or by the Presidium of the Supreme Soviet of the USSR;

to prepare conclusions on questions submitted for the consideration of the Supreme Soviet of the USSR or its Presidium;

to assist state agencies and organizations, as well as deputies of the Supreme Soviet of the USSR, in their work, [insofar as it relates to] carrying out decisions of the Supreme Soviet of the USSR and of its Presidium;

to exercise supervision over the activities of USSR ministries and departments [and] other all-union organizations, as well over republican and local state agencies and organizations, in carrying out the Constitution of the USSR, laws of the USSR, and other decisions of the Supreme Soviet of the USSR and of its Presidium.

In fulfilling the tasks with which they are charged, permanent commissions of the Soviet of the Union and of the Soviet of Nationalities shall be called upon in all their activity, during sessions of the Supreme Soviet of the USSR and in the interval between sessions, to facilitate the uninterrupted and efficient working of the

Supreme Soviet as the highest representative agency of state power of the USSR.

Article 3. Permanent commissions of the Soviet of the Union and of the Soviet of Nationalities, in preparing proposals on questions pertaining to state, economic, or social and cultural construction, shall proceed on the basis of a combination of the interests of the USSR as a whole with the interests of the union republics, the necessity for the rational allocation of productive forces and the integrated development and specialization of the economies of union republics and economic regions, as well as of a consideration of the national and other special features of the union and autonomous republics, autonomous regions, and national areas.

Article 4. Each chamber of the Supreme Soviet of the USSR shall form a Credentials Commission, a Legislative Proposals Commission, a Planning-Budget Commission, and a Foreign Affairs Commission, as well as commissions for branches or groups of branches of state administration (branch commissions).

Article 5. Permanent commissions shall be elected by the Soviet of the Union and by the Soviet of Nationalities from among the deputies of the corresponding chamber for the term of office of the given convocation of the Supreme Soviet of the USSR.

Permanent commissions shall be made up of a president and commission members. The number of members of the commission shall be determined by the chamber. Each permanent commission shall elect from among its members a vice-president and a secretary of the commission.

Presidents and vice-presidents of the chambers, as well as deputies who are members of the Presidium of the Supreme Soviet of the USSR, of the Council of Ministers of the USSR, or of the Supreme Court of the USSR, and the Procurator General of the USSR may not be elected to permanent commissions.

Article 6. Permanent commissions of the Soviet of the Union and of the Soviet of Nationalities shall be responsible to the chamber which elected them and accountable to it.

In the interval between sessions of the Supreme Soviet of the USSR, the activities of permanent commissions of the Soviet of the Union and of the Soviet of Nationalities shall be coordinated by the Presidium of the Supreme Soviet of the USSR.

The President of the Soviet of the Union and the President of the Soviet of Nationalities, being in charge of the internal proceedings of the [respective] chamber, shall provide assistance in organizing the work of the permanent commissions of the chamber.

Article 7. Permenent commissions of the Soviet of the Union and of the Soviet of Nationalities shall operate on the basis of the broad initiative of their numbers, of collegiality, and of public sessions.

In preparing drafts of legislation and other proposals for consideration by the Supreme Soviet of the USSR and by its Presidium [and] in supervising observance of the Constitution and of Soviet legislation, permanent commissions of the chambers shall collaborate with social organizations and shall summarize and discuss proposals of citizens.

II. Questions Related to the Competence of Permanent Commissions

Article 8. The basic direction of activity and questions related to the competence of each permanent commission of the Soviet of the Union and of the Soviet of Nationalities shall be determined by the appropriate chamber of the Supreme Soviet of the USSR and by the present Statute.

Article 9. The Credentials Commissions of the Soviet of the Union and of the Soviet of Nationalities shall be charged with:

(1) verifying the authority of deputies of the appropriate chamber on the basis of Article 50 of the Constitution of the USSR and presenting for its consideration proposals to recognize the authority of deputies who have been elected or to invalidate the election of individual deputies;

(2) preparing and submitting to the Presidium of the Supreme Soviet of the USSR proposals pertaining to elections of deputies to fill vacancies;

(3) preparing conclusions on questions connected with the immunity of a deputy or the recall of a deputy, as provided by Articles 52 and 142 of the Constitution of the USSR.

Article 10. The Legislative Proposals Commissions of the Soviet of the Union and of the Soviet of Nationalities shall be charged with:

(1) working out drafts of laws of the USSR and of decrees of the Supreme Soviet of the USSR [and] edicts and decrees of the Presidium of the Supreme Soviet of the USSR on questions connected with the strengthening of socialist legality and the administration of justice and on other questions of a general nature;

(2) considering in a preliminary way drafts of laws of the USSR and other acts of the Supreme Soviet of the USSR and of its Presidium which have been referred to them for a conclusion, and preparing appropriate conclusions;

(3) taking part, at the request of other permanent commissions, in working out drafts of laws of the USSR and other acts of the Supreme Soviet of the USSR and of its Presidium which are being prepared by the appropriate commissions;

(4) preparing proposals on questions of codification and systematization of the legislation of the USSR;

(5) hearing communications and reports of USSR ministries and departments and of other all-union organizations, as well as of republican and local state agencies and organizations, on questions of strengthening socialist legality and defending the rights and legally protected interests of citizens.

Article 11. The Planning-Budget Commissions of the Soviet of the Union and of the Soviet of Nationalities shall be charged with:

(1) considering in a preliminary way perspective and annual state plans for development of the national economy of the USSR and reports on the fulfillment of state plans submitted by the Government of the USSR for confirmation by the Supreme Soviet of the USSR;

(2) considering in a preliminary way the State Budget of the USSR and the report on fulfillment of the state budget submitted by the Government of the USSR for confirmation by the Supreme Soviet of the USSR;

(3) considering proposals concerning changes in the indicators of the national-economic plan or the State Budget of the USSR submitted to the commissions by USSR ministries or departments, by union-republican Councils of Ministers, and by the All-Union Central Council of Trade Unions, for confirmation by the Supreme Soviet of the USSR;

(4) considering and agreeing upon, in a preliminary way, comments and proposals received from other commissions about the state plan and state budget;

(5) presenting to the corresponding chamber conclusions concerning the State Plan for Development of the National Economy of the USSR and the State Budget

of the USSR [and conclusions concerning] reports about fulfillment of the national-economic plan and execution of the state budget;

(6) working out drafts of USSR laws and other proposals on questions related to planning the national economy and on budgetary and financial questions for consideration by the corresponding chamber and by the Presidium of the Supreme Soviet of the USSR, as well as preparing conclusions on such questions referred to the commission for preliminary consideration;

(7) hearing communications and reports of USSR ministries and departments and of union-republican Councils of Ministers on questions related to the fulfillment of the State Plan for Development of the National Economy of the USSR and execution of the State Budget of the USSR, as well as reports of the All-Union Central Council of Trade Unions on the receipts and expenditures of the state social insurance budget.

Article 12. The Foreign Affairs Commissions of the Soviet of the Union and of the Soviet of Nationalities shall be charged with:

(1) preparing and considering in a preliminary way questions being resolved by the Supreme Soviet of the USSR or by its Presidium related to the development of political, economic, scientific, cultural, and other ties of the USSR with foreign states, with the United Nations, and with other international organizations, as well as presenting proposals and conclusions on such questions to the corresponding chamber or to the Presidium of the Supreme Soviet of the USSR;

(2) considering in a preliminary way, on assignment from the Presidium of the Supreme Soviet of the USSR, treaties, agreements, and conventions of the USSR with other states presented for ratification or denunciation, and working out conclusions on such questions;

(3) hearing communications and reports of USSR ministries and departments and other all-union organizations which carry on political, economic, scientific, cultural, and other ties with foreign states, and of USSR ambassadors, as well as of USSR representatives in international organizations, on questions related to their activity.

Article 13. Branch commissions of the Soviet of the Union and of the Soviet of Nationalities shall be charged with:

(1) preparing drafts of USSR laws and other proposals on questions related to the development of the corresponding branch of state administration for consid-

eration by the chamber or by the Presidium of the Supreme Soviet of the USSR, as well as preparing conclusions on such questions submitted to the commission for preliminary consideration;

(2) considering in a preliminary way the appropriate sections of the State Plan for Development of the National Economy of the USSR [and] of the State Budget of the USSR and reports about their fulfillment;

(3) considering proposals submitted to the commission by USSR ministries and departments and by union-republican Councils of Ministers about amendments and additions to the corresponding sections of the national-economic plan or the State Budget of the USSR [which proposals have been] presented for confirmation by the Supreme Soviet of the USSR;

(4) communicating to the Planning-Budget Commissions comments and proposals on sections of the national-economic plan, of the state budget, and of reports about their fulfillment, and in the event the commission considers it necessary, presenting such comments and proposals directly to the chamber;

(5) hearing communications and reports of the appropriate USSR ministries and departments [and] other all-union organizations, as well as of republican and local state agencies and organizations, concerning the fulfillment of USSR laws and other decisions of the Supreme Soviet of the USSR and of its Presidium.

Article 14. Permanent commissions of one chamber of the Supreme Soviet of the USSR shall in necessary instances coordinate their work with the commission of the same name in the other chamber and shall combine efforts to carry out the tasks with which they are charged.

Article 15. Questions which relate to the competence of several permanent commissions of one or both chambers may be prepared and considered by the commissions jointly, upon the initiative of the commissions as well as upon assignment from the chambers or from the Presidium of the Supreme Soviet of the USSR.

A permanent commission may ask the opinion of other permanent commissions about questions which it is considering.

Article 16. If a permanent commission considers that a question submitted for its consideration relates also to the competence of another permanent commission or deems it necessary to express its opinion on a question being considered by another commission, then it shall have the right to submit a proposal about it to the chamber or to the Presidium of the Supreme Soviet of the USSR.

III. Rights and Duties of Permanent Commissions

Article 17. Permanent commissions of the Soviet of the Union and of the Soviet of Nationalities, when considering questions within their competence, shall enjoy equal rights and have equal duties.

Article 18. Permanent commissions of the Soviet of the Union and of the Soviet of Nationalities shall have in equal measure the right of legislative initiative.

Article 19. Permanent commissions of the Soviet of the Union and of the Soviet of Nationalities may make reports or joint reports at sessions of the Soviet of the Union and of the Soviet of Nationalities or at joint sessions of the chambers on questions within their competence.

Permanent commissions of the Soviet of the Union and of the Soviet of Nationalities shall assign a reporter or co-reporter for questions submitted by them for consideration by the Supreme Soviet of the USSR or for questions referred to the commission for a conclusion.

On questions prepared jointly by permanent commissions, the commissions may make reports or co-reports.

Article 20. Permanent commissions of the Soviet of the Union and of the Soviet of Nationalities shall submit to the respective chamber or to the Presidium of the Supreme Soviet of the USSR proposals to transfer draft laws or other questions of general state significance for nationwide discussion, as well as [proposals] to publish draft laws or other proposals for public discussion.

Proposals and comments made during a discussion shall be summarized and considered by the appropriate permanent commissions, and the results of the discussion shall be reported to the chambers.

Article 21. Permanent commissions of the Soviet of the Union and of the Soviet of Nationalities, on questions within their competence, shall have the right to hear representatives of the USSR government, USSR ministries and departments, and other all-union organizations, as well as representatives of republican and local state agencies and organizations.

Upon the proposal of a permanent commission, directors of USSR ministries and departments and other all-union organizations, as well as directors of republican and local state agencies or organizations, shall be obliged to appear at a commission session and to present explanations on questions being considered by the commission. When this is done, permanent commissions shall in ample time inform directors of the appropriate state agencies and organizations about the forthcoming consideration of questions related to their work.

Article 22. Permanent commissions of the Soviet of the Union and of the Soviet of Nationalities, on questions within their competence, shall have the right to demand presentation of documents, written conclusions, report-data, and other materials from USSR ministries and departments and other all-union organizations, as well as from republican and local state agencies and organizations, [and] from officials. All state agencies and organizations and officials shall be obliged to fulfill the demands of the commissions and to present to them necessary documents, conclusions, and other materials.

Article 23. Recommendations worked out by permanent commissions of the Soviet of the Union and of the Soviet of Nationalities on questions related to the activity of USSR ministries and departments and other all-union organizations, as well as republican and local state agencies and organizations, shall be directed to those state agencies and organizations and shall be communicated to the Presidium of the Supreme Soviet of the USSR, and in necessary instances to the Council of Ministers of the USSR or to the Council of Ministers of a union or autonomous republic.

Recommendations of permanent commissions shall be subject to obligatory consideration by state agencies and organizations. Results of the consideration or measures taken must be communicated to the permanent commission within not more than two months.

Article 24. Permanent commissions of the Soviet of the Union and of the Soviet of Nationalities shall have the right to make proposals to the Council of Ministers of the USSR.

Permanent commissions shall have the right to put questions to the Government of the USSR or to individual members of it.

Article 25. Permanent commissions of the Soviet of the Union and of the Soviet of Nationalities shall have the right to draw into their work deputies of the Supreme Soviet of the USSR who are not members of the commission, as well as representatives of ministries, departments, other state agencies, social organizations, scholarly institutions, and specialists and scholars.

Article 26. Members of permanent commissions of the Soviet of the Union and of the Soviet of Nationalities shall be obliged to participate in sessions of the commission and to fulfill its assignments.

A member of a permanent commission shall be provided with conditions [necessary] for active participation in the resolution of all questions being considered by the commission, and he shall be sent necessary documents and other materials for that purpose.

A member of a permanent commission whose proposals did not receive the support of the commission may bring them up during discussion of the corresponding question in the Supreme Soviet of the USSR or in the Presidium of the Supreme Soviet of the USSR.

Article 27. Members of permanent commissions of the Soviet of the Union and of the Soviet of Nationalities, upon assignment from the commission or on their own initiative, shall study locally questions within the competence of the commission, shall summarize proposals of state agencies, social organizations, and citizens, and shall submit their proposals to the commission.

Article 28. Members of permanent commissions of the Soviet of the Union and of the Soviet of Nationalities shall be freed from their production or service duties with full pay or average wages at their permanent place of work for the period of commission meetings, as well as for fulfillment of commission assignments.

IV. Procedure for the Work of Permanent Commissions

Article 29. Sessions of permanent commissions of the Soviet of the Union and of the Soviet of Nationalities shall be convoked as necessary and may be conducted both during sessions and in the interval between sessions of the Supreme Soviet of the USSR.

Article 30. Sessions of permanent commissions of the Soviet of the Union and of the Soviet of Nationalities shall be authorized [to act] if more than half the members of the commission are present at them.

Article 31. All questions shall be decided in permanent commissions of the Soviet of the Union and of the Soviet of Nationalities by a simple majority of the voters of the members of the commission present at the session.

When joint sessions of several permanent commissions are held, decisions shall be adopted by a simple majority of the votes of each commission.

129

Article 32. Deputies of the Supreme Soviet of the USSR who are not members of the given commission may participate in sessions of permanent commissions of the Soviet of the Union or of the Soviet of Nationalities with the right of a consultative vote.

Article 33. To sessions of permanent commissions of the Soviet of the Union and of the Soviet of Nationalities may be invited representatives of state agencies, social organizations, scholarly institutions, and specialists and scholars, who shall participate in sessions of the commission with the right of a consultative vote.

In case of necessity, a permanent commission may adopt a decision to conduct a closed session.

Article 34. For preparation of questions being considered by them, permanent commissions of the Soviet of the Union and of the Soviet of Nationalities may create subcommissions and working groups from among deputies of the Supreme Soviet of the USSR and representatives of appropriate ministries, departments, other state agencies, social organizations, scholarly institutions, specialists, and scholars.

Permanent commissions of one or of both chambers may form joint subcommissions or working groups.

Article 35. The president of a permanent commission, in directing its work, shall:

convoke sessions of the commission and organize the preparation for sessions;

call upon members of the commission for work in subcommissions or for fulfillment of other commission assignments;

invite representatives of state agencies and other organizations, [and] specialists and scholars to participate in sessions of the commission;

preside at sessions of the commission;

confer in the name of the commission with state and social organizations;

organize the work of carrying out commission decisions;

inform commission members concerning fulfillment of commission decisions and concerning consideration of its recommendations.

Joint sessions of commissions shall be conducted in turn by the presidents of these commissions.

Article 36. Decisions and conclusions of a permanent commission shall be signed by the president of the commission. Decisions adopted by permanent commissions jointly and conclusions prepared jointly by them shall be signed by the presidents of the corresponding commissions.

Protocols of sessions of a permanent commission shall be signed by the secretary of the commission.

Article 37. Permanent commissions of the Soviet of the Union and of the Soviet of Nationalities shall inform the public concerning their activities. To sessions of permanent commissions and of their subcommissions and working groups may be invited representatives of the press, radio, and television.

Communications concerning the work of commissions shall be published in the "Gazette of the Supreme Soviet of the USSR" and in the newspaper "News [Izvestiia] of the Soviets of Working People's Deputies of the USSR."

Article 38. Permanent commissions of the Soviet of the Union and of the Soviet of Nationalities shall be provided services by the apparatus of the Presidium of the Supreme Soviet of the USSR.

7. EDICT ON RURAL SOVIETS

Introductory Note

Those soviets which are not "supreme" soviets are called "local" soviets. Local soviets include not only soviets at the lowest level (city district, city, rural locality, settlement, etc.) but also soviets at intermediate levels (city, district, territory, region, autonomous region, and area). While the supreme soviets are primarily legislative in character, local soviets are primarily agencies of administration. Local soviets have no power to issue "laws" (zakony), though they have the right to pass subordinate types of "legislation" — decisions and regulations.

The edict on the basic rights and duties of rural and settlement soviets, published in April 1968, is the first comprehensive all-union legislation on rural and settlement soviets. It was issued by the Presidium of the USSR Supreme Soviet together with a much longer Model Statute on the Rural and Settlement Soviet of Working People's Deputies. The Model Statute, designed to serve as an example to the union republics in drafting statutes on rural and settlement soviets, covers the same subjects as the edict but is considerably more detailed. Prior to 1968, all the union republics possessed statutes on rural soviets, but only a few had statutes on settlement soviets.

The Law on the Rural and Settlement Soviet of Working People's Deputies of the RSFSR, adopted in July 1968, follows the all-union Model Statute on most basic points. An accompanying RSFSR decree indicated that the supreme soviets of autonomous republics were also expected to draft laws on the rural and settlement soviet which would take into account local conditions. Thus autonomous republic laws, rather than the RSFSR law, will apply in the autonomous republics.

EDICT OF THE PRESIDIUM OF THE SUPREME SOVIET
OF THE USSR ON THE BASIC RIGHTS AND DUTIES OF RURAL AND
SETTLEMENT SOVIETS OF WORKING PEOPLE'S DEPUTIES

(April 8, 1968)

For the purpose of further increasing the role of rural and settlement Soviets of Working People's Deputies in resolving the tasks of economic and social - cultural construction [and] of perfecting the democratic principles of their activities, the Presidium of the Supreme Soviet of the USSR decrees:

Article 1. A rural [or] settlement Soviet of Working People's Deputies as the agency of state power in the territory encompassed by it shall resolve, within the limits of the rights granted by law, all questions of local significance, on the basis of general state interests and of the interests of the working people of the rural locality [or] settlement.

Article 2. A rural [or] settlement Soviet of Working People's Deputies, in accordance with the Constitution of the USSR and the Constitutions of union and autonomous republics, shall direct economic and social-cultural construction in the territory of the Soviet.

In exercising its authority, a rural [or] settlement Soviet of Working People's Deputies shall direct enterprises, institutions, and organizations subordinate to the Soviet and shall also exercise supervision over the work of [the following organizations] located in the territory of the Soviet: collective farms [and] state farms; enterprises of local industry, household services, trade, public dining, and housing and municipal services; institutions of health, education, culture, [and] communications; and other organizations of higher rank directly serving the population; shall organize supervision over observance of legislation by them, shall hear reports of directors of such enterprises, institutions, and organizations, and shall coordinate their activities in the sphere of social-cultural and household servicing of the population.

Decisions and regulations of a rural [or] settlement Soviet of Working People's Deputies, adopted by it within the limits of the rights granted [to it], shall be binding on all collective farms, state farms, enterprises, institutions, and other organizations located in the territory of the Soviet, as well as on officials and citizens.

Article 3. The activities of a rural or settlement Soviet of Working People's Deputies shall be based on collectivity of leadership, publicity of proceedings, regular accountability of deputies to the voters and of the executive committee to the Soviet and the population, and wide-scale enlistment of the working people into participation in the work of the Soviet.

A rural [or] settlement Soviet of Working People's Deputies shall work in close contact with the social organizations of collective farms, state farms, enterprises, institutions, and other organizations located in the territory of the Soviet [and] shall direct the work of agencies of social self-initiative.

Article 4. A rural [or] settlement Soviet of Working People's Deputies shall:
(a) confirm plans of economic and social-cultural construction within its competence, [and] production and financial plans of subordinate enterprises, institutions, and organizations; take part in considering perspective and annual plans of collective farms, state farms, and enterprises of local industry; submit proposals with respect to drafts of production and financial plans of collective farms, state farms, enterprises, institutions, and other organizations of higher rank insofar as they concern housing construction, social-cultural, and household and trade servicing of the population, public services for rural localities and settlements, construction of local roads, and utilization of local raw materials and labor resources;

(b) confirm the rural [or] settlement budget, the liquidity of circulating accounts under the budget, and quarterly distribution of receipts and expenditures; distribute budget funds for expenditures; switch budget funds in necessary instances from one section [of the budget] to another as well as from one article [of the budget] to another (except appropriations for wages); confirm the report on execution of the rural [or] settlement budget; direct surplus funds received in the execution of the rural or settlement budget, as well as amounts by which receipts exceed expenditures at the end of the year as result of over-fulfillment of receipts or economies in expenditures, for the financing of economic and social-cultural measures within its competence, including capital investments   (withdrawal of the funds referred to from a rural [or] settlement Soviet shall not be permitted);

(c) ensure receipt of tax, insurance, and other payments from the population, carry out the work of receiving such payments in the territory of the rural Soviet; exercise supervision over timely submission of payments to the rural or settlement budget by collective farms, state farms, enterprises, and organizations located in the territory of the Soviet, as well as [the timely submission of] collective-farm deductions to the centralized union social insurance fund of collective farmers; organize self-taxation of the rural population;

(d) grant local tax and duty benefits in accordance with Article 2 of the Edict of the Presidium of the Supreme Soviet of the USSR on local taxes and duties, as well as [benefits] with respect to the preliminary conclusion of district [or] city financial agencies regarding the agricultural tax in accordance with Article 18 of the Law of the USSR on the agricultural tax; adopt decisions, in the established procedure, about the granting of money loans for individual housing construction by institutions of the State Bank of the USSR within the limits of the amount set aside for the rural or settlement Soviet;

(e) present to the executive committee of the superior Soviet comments and proposals with respect to the Charters of agricultural artels located in the territory of the Soviet; supervise observance of the Charter of an Agricultural Artel; render assistance to collective farms and state farms in the development of agricultural production, in the fulfillment of production and financial plans [and] of obligations to the state, in the efficient utilization of arable land and of material and labor resources, in the organization and development of auxiliary enterprises, in the raising of labor productivity and the strengthening of labor discipline, in raising the material and cultural level of the life of collective farmers [and] of state farm workers and employees; exercise supervision over the care and correct utilization in collective farms and state farms of agricultural equipment and structures, as well as mineral fertilizers and chemical herbicides, and over the taking of measures to protect crops and plants;

(f) adopt decisions concerning withdrawal of parcels of land from the lands of a rural population center or settlement within the limits and in the procedure established by legislation; exercise supervision over the observance by all land users of the legislation on land use, including [supervision] over correct utilization of the household plot fund

of collective farms and state farms and over observance of the norms of household land plots; resolve land disputes between citizens;

(g) direct the work of subordinate enterprises of local industry and ensure fulfillment   by them of production and financial plans; render assistance to industrial enterprises located in the territory of the Soviet in the development of
production, in the efficient utilization of material and labor resources, in the
increase of labor productivity, and in raising the material and cultural level of
the life of workers and employees;

(h) consider and submit to the executive committee of the superior Soviet
projects for planning and building up population centers; supervise observance of
building plans; suspend construction if it is carried out in violation of building
plans for population centers; exercise supervision over the course of construction
of residences, social and cultural institutions, and municipal enterprises in the
territory of the Soviet; resolve by agreement with collective farms, state farms,
enterprises, and other organizations located in the territory of the Soviet questions concerning joint utilization of their funds set aside for construction and repair of housing and municipal service buildings and, in necessary instances,
[questions] concerning the centralization of such funds;

(i) exercise supervision over fulfillment of plans for construction and repair
of automobile roads by collective farms, state farms, enterprises, and other organizations; supervise the work of transport organizations in servicing the population; give regulations to collective farms, state farms, enterprises, institutions,
and other organizations concerning the providing of transport for the struggle
against natural calamities [and] fires, [and] for the transportation of the sick [and]
visits of medical personnel to the seriously ill and in other exceptional situa-
tions; exercise supervision over the work of communications divisions and agencies in servicing the population;

(j) direct housing and municipal services within its competence and public
services for population centers; allocate the housing fund under the jurisdiction
of the Soviet; confirm joint decisions of the administration and of factory, plant,
and local committees of trade unions concerning the granting of living space in
houses of state, cooperative, and social organizations, with the exception of instances provided by legislation; take measures to provide for fuel, lighting, and
inventory of institutions of education, culture, and health which are on the rural
[or] settlement budget [and] for repair of their buildings and the creation of
necessary housing and living conditions for the personnel of such institutions;

draw collective farms, state farms, enterprises, and other organizations, regardless of their departmental subordination, into taking part in fulfilling the said measures as well as into the work of public services; combine, with the consent of collective farms, state farms, enterprises, and other organizations, assets set aside by them for public services;

(k) exercise supervision over state, cooperative, and collective-farm trade and over household services of the population; confirm plans for the location and specialization of enterprises of trade, public dining, and household services; supervise observance of the Charter of a Consumers' Society;

(l) ensure universal compulsory education; supervise the work of schools, boarding schools, children's pre-school and non-school institutions located in the territory of the Soviet; decide, in accordance with the legislation in force, questions of freeing children from paying for meals in schools (or groups) with a lengthened day operating on the rural [or] settlement budget, and questions of allocating the compulsory education fund among schools;

(m) direct the work of institutions of culture subordinate [to it]; supervise and coordinate the activities of other institutions of culture located in the territory of the Soviet regardless of their subordination; exercise supervision over the correctness of deductions and expenditures from the cultural funds of collective farms and consumers' societies and, by agreement with them, take measures in necessary instances for the centralized utilization of the said funds;

(n) direct the organization of the work of medical institutions operating on the rural [or] settlement budget; exercise supervision over the organization of the work of medical institutions of higher rank located in the territory of the Soviet;

(o) participate jointly with trade union organizations in supervision over the observance of labor legislation and the rules of labor protection and technical safety in collective farms, state farms, and enterprises located in the territory of the Soviet; supervise observance of pension legislation and the work of collective farm councils on social insurance for collective farmers; assign, within the limits of the appropriations provided in the rural [or] settlement budget, support payments to persons who do not have the right to receive a state pension; submit proposals to the executive committee of the superior Soviet for assigning support payments to mothers with many children and to unmarried mothers and for issuing single support payments to citizens who have suffered as a result of natural calamities;

(p) suspend execution of decisions of meetings of collective farmers or of consumers' society shareholders, collective farm boards, or boards of rural consumers' societies, or orders or regulations of directors of enterprises, institutions,
or organizations of higher rank, on questions of land use, public services, building up of population centers, or protection of nature or cultural monuments [when
such decisions, orders, or regulations] contradict legislation, and inform the appropriate superior agencies thereof;

(q) initiate petitions to the executive committee of the superior Soviet to con-
fer the title "Heroine-Mother" and to present [persons] to be awarded orders of
"Glory of Motherhood" and the medals "Motherhood Medal," "For Courage at a
Fire," and "For Saving a Drowning Person;"

(r) carry out in the established procedure the registering and de-registering
of citizens; perform the registration of acts of civil status in accordance with the legislation of the union republic; appoint guardians and tutors;
register divisions of family property of collective farm (or peasant) households;
perform notarial acts in accordance with the Statute on the State Notariat of the
union republic;

(s) ensure strict execution by all citizens of the Law of Universal Military Obligation; keep account in the established procedure of persons obligated to military service and inductees; take measures to organize civil defense.

Article 5. A rural [or] settlement Soviet of Working People's Deputies shall
confirm and remove from office, by agreement with the appropriate superior
agencies of state administration, directors of schools, of children's pre-school
and non-school institutions, of institutions of health and of culture, and of enterprises of municipal and household services which are subordinate to the Soviet.

Article 6. A rural [or] settlement Soviet of Working People's Deputies or
its executive committee may impose administrative sanctions on officials and
citizens for violations of public order, of rules ensuring maintenance of cleanli-
ness in population centers and protection of nature and cultural monuments, [and]
of rules of public services and the building up of population centers and of trade
in alcoholic beverages; for damage to crops caused by the grazing of animals in
collective farms and state farms; and for other violations in those instances and
in the procedure established by the legislation of the union republic.

For consideration of cases of violations of law which entail punishment in administrative procedure, a rural [or] settlement Soviet shall, in necessary instances, with the permission of the executive committee of the superior Soviet, form an administrative commission attached to the executive committee of the rural [or] settlement Soviet.

Article 7. A rural [or] settlement Soviet of Working People's Deputies, in addition to the rights and duties provided by Articles 4, 5, and 6 of the present Edict, may exercise other rights and duties in accordance with the legislation of the USSR and of the union and autonomous republics.

Article 8. For the purpose of further activization of the work of rural [and] settlement Soviets of Working People's Deputies, it shall be deemed necessary to enlarge the circle of questions decided at their sessions and to establish that only at sessions of the Soviets may the following questions be decided:

recognition of the authority of deputies; revocation of deputies' authority upon the personal petition of deputies; the adoption of decisions at the request of deputies; election and modification of the membership of the executive committee and of permanent commissions; reports on the work of the executive committee and of permanent commissions; formation of an administrative commission attached to the executive committee of the Soviet;

confirmation of plans of economic and social-cultural construction within its competence and of plans for measures to fulfill mandates of the voters; confirmation of the rural [or] settlement budget and of the report on its execution; allocation of surplus funds received through over-fulfillment of the receipt portion or economies in the expenditure portion of the rural [or] settlement budget; the combining and allocation of funds set aside by collective farms, state farms, enterprises, and other organizations for construction in housing, municipal services, culture, and household services, and for public services; consideration of comments and proposals with respect to the Charters of Agricultural Artels;

confirmation and removal from office of directors of schools, of children's pre-school and non-school institutions, of institutions of health and of culture, and of enterprises of municipal and household services;

confirmation of recommendations to the executive committee of the superior Soviet concerning the forming, combining, eliminating, or re-naming of the rural [or] settlement Soviet or concerning the establishing or changing of the boundaries of its territory.

The legislation of union and autonomous republics may provide for still other questions to be decided only at sessions of rural [or] settlement Soviets.

Article 9. A deputy of a rural [or] settlement Soviet of Working People's Deputies, during a session or meeting of an executive committee to which he has been elected, shall be freed from fulfillment of his production or service obligations with pay or average wages at his usual place of work.

A deputy of a rural [or] settlement Soviet may not be discharged from his work at an enterprise, institution, or organization at the initiative of the administration or expelled from a collective farm, and also may not be brought to criminal responsibility or arrested in the territory of the Soviet without the consent of the rural [or] settlement Soviet or, in the interval between sessions, without the consent of its executive committee.

Article 10. For discussion of the most important questions concerning the lives of citizens and for explaining to the working people the legislation and major decisions of local Soviets, the executive committee of a rural [or] settlement Soviet shall convoke general meetings and assemblies of citizens residing in the territory of the rural [or] settlement Soviet as a whole or of individual population centers, streets, or blocks, as well as meetings of representatives of residents of the rural locality [or] settlement.

At general meetings or assemblies of citizens of a population center, rural social committees may be elected which shall be accountable in their activities to the [body] which elected them—the meeting or assembly of citizens, or the rural [or] settlement Soviet or its executive committee. Rural social committees, in accordance with the legislation of the union or autonomous republic, may be charged with fulfillment of individual commissions of the executive committee of the rural Soviet in the territory of the population center.

Article 11. The Presidiums of the Supreme Soviets of union republics shall be delegated to bring the legislation of union republics on rural and settlement Soviets of Working People's Deputies into conformity with the present Edict.

Article 12. It shall be established that until the legislation in force in the USSR and union republics is brought into conformity with the present Edict, acts regulating the activities of rural and settlement Soviets of Working People's Deputies shall be applied insofar as they do not contradict the present Edict.

8. STATUTE ON THE CITY SOVIET

Introductory Note

While an all-union edict regulates rural and settlement soviets (Document 7), no comprehensive all-union legislation has yet been passed for other soviets. Legislation on such soviets has until now been left to the individual union republics. However, only two republics have enacted statutes on regional soviets, six have statutes on district soviets, and six have statutes on city soviets. The Azerbaijan SSR, whose city soviet statute is here translated, also has enacted a statute to govern its district soviets.

STATUTE ON THE CITY SOVIET OF WORKING PEOPLE'S
DEPUTIES OF THE AZERBAIJAN SSR

(confirmed by an edict of the Presidium of the Supreme Soviet
of the Azerbaijan SSR, December 29, 1958)

CHAPTER I

General Provisions

Article 1.   A city Soviet of Working People's Deputies, on the basis of Article 86 of the Constitution of the Azerbaijan   SSR, shall be the agency of state power in the city.

Article 2.   On the basis of Articles 87 and 141 of the Constitution of the Azerbaijan SSR, a city Soviet of Working People's Deputies shall be elected by the working people of the city on the basis of universal, equal, and direct suffrage by secret ballot for a term of two years.

Electoral norms and the procedure for conducting elections shall be determined by the "Statute on Elections to a Regional (the Nagorno-Karabakh Autonomous Region), District, City, Rural, and Settlement Soviets of Working People's Deputies of the Azerbaijan SSR."

Article 3.   A city Soviet of Working People's Deputies, in accordance with Article 88 of the Constitution of the Azerbaijan SSR, shall direct cultural-political and economic construction in its territory, shall establish the budget of the city, shall direct the activities of agencies of administration subordinate to it, shall ensure protection of state order, shall foster the strengthening of the defense capacity of the country, and shall ensure observance of the laws and protection of the rights of citizens.

Article 4. A city Soviet of Working People's Deputies shall:

(a) direct enterprises, institutions, and organizations within its jurisdiction;

(b) oversee the activities of enterprises, institutions, and organizations of republican and union-republican rank located in the territory of the city; have the right to hear reports of their directors, to recommend to them measures to improve the work of such enterprises, institutions, and organizations, and in necessary instances to raise questions about their work before appropriate superior agencies;

(c) foster the fulfillment of measures being carried out in the territory of the city by state agencies and social organizations;

(d) discuss questions of district, regional, republican, and all-union importance and present its proposals to superior agencies.

Article 5. A city Soviet of Working People's Deputies shall be governed in its activities by the Constitution and laws of the USSR and the Azerbaijan SSR, edicts of the Presidium of the Supreme Soviet of the USSR and the Presidium of the Supreme Soviet of the Azerbaijan SSR, decrees and regulations of the Council of Ministers of the USSR and the Council of Ministers of the Azerbaijan SSR, and decisions and regulations of its superior Soviets of Working People's Deputies and their executive committees.

Article 6. A city Soviet of Working People's Deputies shall adopt decisions and issue regulations within the limits of the rights granted it by the laws of the USSR and the Azerbaijan SSR.

Article 7. A city Soviet of Working People's Deputies shall have the right to annul decisions and regulations of inferior Soviets of Working People's Deputies and of their executive committees.

Article 8. A city Soviet of Working People's Deputies shall enjoy the rights of a legal person.

Article 9. District Soviets of Working People's Deputies in cities shall operate on the basis of the present Statute, with the exception of point "b" of Article 14, points "b," "d," "e," "h," "i," "j," "k," and "l" of Article 15, point "i" of Article 21, points "c" and "f" of Article 25, and Article 50.

Article 10. The activities of the city Soviets of Working People's Deputies of the Nakhichevan Autonomous Soviet Socialist Republic shall be defined by the Statute on the City Soviet of Working People's Deputies of the Nakhichevan ASSR.

CHAPTER II

Rights and Duties of a City Soviet of Working People's Deputies

Article 11.   In the sphere of planning a city Soviet of Working People's Deputies shall:

(a) confirm current and perspective plans for the development of [that portion of] the national economy which is within the jurisdiction of the city Soviet of Working People's Deputies and ensure their fulfillment;

(b) confirm production and financial plans as well as plans for capital construction work for enterprises of city rank and supervise their fulfillment;

(c) coordinate the working out, and supervise the fulfillment of, plans for the development of housing [and] municipal services, social and cultural construction, road construction, and public services, carried out by enterprises, institutions, and organizations not within its jurisdiction;

(d) uncover surplus resources of the city for the purpose of utilizing them rationally in the national economy;

(e) foster the discovery and study of natural resources and adopt measures to utilize them efficiently;

(f) ensure the carrying out of national-economic accounting; render assistance in the work of state statistical agencies.

Article 12.   In the sphere of budgetary and financial work a city Soviet of Working People's Deputies shall:

(a) confirm the budget of the city and the report on its execution;

(b) organize execution of the budget of the city;

(c) ensure timely financing of branches of the national economy and of social and cultural measures in accordance with the budget which has been confirmed, and [ensure] payment in the established time periods of wages to personnel of budget institutions and supervise the correctness of utilization of budget funds;

(d) exercise supervision over the observance of financial and staffing discipline and fulfillment of financial plans by enterprises, institutions, and organizations located in the territory of the city;

(e) confirm a budget for special funds of institutions which are on the city

144

budget and supervise the correctness of their utilization;

(f) direct the work of calculating and exacting, within the limits of the law, state and local taxes from enterprises, organizations, and the population, and also decide questions of granting tax benefits;

(g) direct the work of city agencies of state insurance;

(h) direct the work of state labor savings banks;

(i) foster the work of institutions of the State Bank and of special banks.

Article 13. In the sphere of industry a city Soviet of Working People's Deputies shall:

(a) direct the development of local industry of city rank;

(b) ensure fulfillment of production and construction plans by enterprises within the jurisdiction of the city Soviet, improvement of quality, observance of product mix, and lowering of the production cost of products being produced by them;

(c) oversee the activities of enterprises located in the territory of the city which are subordinate to the Council of the National Economy [or] to republican or union-republican ministries, hear reports of directors of such enterprises concerning the fulfillment of the production plans of the enterprises, [and] concerning housing construction, public services, [and] cultural and household servicing of workers and employees, and render assistance to the said enterprises in their work;

(d) confirm plans for the construction of buildings of local importance and oversee fulfillment of plans of capital construction in the city;

(e) adopt measures to increase the production of consumer goods and construction materials through use of local raw materials and by-products of industrial enterprises; ensure expansion of the network and further improvement of the work of enterprises providing household services to the population;

(f) oversee correct utilization of production capacities [and] economical expenditure of raw materials, other materials, fuel, and electrical power at enterprises within the jurisdiction of the city Soviet, as well as at enterprises of republican and union-republican rank; supervise the creation at such enterprises of proper production conditions and the observance of the rules of labor protection and technical safety;

(g) adopt measures to develop local trades and crafts, supervise the work of cooperative trade artels;

(h) ensure the wide-scale introduction of advanced labor methods and of new equipment, foster the development, by all possible means, of socialist competition for fulfillment of production plans ahead of schedule, facilitate the development of the creative initiative of workers, engineering and technical personnel, and employees at enterprises and construction projects in the further raising of labor productivity.

Article 14. In the sphere of trade a city Soviet of Working People's Deputies shall:

(a) exercise direction and supervision over state and cooperative trade and over public dining, confirm a plan for goods turnover (except for city Soviets of cities of district rank) and ensure its fulfillment;

(b) establish retail prices for goods put out by enterprises of city rank from local raw materials and from by-products of industrial enterprises when such prices are not established in the centralized procedure, with subsequent registration of the prices so established in the Council of Ministers of the Azerbaijan SSR;

(c) ensure the correct location of enterprises of trade and public dining (stores, stands, cafeterias, restaurants, buffets, and others); bring industrial goods and foods prepared from local raw materials into the goods turnover by all possible means, watch over the correct distribution of goods and their delivery into the trade network, taking into account seasonal demand and the special national and household features of the population;

(d) exercise supervision over the uninterrupted sale to the population of industrial goods and foods and of goods of prime necessity;

(e) organize the work of state and cooperative trade enterprises in the purchase, working up, and sale of agricultural products and raw materials, [and] exercise supervision over the observance of purchase and sale prices by them;

(f) ensure the development of collective farm trade [and] the expansion of the network of collective farm markets and commission stores for the sale of agricultural products;

(g) exercise supervision over the observance by trading organizations of the rules of Soviet trade [and] the established prices and over the polite servicing of purchasers in the trade network, [and] wage a struggle against speculation;

(h) exercise systematic supervision over the work of public dining enterprises; consider proposals of agencies of social supervision and adopt necessary measures with respect to them.

Article 15. In the sphere of housing and municipal services and of public
services a city Soviet of Working People's Deputies shall:

(a) direct housing and municipal services within its jurisdiction; organize the
construction, exploitation, and capital and current repair of residences and municipal enterprises (hotels, electric power stations, sewers, baths, laundries, etc.),
administrative buildings, [and] trade and warehouse and other non-residential
premises;

(b) work out a plan for building up the city, [and] exercise supervision over
the construction and the architectural composition of the city in accordance with
the plan for building it up;

(c) supervise the correct exploitation of the housing fund and of municipal enterprises, regardless of which department they belong to;

(d) exercise supervision over the construction of residences, civic buildings,
and structures, regardless of which department they belong to, and also issue
permits to commence exploitation of these buildings;

(e) allocate living space in accordance with the law and exercise supervision
over the corrrect distribution of living space in houses whose exploitation is being begun by enterprises, institutions, and organizations;

(f) foster by all possible means the development of individual and collective
housing construction in the city;

(g) organize the work of electrification and gasification of the city;

(h) have charge of all lands within the limits of the city border, no matter who
has the use of them;

(i) set aside, in agreement with agencies of state sanitary supervision, parcels of land for industrial, housing, social and cultural, and administrative construction; plan and subdivide parcels of land for the construction of individual
houses for the working people in accordance with the projects for planning and
building up the city;

(j) set aside, in agreement with agencies of state sanitary supervision, parcels of land for city cemeteries and show care for their servicing and protection,
[and] ensure that communal graves are kept in proper condition;

(k) set aside, in agreement with agencies of state sanitary supervision, parcels of land for dumps, sanitation areas, and other needs of the city economy,
[and] ensure their correct utilization and proper condition;

(l) confer names on squares, streets, lanes, alleys, gardens, boulevards, [and] parks, and establish a numbering system for houses;

(m) direct the services of population centers, the protection and expansion of greenery, facilitate the development of social initiative in the provision of services and the planting of greenery, widely drawing into this work enterprises, institutions, organizations, and the population.

Article 16. In the sphere of agriculture a city Soviet of Working People's Deputies shall:

(a) direct the development of all branches of agricultural production in the rural area attached to the city; render assistance to collective farms, state farms, and auxiliary economic undertakings in increasing the production of products of crop cultivation and animal husbandry, in raising labor productivity and strengthening labor discipline, [and] in the further raising of the material and cultural level of life of toilers in agriculture;

(b) carry out the registration (with the exception of city Soviets of cities of district rank) of Charters of Agricultural Artels and ensure that they are strictly executed; adopt measures to strengthen collective farms organizationally and economically, [and] supervise the creation and correct utilization of indivisible funds in collective farms, on the basis of a proper balance of social interests of the collective farms and personal material interests of the collective farmers;

(c) consider (with the exception of city Soviets of cities of district rank) annual and perspective production plans adopted by general meetings of collective farmers, receipt-expenditure estimates, and annual reports of collective farms;

hear reports of governing boards of collective farms on fulfillment of plans of development of agriculture, on the course of agricultural work, and on other questions, as well as reports on the work of inspection commissions of collective farms;

(d) on the basis of the state plan for the development of agriculture, transmit (with the exception of city Soviets of cities of district rank) to collective farms planning assignments for the volume of state purchases of products of crop cultivation and animal husbandry and ensure timely fulfillment by collective farms of such assignments;

bear responsibility for the organization and fulfillment of the plan for purchases of agricultural products and raw materials, and also exercise supervision over the work of purchasing organizations and enterprises in receiving agricultural products and raw materials from collective farms and state farms and in ensuring their safekeeping;

(e) supervise the work of state farms, auxiliary economic undertakings, and other agricultural enterprises, assist them in fulfilling production plans and turning them into model economic undertakings of high productivity; hear reports of managers of state farms and auxiliary economic undertakings on the fulfillment of plans of development of agriculture, on the course of agricultural work, and on other questions;

(f) organize socialist competition among collective farms and state farms for raising labor productivity, for developing by all possible means all branches of agriculture, and for receiving large harvests of agricultural crops and high productivity in animal husbandry;

(g) supervise the work of technical repair, machine-tractor, and other specialized stations, [and] register contracts concluded between them and collective farms and watch over their fulfillment; hear reports of managers of the said enterprises on the fulfillment of production plans, on cultural and household servicing of workers and employees, and on other questions;

(h) direct veterinary and zootechnical work; organize veterinary services for collective farms, state farms, and other enterprises and institutions, as well as veterinary services for livestock and poultry in the personal ownership of the population.

Article 17. In the sphere of road construction and transport a city Soviet of Working People's Deputies shall:

(a) direct the construction of roads, ensure the servicing and repair of roads of local significance; oversee the condition of roads of republican and union significance in the territory within its jurisdiction;

(b) organize a road service to protect and maintain in proper condition roads, bridges, river crossings and other structures, and road signs;

(c) direct city transport; ensure the development and proper exploitation of tramway, trolley-bus, and other types of city transport; foster the work of rail, water, and air transport;

(d) organize transport for communication with factories, plants, state farms, and collective farms located in the territory of the city.

Article 18. In the sphere of communications a city Soviet of Working People's

Deputies shall:

(a) supervise and oversee the work of local communications agencies, render them aid and assistance in the development and improvement of all types of communications, in the dissemination of printed matter, in the delivery of correspondence, and in the preservation of structures used in communications;

(b) carry out measures to develop radiofication, telephonization, and television in the city;

(c) organize local radio broadcasts.

Article 19. In the sphere of public education a city Soviet of Working People's Deputies shall:

(a) direct public education in the city;

(b) ensure fulfillment of the law on universal compulsory education;

(c) direct the work of schools, boarding schools, and children's homes, [and] ensure expansion of their network; exercise supervision over instructional and educational work in schools, boarding schools, and children's homes, ensure the organization of labor education and polytechnical education, and exercise supervision over the status of polytechnization and instructional and educational work in schools [and] the preparation of students for practical activity; keep (with the exception of city Soviets of cities divided into districts) a record of children of school and pre-school age;

(d) direct the work of schools of working and rural youth;

(e) direct the work of kindergartens, adopt measures to expand the network of kindergartens, both those which are on the city budget and those funded by collective farms, state farms, and industrial enterprises, [and] facilitate enlargement of the seasonal network of pre-school institutions;

(f) direct non-school and pre-school education of children [and] adopt measures to expand the network of children's non-school institutions; organize children's libraries, children's technical stations, pioneer camps, [and] children's playgrounds, [and] ensure direction of their work;

(g) organize the work of making arrangements for children left without parents to live in children's homes or to be educated in families of the working people;

(h) organize and finance schools, organize the construction and repair of the buildings of schools, boarding schools, study workshops, pre-school, and other children's institutions which are on the city budget, [and] provide these schools and other children's institutions with furniture, textbooks, study aids, equipment, [and] fuel.

Article 20. In the sphere of culture and enlightenment a city Soviet of Working People's Deputies shall:

(a) direct the activities of institutions of culture and enlightenment located in the territory of the city;

(b) ensure expansion of the network of institutions of culture and enlightenment and improvement of their servicing the population; direct the spreading of motion picture theaters;

(c) facilitate the development of popular creative activity, of musical and choral collectives, of ensembles, and of other types of amateur artistic activities, [and] organize exhibitions, contests, and competitions;

(d) provide institutions of culture and enlightenment which are on the city budget with equipment, goods, and fuel, [and] organize repair of their buildings, carry out construction of new institutions of culture and enlightenment;

(e) foster the work of the city division of the Society for the Dissemination of Political and Scientific Knowledge of the Azerbaijan SSR; organize the regular holding of lectures, talks, and reports for the population;

(f) ensure the protection of historical monuments, monuments of culture, and nature preserves;

(g) direct the development of trade in books and foster the dissemination of newspapers and magazines among the city pupulation;

(h) organize improvement of the qualifications of the personnel of institutions of culture and enlightenment.

Article 21. In the sphere of health a city Soviet of Working People's Deputies shall:

(a) direct the care of health and the taking of measures for sanitation and disease prevention and epidemic control in the city;

(b) organize the servicing of the population with free medical help in hospitals, out-patient clinics, and at home. [and] ensure the normal functioning of hospitals, out-patient clinics, first-aid stations, medical centers, medical assistant and midwife centers, maternity homes, pharmacies, and other medical institutions.

(c) organize the construction and repair of premises for healthcare institutions, [and] provide institutions of healing and disease prevention which are on the city budget with equipment, goods, and fuel;

(d) foster the development and servicing of local health resorts and rest homes;

(e) ensure the taking of measures to protect motherhood and childhood [and] the expansion of the network of children's nurseries, playgrounds, [and] milk kitchens, [and] carry out health measures among children; exercise supervision over the work of children's hospitals, nurseries, and children's sanitoria; supervise the proper handling of medical service for children in schools, children's homes, kindergartens, [and] in pioneer camps;

(f) exercise supervision over observance of the sanitary condition of the city, settlements, rural population centers, industrial, municipal, [and] trade enterprises and enterprises of public dining, of markets, housing, schools, children's institutions, places of public use, and other social and cultural institutions;

(g) exercise supervision over the sanitary condition of sources of water supply and reservoirs, adopt measures against the pollution of air and soil, wage a struggle against pollution by stagnant waters of sources of the drinking water supply for the economy; organize in the city sanitary and epidemic stations and anti-epidemic units; ensure the taking of sanitary and health measures and adopt measures to prevent and liquidate epidemic diseases;

(h) direct the organization of medical and sanitation enlightenment among the population;

(i) ensure the taking of measures to train and retrain junior medical personnel.

Article 22.　In the sphere of physical culture and sports a city Soviet of Working People's Deputies shall:

(a) ensure mass development of physical culture and sports, [and] collaborate with industrial enterprises, organizations, and institutions in organizing physical education among the population;

(b) organize the conducting of sports competitions, meets, tournaments, and other mass physical culture measures;

(c) foster the work of city Councils of Voluntary Sports Societies.

Article 23.　In the sphere of social insurance a city Soviet of Working People's Deputies shall:

(a) direct social insurance work for the working people in the city;

(b) ensure the correct and timely granting and paying of state pensions established by law;

(c) foster the finding of jobs and labor training for invalids of war and labor [and] for members of the families of military personnel and of soldiers and partisans who have perished;

(d) exercise supervision over the granting of benefits and priorities established by law for invalids of war and labor, for families of soldiers of the Soviet Army and partisans who have perished, for families of military personnel, and for pensioners; adopt measures to improve their material and living conditions;

(e) exercise direction of the work of institutions of social insurance (invalids' homes, homes for the aged, and others); appoint guardians and curators for the aged and for invalids [and] adopt measures to improve their material and living conditions;

(f) ensure the correct granting and timely paying of state aid to mothers with many children and to unmarried mothers;

(g) organize the construction and repair of institutions and enterprises which are on the city budget [and] provide such institutions and enterprises with fuel, furniture, and equipment;

(h) render assistance in the work of primary organizations of the Azerbaijan Society of the Blind and the Azerbaijan Society of the Deaf and Dumb;

(i) organize and supervise the work of medical-labor expert commissions [and] ensure their normal functioning.

Article 24. In the sphere of labor and training of cadres a city Soviet of Working People's Deputies shall:

(a) in accordance with Article 12 of the Constitution of the Azerbaijan SSR, foster by all possible means the participation of every able-bodied citizen in socially useful labor;

(b) exercise supervision over the observance of labor laws;

(c) facilitate by all possible means the strengthening of state and labor discipline in enterprises, institutions, and organizations;

(d) direct the work of recruiting youth for agriculture mechanization academies, trade, railroad, and technical academies, [and] factory and plant training schools;

(e) ensure the carrying out of organized recruitment of workers for industry, construction, and transport and also ensure the finding of jobs for youth who have completed general education schools;

(f) foster the finding of jobs and arranging of living conditions for citizens de-
mobilized from the ranks of the Armed Forces of the USSR;

(g) exercise direction of the training and retraining of cadres in mass occupa-
tions.

Article 25. In the sphere of protection of state order [and] the rights of citizens and of observance of socialist legality, a city Soviet of Working People's
Deputies shall:

(a) secure protection of state order [and] of the rights and interests of state
institutions and enterprises, cooperative and social organizations, and societies
of the working people, as well as of the rights and interests of citizens, in accordance with the Constitution of the Azerbaijan SSR and the legislation in force;

(b) ensure observance of socialist legality by all institutions, enterprises, organizations, collective farms, and citizens, [and] strict execution by them of laws,
edicts, decrees, decisions, and regulations of superior agencies of state power
and administration, as well as of its own decisions and regulations;

(c) exercise supervision over the legality of decisions and regulations adopted
by district (i.e., districts within a city), rural, and settlement Soviets and their
executive committees;

(d) annul decisions of governing boards and general meetings of members of
collective farms and consumers' societies in the event that such decisions do not
conform to law;

(e) secure protection of socialist ownership, of public order, of the person and
property of citizens; assist agencies of the procuracy and people's courts in their
work;

(f) exercise supervision over the activities of corrective-labor institutions
located in the territory of the city;

(g) ensure timely consideration and correct resolution of petitions and complaints of citizens by all enterprises, institutions, and organizations located in
the territory of the city;

(h) in accordance with the legislation in force, exercise the functions of guard-
ianship and curatorship; decide questions of adoption (except for city Soviets of
cities divided into districts); direct the work of agencies of registration of acts
of civil status;

(i) supervise the condition of protection of crops and plants in collective farms, state farms, and other state and social economic undertakings located in the rural area attached to the city;

(j) adopt measures to prevent natural calamities and to liquidate their consequences; direct fire prevention work in the territory of the city; ensure supervision over the observance of fire prevention rules by enterprises, institutions, and organizations, as well as by the population; foster the work of the voluntary fire society;

(k) adopt, in the established procedure, decisions which provide for administrative responsibility for their violation.

Article 26. In the sphere of defense work a city Soviet of Working People's Deputies shall:

(a) ensure execution of the law on universal military obligation by all citizens, enterprises, institutions, and organizations;

(b) render assistance in the preparation and conduct of induction of citizens for military service and reserve training; ensure the carrying out of pre-induction training of citizens;

(c) direct local anti-aircraft defense, exercise supervision and render assistance in the preparation of enterprises, institutions, organizations, and the population for anti-aircraft defense;

(d) assist by all possible means in the work of city organizations of the Voluntary Army, Aviation, and Navy Auxiliary Society (DOSAAF) and the society of the Red Crescent of the Azerbaijan SSR.

Article 27. A city Soviet of Working People's Deputies shall, in the procedure established by law, make economic use of enterprises, buildings, structures, and other property within its jurisdiction through direct exploitation or by renting them out.

CHAPTER III

Sessions of a City Soviet of Working People's Deputies

Article 28. In accordance with Article 94 of the Constitution of the Azerbaijan SSR, sessions of a city Soviet of Working People's Deputies shall be convoked at least six times a year, that is, at least once every two months; sessions of a city Soviet of Working People's Deputies in a city divided into districts [shall be convoked] at least four times a year, that is, at least once every three months.

Article 29. Sessions of a city Soviet of Working People's Deputies shall be convoked by the executive committee of a city Soviet of Working People's Deputies by its own decision as well as upon the demand of not less than one third of the deputies of the city Soviet.

Questions submitted for the consideration of the city Soviet and the place and time of convocation of a session of the city Soviet shall be communicated to the deputies not later than ten days before the session.

Article 30. A session of a city Soviet of Working People's Deputies shall be authorized [to act] if there are present at it not less than two thirds of the total number of deputies of the city Soviet.

A city Soviet of Working People's Deputies shall elect for the period of its session a president and secretary to conduct meetings of the session.

Article 31. Questions for consideration by the city Soviet of Working People's Deputies shall be submitted by its executive committee, permanent commissions, and deputies of the city Soviet. Inclusion of a particular question in the agenda of the session shall be decided at the session by a simple majority of the votes.

Article 32. A city Soviet of Working People's Deputies shall elect for the term of authority of the Soviet a credentials commission, which shall verify the authority of deputies of the city Soviet.

Upon the recommendation of the credentials commission the city Soviet shall decide either to recognize the authority or to annul the elections of individual deputies.

Article 33. Decisions of a city Soviet of Working People's Deputies shall be adopted by a simple majority of votes and signed by the president and secretary of the executive committee of the city Soviet. A protocol of a session of a city Soviet of Working People's Deputies shall be signed by the president and secretary of the session.

Article 34. Decisions of a city Soviet of Working People's Deputies shall enter into force from the time they are made known to the appropriate institutions, enterprises, organizations, or citizens if no other time is established in the decision itself.

Article 35. On the basis of Articles 98 and 99 of the Constitution of the Azerbaijan SSR, decisions and regulations of a city Soviet of Working People's Deputies may be suspended by the executive committee of a superior Soviet and annulled by the superior Soviet of Working People's Deputies.

Article 36. Deputies of superior and inferior Soviets may take part in meetings of sessions of a city Soviet of Working People's Deputies with the right of a consultative vote. Representatives of state institutions and enterprises and of collective farms and cooperative and social organizations, workers, collective farmers, and employees may also be invited to meetings of a session.

CHAPTER IV

The Executive Committee of a City Soviet of Working People's Deputies

Article 37. The executive and administrative agency of a city Soviet of Working People's Deputies shall be an executive committee elected at a session of the Soviet from among the deputies of the city Soviet and composed of a president, vice-president, secretary, and members of the executive committee.

Article 38. The executive committee of a city Soviet of Working People's Deputies shall be responsible to the Soviet which elected it and accountable to it, and also accountable to the executive committee of the superior Soviet of Working People's Deputies.

The executive committee of a city Soviet of Working People's Deputies of a city of republican rank shall be responsible to the city Soviet which elected it and accountable to it, and also accountable to the Council of Ministers of the Azerbaijan SSR.

Article 39. In accordance with Article 92 of the Constitution of the Azerbaijan SSR, the executive committee of a city Soviet of Working People's Deputies shall exercise direction over cultural-political and economic construction in its territory on the basis of decisions of the city Soviet and of superior state agencies.

The executive committee of a city Soviet of Working People's Deputies may decide all questions of cultural-political and economic construction referred by the present Statute to the competence of the city Soviet, except questions subject to compulsory consideration at sessions of the city Soviet—confirmation of the budget of the city and of the report on its execution, confirmation of the national-economic plan, formation of sections of the executive committee of the city Soviet of Working People's Deputies, and confirmation of heads of sections.

Article 40. The executive committee of a city Soviet of Working People's Deputies shall foster the work of inferior Soviets of Working People's Deputies and direct their executive committees, hear and discuss reports of inferior Soviets of Working People's Deputies, [and] summarize and disseminate favorable experience of their work.

Article 41. The executive committee of a city Soviet of Working People's Deputies shall adopt decisions and issue regulations on the basis of and in execution of the Constitutions of the USSR and Azerbaijan SSR, laws, edicts, decrees, decisions, and regulations of superior state agencies, as well as of decisions and regulations of the Soviet which elected it.

Article 42. Sessions of the executive committee of a city Soviet of Working People's Deputies shall be convoked at least twice a month and shall be authorized [to act] if a majority of the membership of the executive committee is present at them.

Article 43. Representatives of permanent commissions, deputies of the city Soviet, and representatives of interested institutions, enterprises, and organizations may take part in sessions of the executive committee of a city Soviet of Working People's Deputies.

Article 44. Decisions of the executive committee of a city Soviet of Working People's Deputies shall be adopted by a simple majority of the votes, and shall be signed [as follows]: decisions, by the president and secretary of the executive committee of the city Soviet; and regulations, by the president of the executive committee of the city Soviet.

Article 45. Decisions and regulations of the executive committee of a city Soviet may be annulled by a superior Soviet or its executive committee, as well as by the city Soviet of Working People's Deputies.

Article 46. The executive committee of a city Soviet of Working People's Deputies shall have the right to annul decisions and regulations of executive committees of inferior Soviets of Working People's Deputies and to suspend decisions and regulations of inferior Soviets of Working People's Deputies, and also to annul orders and instructions of section heads and of other agencies subordinate to the executive committee.

Article 47. The president of the executive committee of a city Soviet of Working People's Deputies shall organize the fulfillment of decisions of the city Soviet and of its executive committee and shall inform the city Soviet about fulfillment of mandates and proposals of the voters [and] of decisions adopted by previous sessions.

The president of the executive committee of a city Soviet of Working People's Deputies shall be the manager of credits for the city budget and the manager of the current account of the city Soviet in institutions of the State Bank.

Article 48. The secretary of the executive committee of a city Soviet of Working People's Deputies shall organize the preparation of materials for sessions of the city Soviet and sessions of the executive committee.

Article 49. The executive committee of a city Soviet of Working People's Deputies must render help to deputies in the fulfillment of their duties as deputies, in the conduct of organizational work among the population by electoral areas, in the preparation and making of reports to the voters, [and] in the carrying out of mandates and proposals of the voters, and [must] familiarize deputies with the legislation in force and with decisions of the party and government [and] draw deputies into active participation in accomplishing the tasks of economic and cultural construction.

Article 50. The executive committee of a city Soviet of Working People's Deputies (except cities of district rank) shall, in case of necessity, make proposals to the Council of Ministers of the Azerbaijan SSR to change the borders of a city, city-type settlement, or rural Soviet, to form new settlements or rural Soviets, to change administrative centers, to transfer population centers from one category to another, as well as to merge or split up rural Soviets. The Council of Ministers of the Azerbaijan SSR shall make recommendations on such questions to the Presidium of the Supreme Soviet of the Azerbaijan SSR.

Article 51. In accordance with the Statutes on Elections, the executive committee of a city Soviet of Working People's Deputies shall carry out in its territory necessary measures with respect to elections to the Supreme Soviet of the USSR, Supreme Soviet of the Azerbaijan SSR, local Soviets of Working People's Deputies, and people's courts.

Article 52.   Upon the expiration of the authority of a city Soviet of Working People's Deputies, the executive committee of the city Soviet of Working People's Deputies shall preserve its authority until the formation of a new executive committee by the newly elected city Soviet.

Article 53.   The newly elected city Soviet of Working People's Deputies shall be convoked by the executive committee of the previous convocation's city Soviet not later than fifteen days after the elections.

Article 54.   The executive committee of a city Soviet of Working People's Deputies shall have a seal conforming to a model confirmed by the Presidium of the Supreme Soviet of the Azerbaijan SSR.

Article 55.   On the basis of Article 103 of the Constitution of the Azerbaijan SSR, the executive committee of a city Soviet shall have sections formed by the city Soviet of Working People's Deputies.

Article 56.   Sections of the executive committee of a city Soviet of Working People's Deputies shall be in charge of individual branches of economic and cultural construction [and] shall give direction to the work of enterprises, institutions, and organizations subordinate to them.

Article 57.   Sections of the executive committee of a city Soviet of Working People's Deputies shall be subordinate in their activities both to the city Soviet and its executive committee and to the corresponding section of the executive committee of the district Soviet of Working People's Deputies.

Sections of the executive committee of a city Soviet of Working People's Deputies (of cities of republican rank) shall be directly subordinate in their activities both to the city Soviet and its executive committee and to the corresponding Ministries of the Azerbaijan SSR.

Article 58.   Sections of the executive committee of a city Soviet of Working People's Deputies shall be under the charge of heads confirmed by the city Soviet of Working People's Deputies.

The executive committee of a city Soviet of Working People's Deputies in the interval between sessions shall appoint and remove heads of sections with subsequent confirmation at a session of the city Soviet.

Heads of sections of the executive committee of a city Soviet shall issue, within the limits of the competence of the respective section, orders and instructions and shall verify their execution.

CHAPTER V

Permanent Commissions of a City Soviet of Working People's Deputies

Article 59. Permanent commissions of a city Soviet of Working People's Deputies shall be agencies of the Soviet formed from among the deputies by individual branches of the activities of the Soviet and shall function on the basis of the Statute on Permanent Commissions.

Article 60. The following permanent commissions of a city Soviet of Working People's Deputies may be formed on the basis of local conditions and depending on the number of deputies: budget and financial, for agriculture, for industry, for public education, for health, for socialist legality and public order, for social insurance, for culture, for trade, for housing and municipal services, for public services, and others.

Article 61. Permanent commissions of a city Soviet of Working People's Deputies shall:

(a) participate in preparing questions of economic and cultural construction submitted for the consideration of the city Soviet or its executive committee, give their proposals and comments on such questions, and designate their reporters or co-reporters;

(b) take part in verifying execution of decisions of the city Soviet, as well as decisions of superior Soviets and their executive committees; conduct organizational work among the population for the practical realization of such decisions;

(c) upon assignment from the city Soviet or on its own initiative verify, within the limits of its competence, the work of sections of the executive committee, institutions, enterprises, and organizations located in the territory of the city, without interfering in their operational activities; transmit their proposals on the results of the verification to directors of enterprises, institutions, and organizations, for decision, or submit them for the consideration of the city Soviet or its executive committee.

Article 62.   Permanent commissions of a city Soviet of Working People's Deputies, in order to fulfill the tasks with which they are charged, shall draw into their work a large number of activists from the workers, employees, intelligentsia, collective farmers, [and] housewives.

Article 63.   Permanent commissions of a city Soviet of Working People's Deputies shall be accountable in their activities to the Soviet of Working People's Deputies which elected them.

Article 64.   The executive committee of a city Soviet of Working People's Deputies shall by all possible means render help to permanent commissions in the organization of their work [and] shall consider their proposals and adopt practical measures with respect to them.

CHAPTER VI

Deputies of a City Soviet of Working People's Deputies

Article 65.   Deputies of a city Soviet shall be obliged to participate actively in the work of the city Soviet of Working People's Deputies, to maintain a continual tie with the voters, to fulfill mandates and proposals of the voters, to consider complaints and petitions of citizens and to foster their proper resolution, and to fulfill assignments of the Soviet or its executive committee or a permanent commission.

A deputy of a city Soviet must carry on organizational work in his electoral area, facilitate the strengthening of state and labor discipline in production, explain to the voters and to all the working people decisions of the city Soviet as well as decrees of superior party and state agencies, drawing the broad masses of the population into the work of fulfilling them.

A deputy of a city Soviet shall be obliged to report regularly to the voters on his own work and on the work of the city Soviet of Working People's Deputies.

Article 66. A deputy of a city Soviet shall have the right to submit for consideration by the Soviet or its executive committee any questions arising in the course of his activities as deputy.

Article 67. A deputy of a city Soviet shall have the right of questioning the executive committee of the city Soviet as well as heads of its sections. Questioning may be done both at a session itself and also from the day the convocation of a session is announced, that is, ten days before a session. Questioning may be done on any matter which comes within the competence of the city Soviet regardless of the agenda of the session.

The executive committee of a city Soviet or heads of its sections to whom a question of a deputy is addressed shall be obliged to answer the deputy's question at the given session. In exceptional cases, with permission of the Soviet, an answer to a question may be given at the following session. The city Soviet shall adopt a decision with respect to the question of a deputy.

Article 68. Deputies of a city Soviet shall have the right to approach directors of institutions, organizations, and enterprises located in the territory of the city on questions connected with their activities as deputy. Directors of such institutions, organizations, and enterprises shall be obliged to give an answer to the deputy within seven days.

Article 69. A deputy of a city Soviet who is not a member of the executive committee of the city Soviet may participate in sessions of the executive committee with the right of a consultative vote.

Article 70. A deputy of a city Soviet may not be brought to responsibility in court or arrested without the consent of the city Soviet, and in the interval between sessions of the city Soviet without the consent of the executive committee of the city Soviet of Working People's Deputies.

Article 71. A deputy of a city Soviet who has not justified the trust of the voters may, in accordance with Article 150 of the Constitution of the Azerbaijan SSR, be recalled at any time upon a decision of the majority of the voters in the procedure established by law.

Article 72. In the event that a deputy of a city Soviet departs to another locality or is unable for other reasons to fulfill his duties as deputy in the particular electoral area, the deputy shall petition the city Soviet to remove his authority as deputy, [and the Soviet] at its next session shall consider such petition and shall deem the deputy to have ceased to be a member of the city Soviet.

Article 73.   On the basis of Article 120 of the Statute on Elections to Local Soviets of the Azerbaijan SSR, in the event of the departure of a deputy from the membership of a city Soviet, the executive committee of the superior Soviet* not later than two months after the departure of the deputy shall order elections for a new deputy in the appropriate electoral area.

*By an edict of January 11, 1961, a change has been made in Article 120 according to which the ordering of new elections to replace a deputy who has departed is done by the executive committee of the Soviet from the membership of which the deputy departed. [Footnote in the 1966 Collection of Azerbaijan laws — Translators.]

164

9. STATUTE ON PERMANENT COMMISSIONS OF LOCAL SOVIETS

Introductory Note

Since local soviets are primarily administrative (rather than legislative) agencies, permanent commissions of local soviets (unlike permanent commissions of supreme soviets) are concerned chiefly with problems of administration and checking on the execution of state policies. In 1967, a total of 301,760 permanent commissions operated in the 48,770 local soviets of the USSR, an average of six permanent commissions per local soviet.

STATUTE ON PERMANENT COMMISSIONS OF LOCAL SOVIETS OF
WORKING PEOPLE'S DEPUTIES OF THE UKRAINIAN SSR

(approved by a decree of the Presidium of the Supreme Soviet
of the Ukrainian SSR, May 31, 1957)

SECTION I

General Provisions

Article 1.   Permanent commissions of regional, district, city, city district,
rural, and settlement Soviets of Working People's Deputies shall be agencies of
the respective Soviet of Working People's Deputies.

Permanent commissions of local Soviets of Working People's Deputies shall
be called upon to take an active and obligatory part in preparing proposals and
drafts of decisions at session[s] of the Soviet, to foster the carrying out of decisions of Soviets and their executive committees and of decrees of superior state
agencies, to carry on organizational work among the broad masses of the working people, and to help executive committees in organizing prompt fulfillment of
the concrete tasks of economic and cultural construction, observance of socialist
legality, and protection of state order and the rights of citizens.

Article 2.   Permanent commissions in their practical activity shall be governed by the Statute on the Soviet of Working People's Deputies which elected them
and by decisions of the Soviet and its executive committees.

Article 3.   Permanent commissions of local Soviets of Working People's Deputies shall be accountable to the Soviets which elected them.

Article 4.   Depending on the number of deputies and taking into account the
special features of the region, district, city, settlement, or rural locality, Soviets
of Working People's Deputies may form permanent commissions for the [follow-
ing] questions: budget, local industry, agriculture, public education, health, cul-

166

ture, social insurance, trade, municipal services, public services, road construction, transport, communications, and others.

SECTION II

Procedure for Forming Permanent Commissions of a Local Soviet of Working People's Deputies

Article 5. Permanent commissions shall be formed at the first session of the respective Soviet of Working People's Deputies from among the deputies for the term of office of the Soviet and shall include a president and members of the commission in a number established by the Soviet itself.

Article 6. It is not recommended to elect to membership in permanent commissions members of the executive committee or members of other permanent commissions of the given Soviet of Working People's Deputies.

Deputies who are heads of sections or are chiefs of administrations of the executive committee may serve as members of permanent commissions which are not concerned with the work of the sections or administrations which they head.

Article 7. Permanent commissions of a Soviet of Working People's Deputies shall elect from their own membership a vice-president and a secretary of the commission.

Article 8. In the event of departure of a member of a permanent commission from the office of deputy, the president of the commission shall submit for resolution by the next session of the Soviet the question of electing a new member of the commission; the question of electing a president of a permanent commission to replace one who has departed shall be submitted by the executive committee for consideration by a session of the Soviet.

SECTION III

Rights and Duties of Permanent Commissions of a Local Soviet of Working People's Deputies

Article 9. Permanent commissions shall take an active part in working out proposals, drafts of decisions, and conclusions with respect to questions of economic and cultural construction and strengthening of the state legal order and shall submit them for consideration by the Soviet or its executive committee, shall make co-reports at sessions, shall take part in discussion of economic plans and assignments, and shall exercise supervision over the activity of enterprises, institutions, and organizations subordinate to the Soviet of Working People's Deputies.

Executive committees and their sections and administrations must consider proposals. and conclusions of permanent commissions and adopt practical measures with respect to them.

In the event of disagreement with a decision of the executive committee, a permanent commission shall have the right to transfer the question for consideration by the Soviet of Working People's Deputies.

Article 10. Permanent commissions, upon assignment from the Soviet or on its own initiative, shall study and prepare for consideration by the Soviet proposals and drafts of decisions with respect to the [following] questions:

(a) fulfillment of the budget, verification of the work of enterprises of industry and agriculture and of institutions of public education, health, the work of culture and enlightenment, trade, public services, and cultural and household servicing of the population;

(b) they shall present conclusions with respect to questions submitted by the executive committee and other state institutions and organizations for consideration by the Soviet;

(c) they shall organize the working people to fulfill decisions of the Soviet;

(d) they shall conduct verification of the execution of decisions of the Soviet and of decrees of superior state agencies by sections and administrations of the executive committee and by other institutions and organizations;

(e) they shall report regularly to the Soviet on work which has been accomplished.

Article 11. Permanent commissions of a Soviet of Working People's Deputies shall systematically check the work of sections and administrations of the executive committee and of enterprises, institutions, collective farms, state farms, MTS [machine-tractor stations], and other organizations subordinate to the Soviet and shall expose inadequacies in their work and help eliminate them. In case of necessity permanent commissions shall have the right to demand from their directors necessary information and clarifications with respect to questions submitted for the consideration of the Soviet or the executive committee.

Article 12.   Permanent commissions may hear informational reports of heads of sections and chiefs of administrations of the executive committee of the Soviet of Working People's Deputies, as well as of directors of enterprises, institutions, and organizations located in the territory of the Soviet, and may draw into participation in their work and for consultations specialists of various branches of the national economy and representatives of state institutions and scholarly and social organizations.

Article 13.   Permanent commissions may draw into their work deputies of the Soviet who are not members of such commissions and broad groups of activists of workers, collective farmers, and intelligentsia. Two or several permanent commissions, in studying and considering questions common to them, may conduct their work jointly.

Article 14.   Deputies of the Soviet who are not members of commissions and persons brought in to participate in the work of permanent commissions may take part in sessions of permanent commissions with the right of a consultative vote.

Article 15.   Representatives of permanent commissions may take part in sessions of the executive committee of the Soviet of Working People's Deputies with the right of a consultative vote.

Article 16.   Permanent commissions shall carry out their activity in close connection with the executive committee of the Soviet of Working People's Deputies; permanent commissions shall conduct sessions, as well as conferences, with participation of representatives of sections of the executive committee, of institutions, and of economic organizations.

Article 17.   Sessions of permanent commissions of Soviets of Working People's Deputies shall be convoked at least once every two months, during non-work hours.

If he finds it necessary to leave his usual place of residence to fulfill service duties, a member of a permanent commission shall be freed from his basic work with average pay at his place of work.

Article 18.   Sessions of a permanent commission shall be authorized [to act] if not less than half the members of the commission is present at them.

Article 19. At sessions of permanent commissions a protocol shall be kept in which shall be entered proposals which have been worked out and submitted for the consideration of the appropriate Soviet or of its executive committee.

Article 20. A permanent commission may adopt decisions with respect to questions not requiring consideration by the Soviet or its executive committee, namely: for elections of a vice-president or secretary, confirmation of its work plan, or allocation of duties among members of the commission or making assignments to them, as well as for hearing reports of members of the commission on fulfillment of assignments or on the results of investigations.

Article 21. All questions at sessions of permanent commissions shall be decided by a simple majority of the votes.

Members of permanent commissions who are not in agreement with decisions of commissions may speak in defense of their proposals during discussion of the given question in the Soviet or at a session of the executive committee.

Article 22. The president of a permanent commission shall organize and give direction to the work of the commission [and] shall maintain contact with the executive committee of the Soviet of Working People's Deputies and its sections and administrations, as well as with state and social organizations, enterprises, and collective farms; shall make reports and co-reports at sessions of the Soviet on questions under discussion and shall report to the Soviet on the work of the commission.

Article 23. Permanent commissions of a Soviet of Working People's Deputies shall not enjoy the rights of a legal person.

Article 24. Permanent commissions shall work in contact with the executive committee of the Soviet of Working People's Deputies, which shall:

(a) acquaint them with decisions and work plans of the executive committee and of its sections and administrations; inform them about measures adopted with respect to questions submitted by permanent commissions;

(b) invite to its sessions those permanent commissions to whose activity questions under discussion are related;

(c) pose the question of including in the agenda of sessions of the Soviet and sessions of the executive committee proposals prepared or submitted by permanent commissions;

(d) summarize and disseminate the best forms and methods of work of permanent commissions;

(e) secure organizational and technical servicing for permanent commissions and provide them with buildings necessary for their work;

(f) keep in its office a record of the proceedings of permanent commissions.

10. STATUTE ON THE COMMITTEE OF PARTY-STATE CONTROL

Introductory Note

In the earliest days of Soviet power, agencies were established to supervise the work of the state bureaucracy and to check on execution of party and government policy. The People's Commissariat of State Control, established December 5, 1917 (old style), was merged in 1920 with the network of worker control agencies which supervised the activities of factory executives; the reorganized commissariat was named the People's Commissariat of Worker-Peasant Inspection (Rabkrin). With the formation of the Soviet Union in December 1922, a corresponding commissariat was established in the newly-organized Council of People's Commissars of the USSR.

Beginning in 1920, a hierarchy of control agencies, called control commissions, also functioned within the Communist Party. The Central Control Commission, at the top of this hierarchy, enjoyed a status almost equal to that of the Party Central Committee. In the course of 1923 and 1924 the hierarchies of the Worker-Peasant Inspection and the party control commissions were gradually merged, forming a united agency of party-state control.

In 1934 the united organization was abolished and separate control agencies for party and government re-established. The government control organization was named the Commission of Soviet Control, and the party agency was re-named the Party Control Commission. In 1940 the Commission of Soviet Control was re-organized into the People's Commissariat of State Control, which in 1946 was re-named the Ministry of State Control. (At that time all people's commissariats were re-named ministries.) The Party Control Commission was re-named the Party Control Committee in 1952. In 1957 the Ministry of State Control was abolished and replaced by the Commission of Soviet Control.

In 1962 the party and government control agencies were once again merged, as they had been in 1923, this time into an organization called the Committee of

Party-State Control of the Central Committee of the CPSU and the USSR Council of Ministers. A separate party control organization, called the Party Commission, was retained, however, to handle appeals from imposition of party penalties.

In 1965 control work was once again split between party and government agencies. The government control agency was named the Committee of People's Control and was made subordinate solely to the USSR Council of Ministers; the Party Commission was re-organized into the Party Control Committee.

Despite these numerous organizational changes, the functions and powers of the control agencies have changed only slightly since 1934. Prior to that time, the agencies had enjoyed more extensive powers.

The Statute on the Committee of Party-State Control, here translated, is still in effect for the agencies of People's Control, except that they are subordinate to the USSR Council of Ministers alone, and not to the party's Central Committee, as was the Committee of Party-State Control. With the abolition of the Committee of Party-State Control in 1965, it was planned to issue a new statute to govern People's Control agencies, but as of October 1, 1968 no draft had been made public.

The Russian word kontrol', which the translators elsewhere have rendered as "supervision," is translated in this Statute as "control," since the phrase "party control" is widely used in English-language literature on the Soviet Union. It should be emphasized, however, that like its German and French equivalents, kontrol' connotes more the idea of supervision than of actual direction or management.

STATUTE ON THE COMMITTEE OF PARTY-STATE CONTROL OF THE CENTRAL COMMITTEE OF THE CPSU AND THE COUNCIL OF MINISTERS OF THE USSR AND ON THE CORRESPONDING LOCAL AGENCIES

(confirmed by a decree of the Central Committee of the CPSU
and the Council of Ministers of the USSR, December 20, 1962)

I.

The correct organization of control and verification of performance is a most important Leninist principle of the activity of the Communist Party and the Soviet state in the construction of the new society and a powerful means for improvement of party and state leadership, for the strengthening of the tie of the party with the people, for the enlistment of the masses in the administration of the affairs of society. In proportion to the further movement of our country forward toward communism, to the complexity of the direction of economic construction and to the gigantic development of productive forces, the role of mass control will grow still more and more.

In execution of the directive of the XXII Congress of the CPSU, the November (1962) Plenum of the Central Committee of the CPSU adopted a decision on the radical reorganization of the system of control in the country, placing at its foundation the Leninist idea of the combination of party and state control, of the creation of a system of single, all-embracing, permanently functioning control with the participation therein of the broad masses of communists and of all working people. V. I. Lenin saw in the flexible combination of the soviet and the party a guarantee of successful work, a source of extraordinary force for our policy.

Proceeding from this, the Central Committee of the CPSU, the Presidium of the Supreme Soviet of the USSR, and the Council of Ministers of the USSR have formed a single agency——the Committee of Party-State Control of the Central Committee of the CPSU and the Council of Ministers of the USSR (CPSC).

What is most important in the activity of the Committee of Party-State Control of the Central Committee of the CPSU and the Council of Ministers of the USSR, and of its local agencies, is the rendering of aid to the party and the state

in the fulfillment of the Program of the CPSU, in the organization of systematic
verification of actual execution of directives of the party and government, in the
further improvement of leadership in communist construction, in the struggle
for the development by all possible means of the socialist economy, in the observance of party and state discipline and of socialist legality.

Agencies of party-state control must look deeply into our entire socialist
economy, must be well informed on the state of affairs, and must give a correct
objective evaluation of the course of fulfillment of party and government decrees.

The task of control agencies is to govern themselves undeviatingly in their
work by V. I. Lenin's instruction: "Verify people and verify the actual performance of things — in this, yet again in this, and only in this is the crux of all
work and of all policy."

Decisive conditions for the successful activity of agencies of party-state control are: the broadest and most active enlistment both of communists and of the
non-party masses, of women, [and] of youth, in the business of control; broad
publicity in this work, carried out through meetings of the working people,
[through] the press, radio, television, motion pictures; an attentive attitude
toward letters and complaints, warnings, and proposals of the Soviet people.

Agencies of party-state control shall act as practical organizers of a mass
people's control of the most democratic type, the likes of which are not known to
a single capitalist state, where the working people are completely deprived of
this right.

Committees of party-state control, being agencies of the party and government,
shall not only verify and punish, but, chiefly, prevent mistakes and the possibility
of any kind of abuses, shall help the Central Committee of the CPSU and the Council of Ministers of the USSR to educate and warn cadres against shortcomings and
blunders in their work, shall orient them toward the successful resolution of political and economic tasks.

Committees of party-state control [and] the whole huge army of their activists must construct their work in such a way that bureaucrats and red-tape artists, parasites, bribe-takers, thieves, speculators, and cheats will sense the in-
evitability of punishment, will tremble before the great force of the Soviet public.

Agencies of party-state control must actively support, reward, and develop
everything new, advanced, and progressive that arises in all spheres of our life,
must decisively and persistently achieve the elimination of hidden shortcomings,

must adopt real measures to the end that, as a result of verifications, the state of affairs improves and unconditional fulfillment of the directives of the party and government is secured.

The assignment of these tasks to agencies of party-state control shall not remove from party, soviet, and economic organizations responsibility for the verification of exeuction of decisions of the party and government. On the contrary, it is essential to increase the responsibility of party, soviet, economic, planning, and other agencies of the entire party and state apparatus from top to bottom for the organization of absolute execution of the directives of the party and government.

II.

1. The Committee of Party-State Control of the Central Committee of the CPSU and the Council of Ministers of the USSR, being a union-republican agency, shall include a president of the Committee, vice-presidents, and members of the Committee, who shall be leading workers of the Committee and of local commit tees of party-state control, representatives of trade unions, of the komsomol, of the press, of workers, of collective farmers, and of the intelligentsia, who enjoy general confidence.

The Committee shall be confirmed by the Central Committee of the CPSU and by the Council of Ministers of the USSR, and executive personnel of the Committee staff by the Central Committee of the CPSU.

The Committee of Party-State Control shall carry out all its activity under the direct guidance of the Central Committee of the CPSU and the Council of Ministers of the USSR and shall be accountable to them.

2. Republican, territorial, and regional committees of party-state control shall be agencies of the central committees of union-republican party organizations and of the councils of ministers of the republics, of territorial and regional committees of the party, and of executive committees of territorial and regional Soviets of Working People's Deputies.

The membership of republican, territorial, and regional committees of party-state control shall include the leading personnel of such committees, representatives of inferior control agencies, of trade union and komsomol organizations, and of the press, and authoritative comrades from among workers, collective farmers, and the intelligentsia.

In territories and regions where two independent territorial or regional committees of the party and two territorial or regional Soviets of Working People's Deputies have been created, two committees of party-state control shall be formed.[*]

Republican, territorial, and regional committees of party-state control shall be confirmed at plenums of the respective party committees. Presidents of republican, territorial, and regional committees of party-state control and their deputies shall be confirmed by the Central Committee of the CPSU and by the Council of Ministers of the USSR, upon recommendation of the Committee of Party-State Control of the Central Committee of the CPSU and the Council of Ministers of the USSR.

The Committee of Party-State Control of the Bureau of the Central Committee of the CPSU for the RSFSR and the Council of Ministers of the RSFSR shall be confirmed by the Central Committee of the CPSU.

3.　City and district committees of party-state control and committees of party-state control for collective and state farm production administrations and for industrial zones shall be agencies of republican, territorial, and regional committees of party-state control. The membership of the said committees shall be confirmed at plenums of the respective party committees. The committees shall include representatives of trade union, komsomol, and other social organizations, and of the press, and authoritative comrades from among workers, collective farmers, and the intelligentsia.

The presidents of such committees shall be confirmed by superior party and control agencies and shall be authorized representatives of republican, territorial, and regional committees of party-state control.

4.　At enterprises and construction sites, on collective and state farms, in institutions, and in housing administrations, groups for the assistance of

---

[*]In accordance with the decree of the November (1964) Plenum of the Central Committee of the CPSU "On uniting industrial and rural regional and territorial party organizations," the Central Committee of the CPSU adopted the proposal of the Committee of Party-State Control of the Central Committee of the CPSU and the Council of Ministers of the USSR to unite industrial and rural regional and territorial committees of party-state control. [Footnote in Handbook of a People's Controller— Translators.]

committees of party-state control shall be formed by means of delegating to them representatives from party, trade union, komsomol, and other social organizations, elected at meetings of such organizations as well as at general meetings of collective farmers and residents of housing administrations. The most active and authoritative comrades, both communists and non-party workers, collective farmers, specialists, employees, scholars, persons active in literature and art, pensioners, and housewives must be brought into the assistance groups. In the largest assistance groups, a group bureau may be elected.

The presidents of the assistance groups and their deputies shall be elected at a general meeting of the members of the group and shall be confirmed by the party committee or bureau of the primary party organization and by the superior agency of party-state control.

In shops, divisions, sectors, and brigades of enterprises, construction projects, and collective and state farms, groups or posts for the assistance of party-state control shall be formed from representatives delegated to their membership from party, trade union, and komosol organizations and from meetings of collective farmers.

Assistance groups shall work under the direction of party organizations and of the appropriate local agencies of party-state control and shall be organizing centers around which shall be united all social control.

Assistance groups shall be granted a broad opportunity for placing questions before the administration, before party, trade union, and komsomol organizations, and before committees of party-state control concerning the elimination of shortcomings discovered by them and concerning the bringing of the guilty to responsibility. The proposals of assistance groups shall be considered by the directors of enterprises, construction projects, collective farms, state farms, and institutions, and by primary party, trade union, and komsomol organizations.

Assistance groups shall periodically make reports on the work they have carried out at party, trade union, and komsomol meetings and at meetings of the working people.

5.   The Committee of Party-State Control of the Central Committee of the CPSU and the Council of Ministers of the USSR and its agencies shall directly and, in necessary instances, jointly with the sections of the Cen-

tral Committee of the CPSU, with the staff of the Council of Ministers of
the USSR, and with local party committees and party and soviet organizations:

(a)   carry out a verification of the actual execution of directives of the
party and government by ministries, state committees, departments, organizations, enterprises, construction projects, collective farms, state farms,
and institutions;

(b)   control the fulfillment of national-economic plans, uncover internal
reserves and unused possibilities for expanding production in industry and
agriculture, for improving the quality of products, for reducing their production cost, and for increasing labor productivity; wage a struggle for the
strictest regime of economy [and] for the correct and most expedient expenditure of means and of material valuables;

(c)   render aid to the party in the improvement of the work of the state
and administrative apparatus, and in its further economization and improvement;

(d)   decisively suppress violations of party and state discipline, manifestations of localist tendencies, a departmental approach to affairs, cheat-
ing, falsification, mismanagement, and squandering;

(e)   wage a ruthless struggle against bureaucratism and red tape, bribery, speculation, abuse of official posision, and against any infringements
of socialist ownership; exercise control over the amount of labor and the
amount of consumption, over observance of the socialist principle: "He who
does not work, neither shall he eat;" speak out against any other actions
that cause harm to communist construction;

(f)   the committee of Party-State Control of the Central Committee of
the CPSU and the Council of Ministers of the USSR shall place before the
Central Committee of the CPSU and the Council of Ministers of the USSR
questions having a general party and general state significance, on the basis of summaries of the results of verifications of the fulfillment of the
directives of the party and the government.

6.   The Committee of Party-State Control of the Central Committee
of the CPSU and the Council of Ministers of the USSR and its local agencies shall have the right:

(a)   to give to the appropriate directors of ministries, state committees,
departments, organizations, enterprises, construction projects, collective

farms, and institutions, instructions concerning the elimination of shortcomings and violations in the fulfillment of decrees of the party and government. Directors of soviet and economic organizations, enterprises, construction projects, collective farms, and institutions shall be obliged to eliminate without delay violations and shortcomings discovered by committees of party-state control and to report the results to the appropriate agencies of party-state control;

(b) to hear reports, and to demand explanations as well as necessary documents and materials from directors who fulfill the decrees and instructions of the party and the government poorly or allow bureaucratism or red tape; to impose penalties on persons guilty of presenting incorrect or false information or conclusions;

(c) to recommend to the appropriate agencies and organizations that reports of directors be heard in executive committees and at sessions of Soviets of working People's Deputies, collegia of ministries, state committees and departments, sessions of party committees, [and] at general meetings of workers, collective farmers, and employees, on questions connected with the elimination of shortcomings in the fulfillment of decrees of the party and government;

(d) to suspend regulations and actions of organizations, institutions, and officials that are illegal and could cause harm to the interests of the state;

(e) to set for persons guilty of unsatisfactory fulfillment of decisions of the party and government time limits for correction; in necessary instances to transfer cases for consideration by comrades' courts; to assess monetary deductions against officials who have caused material harm to the state [or] to cooperative or social organizations;

(f) to bring the guilty to responsibility, to impose disciplinary penalties, to reduce in office, to dismiss from positions occupied, to refer materials on abuses and other criminal acts to agencies of the procuracy for bringing the guilty to criminal responsibility.

Agencies of party-state control shall be obliged to use wisely the rights granted to them, not to overbear in the application of penalties, but also not to spare those persons who by their actions bring harm to the cause of communist construction.

7.   The committees of party-state control, from the top to the bottom, along with their staff, shall create auxiliary sections, permanent and temporary

social commissions, shall have auxiliary inspectors and controllers brought into the work of agencies of party-state control on the recommendations of party, soviet, and social organizations.

Agencies of party-state control may enlist for verifications, investigations, and inspections personnel of the staff of party, soviet, and economic agencies, of enterprises, construction projects, collective farms, state farms, and institutions, and members of inspection commissions and the control and inspection staff of ministries, state committees, and departments.

Republican, territorial, and regional committees of party-state control may enlist for fulfillment of their assignments auxiliary personnel, as a rule on a social service basis, but in necessary instances (on the basis of a special instruction confirmed by the Council of Ministers of the USSR) with release from basic work in production or in an institution for a term of up to two weeks a year and with preservation of average monthly wages at the place of work.

Agencies of party-state control shall educate their staff and auxiliary personnel and members of groups and posts for the assistance of committees of party-state control in the spirit of genuinely Leninist qualities and traits of character and of high responsibility to the party and state for fulfillment of their honorable duties.

8. For the purpose of the wide publicity of their work, agencies of party-state control shall actively use the press, motion pictures, radio, and television, shall systematically publish the results of verifications and of measures adopted with respect to them; [and] shall draw into the business of control worker and rural correspondents, journalists, writers, poets, [and] artists.

PART TWO

11. STATUTE ON PROCURACY SUPERVISION

Introductory Note

Although the Soviet Procuracy was established in 1922, the 1955 Statute on Procuracy Supervision is the first comprehensive legislation defining its structure and activities. From 1922 to 1933, the procuracy was organized on a republican basis, first in the RSFSR and later in the other Soviet republics. After the formation of the Soviet Union (December 30, 1922), a special procurator's office was established to handle cases in the new all-union supreme court, but the republican procuracies remained free of federal supervision. The republican procuracies were subordinate to the republican ministries of justice.

In 1933, a federal procuracy was established, and a statute on the federal procuracy was enacted. While this statute gave the federal procurator extensive powers over the republican procuracies, the latter remained subordinate also to the republican ministries of justice. This dual subordination was ended in 1936, when the republican procuracies were separated from the ministries of justice and made subordinate to the federal procuracy alone. It was just in that period, however, that the procuracy was in fact, though not in theory, brought under the domination of the state security agencies.

The procuracy's rights and duties are set forth in the 1955 Statute in much greater detail than ever before. Of particular significance are the detailed provisions on procuracy supervision of places of confinement. Perviously, the procuracy's supervisory powers over places of confinement had been stated only in general terms and had, in fact, rarely been exercised.

STATUTE ON PROCURACY SUPERVISION IN THE USSR

(confirmed by an edict of the Presidium of the Supreme Soviet of the USSR,
May 24, 1955, and amended by edicts of the Supreme Soviet of the USSR,
February 27, 1959, March 3, 1960, February 14, 1964, and December 14, 1966)

CHAPTER I

General Provisions

Article 1. In accordance with Article 113 of the Constitution of the USSR, the Procurator General of the USSR shall be charged with supreme supervision over strict execution of the laws by all ministries and their subordinate institutions and by individual officials, as well as by citizens of the USSR.

Article 2. The task of supreme supervision over strict execution of the laws shall be to strengthen socialist legality in the USSR and to protect from any infringements:

(1) the social and state system of the USSR secured by the Constitution of the USSR and by the Constitutions of union and autonomous republics, the socialist system of economy, and socialist ownership;

(2) the political, labor, housing, and other personal and property rights and legally protected interests of citizens of the USSR guaranteed by the Constitution of the USSR and by the Constitutions of union and autonomous republics;

(3) the rights and legally protected interests of state institutions and enterprises, collective farms, and cooperative and other social organizations.

The Procurator General of the USSR and procurators subordinate to him shall be obliged to watch over proper and uniform application of the laws of the USSR and of the union and autonomous republics, notwithstanding any local differences and despite any local influences.

Article 3. The Procurator General of the USSR and procurators subordinate to him shall carry out the tasks with which they are charged through:

(1) supervision over strict execution of the laws by all ministries and departments and their subordinate institutions and enterprises, by executive and administrative agencies of local Soviets of Working People's Deputies, and by cooperative and other social organizations, and also supervision over strict observance of the laws by officials and citizens;

(2) bringing to criminal responsibility persons guilty of committing crimes;

(3) supervision over observance of legality in the activity of agencies of inquiry and preliminary investigation;

(4) supervision over the legality and justification of judgments, decisions, rulings, and decrees of judicial agencies;

(5) supervision over the legality of execution of judgments;

(6) supervision over the observance of the legality of the keeping of persons confined in places of deprivation of freedom.

Article 4. The Procurator General of the USSR and procurators subordinate to him, exercising supervision over legality on behalf of the state, shall be obliged to take prompt measures to eliminate any violations of the laws, regardless of who has committed such violations.

Article 5. Agencies of the procuracy in the USSR shall constitute a single centralized system headed by the Procurator General of the USSR with subordination of inferior procurators to superiors.

Article 6. On the basis of Article 117 of the Constitution of the USSR, agencies of the procuracy shall exercise their functions independently of any local agencies whatsoever, being subordinate only to the Procurator General of the USSR.

Article 7. The Procurator General of the USSR shall be responsible to the Supreme Soviet of the USSR and accountable to it, and in the interval between sessions of the Supreme Soviet of the USSR to the Presidium of the Supreme Soviet of the USSR, to which it shall also be accountable.

Article 8. The Procurator General of the USSR, on the basis of and in execution of the laws in force, shall issue orders and instructions, which shall be binding on all agencies of the procuracy.

Orders and instructions of the Procurator General of the USSR may be annulled by the Presidium of the Supreme Soviet of the USSR if they do not conform to law.

Article 9. The Procurator General of the USSR may make recommendations to the Presidium of the Supreme Soviet of the USSR concerning questions which are subject to resolution by legislation or which require interpretation of the law under section "c" of Article 49 of the Constitution of the USSR.

CHAPTER II

Supervision over Execution of the Laws by Institutions, Organizations, Officials, and Citizens of the USSR

Article 10. The Procurator General of the USSR and procurators subordinate to him, within the limits of their competence, shall exercise supervision:

(1) over the strict conformity of acts issued by ministries and departments and their subordinate institutions and enterprises, as well as by executive and administrative agencies of local Soviets of Working People's Deputies and by cooperative and other social organizations, to the Constitution and laws of the USSR, to the Constitutions and laws of union and autonomous republics, and to decrees of the Council of Ministers of the USSR and Councils of Ministers of union and autonomous republics;

(2) over strict execution of the laws by officials and citizens of the USSR.

Article 11. The Procurator General of the USSR, procurators of union and autonomous republics, procurators of territories, regions, autonomous regions, national areas, districts, and cities, as well as military procurators, within the limits of their competence, shall have the right:

(1) to demand and obtain orders, instructions, decisions, regulations, decrees, and other acts issued by ministries and departments and their subordinate institutions and enterprises, as well as by executive and administrative agencies of local Soviets of Working People's Deputies, by cooperative and other social organizations, and by officials, in order to check the conformity of such acts to the law;

(2) to require from directors of ministries, departments, institutions, enterprises, executive and administrative agencies of local Soviets of Working People's Deputies, cooperative and other social organizations, and officials, presentation of necessary documents and information;

(3) to perform on-the-spot checks of execution of the laws in connection with petitions, complaints, and other information concerning violations of the law;

(4) to require, in connection with available data concerning violations of the law, from directors of ministries, departments, institutions, enterprises, executive and administrative agencies of local Soviets of Working People's Deputies, cooperative and other social organizations, and officials, performance of checks and reviews of the activity of their subordinate institutions, enterprises, and organizations and their subordinate officials;

(5) to require from officials and citizens personal explanations concerning violations of the law.

Article 12. Ministries, departments, institutions, enterprises, executive and administrative agencies of local Soviets of Working People's Deputies, cooperative and other social organizations, as well as officials, shall be obliged upon demand of a procurator to send to him orders, instructions, decisions, regulations, decrees, and other documents, as well as to present necessary information and explanations.

Article 13. The Procurator General of the USSR and procurators subordinate to him shall protest orders, instructions, decisions, regulations, decrees, and other acts which contradict the law, to the agency which issued the relevant act or to [its] superior agency.

A procurator's protest must be considered within ten days. The procurator who lodged the protest shall be notified of the decision adopted with respect to the protest.

The lodging by a procurator of a protest against a decree to bring a person to administrative responsibility issued by an agency authorized [to issue the decree] shall suspend execution of the administrative sanction until consideration of the protest by the respective agency.

Article 14. A procurator shall be obliged to accept and consider petitions and complaints of citizens concerning a violation of a law, to verify such petitions and complaints within the time periods established by law, and to take measures to restore rights which have been violated and to defend the legal interests of citizens.

Article 15. In regard to officials or citizens who have violated the law, a procurator, depending on the nature of the violation, shall either bring the guilty persons to criminal responsibility or shall take measures to bring the offender to administrative or disciplinary responsibility.

In necessary instances a procurator shall take measures to ensure compensation for material damage caused by a violation of the law.

Article 16. The Procurator General of the USSR and procurators subordinate to him shall have the right to submit recommendations to state agencies and social organizations for eliminating viplations of a law and the causes which make violation of the law possible.

A state agency or social organization shall be obliged within one month to consider the recommendation of a procurator and to take necessary measures to eliminate violations of the law and the causes which make violation of the law possible.

CHAPTER III

Supervision over Execution of the Laws in the Activity
of Agencies of Inquiry and Preliminary Investigation

Article 17. The Procurator General of the USSR and procurators subordinate to him, in exercising supervision over strict execution of the laws in the activity of agencies of inquiry and preliminary investigation, shall be obliged:

(1) to bring to criminal responsibility persons guilty of committing crimes, to take measures to the end that not a single crime should remain unsolved and that not a single criminal should evade responsibility;

(2) to watch closely that no citizen should be subjected to being brought illegally or without justification to criminal responsibility or [be subjected] to any other illegal restriction of his rights;

(3) to watch over the undeviating observance by agencies of inquiry and preliminary investigation of the procedure established by law for investigation of crimes.

Article 18. A procurator shall exercise supervision to the end that no one should be arrested without a court decree or the sanction of a procurator.

In deciding the question of sanctioning an arrest, a procurator shall be obliged to familiarize himself thoroughly with all materials which form the basis for the necessity of arrest and in necessary instances personally to question the person subject to arrest.

Article 19. A procurator, in exercising supervision over the investigation of crimes, shall have the right:

(1) to give instructions to agencies of inquiry and of preliminary investigation concerning the investigation of crimes, the selection, modification, or annulment of measures of restraint with respect to an accused person, as well as the searching for criminals in hiding;

(2) to demand from agencies of inquiry and of preliminary investigation the files of criminal cases, documents, materials, and other information concerning crimes which have been committed, in order to verify them;

(3) to participate in performing the preliminary investigation or inquiry in criminal cases and, in necessary instances, personally to investigate any type of case;

(4) to return criminal cases to agencies of inquiry or of preliminary investigation with his directives concerning the performing of additional investigation;

(5) to annul illegal or unjustified decrees of agencies of inquiry or of preliminary investigation;

(6) to remove an investigator or person performing an inquiry in a case from further conduct of the investigation or inquiry if such persons have allowed a violation of the law in investigating the case;

(7) to withdraw any case from an agency of inquiry and to transfer it to an agency of preliminary investigation, as well as to transfer a case from one agency of preliminary investigation to another, with the aim of ensuring the fullest and most objective possible investigation of the case;

(8) to commission agencies of inquiry to perform individual investigative acts in cases being handled by investigators of agencies of the procuracy, in particular [to secure] the detention, appearance, or arrest of an accused person, to perform a search or seizure, or to search for criminals in hiding;

(9) to terminate criminal cases on the grounds indicated in the law.

Article 20. Directives of a procurator to agencies of inquiry and of preliminary investigation in connection with the investigation by them of criminal cases and given in the procedure provided by the procedural law shall be binding on such agencies.

Article 21. A procurator shall be obliged, within the time periods established by law to consider complaints addressed to him or received by him against actions of agencies of inquiry or of preliminary investigation and to inform complainants of decisions with respect to complaints.

CHAPTER IV

Supervision over the Legality and Grounds for Judgments,
Decisions, Rulings, and Decrees of Judicial Agencies

Article 22. The Procurator General of the USSR and procurators subordinate to him shall be obliged to exercise supervision over the legality and grounds for judgments, decisions, rulings, and decrees rendered by judicial agencies.

Article 23. The Procurator General of the USSR and procurators subordinate to him shall:

(1) participate in administrative sessions of a court;

(2) participate in consideration of criminal and civil cases in judicial sessions and give conclusions on questions arising during judicial consideration;

(3) support the state accusation in court during consideration of criminal cases;

(4) present claims [by instituting] either civil cases or civil suits in criminal cases, and support the suits in court, if such is required for protection of state or social interests or of the rights or legal interests of citizens;

(5) lodge protests, in the procedure established by law, against illegal or unjustified judgments, decisions, rulings, or decrees of judicial agencies;

(6) give conclusions with respect to criminal and civil cases being considered by a higher court on appeal or on protest;

(7) exercise supervision over execution of judgments of a court.

Article 24. The Procurator General of the USSR and all procurators subordinate to him shall have the right, within the limits of their competence, to demand and obtain by way of supervision the file of any civil or criminal case from judicial agencies for verification.

Article 25. The right of lodging protests against judgments, decisions, rulings, and decrees of a court which have taken legal effect shall belong:

to the Procurator General of the USSR and his deputies, with respect to judgments, decisions, rulings, and decrees of any court of the USSR or of union or autonomous republics;

to the procurator of a union republic and his deputies, with respect to judgments, decisions, rulings, and decrees of courts of the union republic and of autonomous republics forming part of it, except for decrees of the Presidium of the Supreme Court of the union republic;

to the procurator of an autonomous republic, with respect to judgments, decisions, and rulings of people's courts of the autonomous republic, as well as the rulings of judicial divisions of the Supreme Court of the autonomous republic as a court of second instance;

to the procurator of a territory, region, or autonomous region, with respect to judgments, decisions, and rulings of people's courts, as well as rulings of judicial divisions of the territorial or regional court, or court of the autonomous region, respectively, as a court of second instance;

to the Chief Military Procurator, with respect to judgments and rulings of any military tribunal;

to the military procurator of a military area (or fleet), with respect to judgments and rulings of inferior military tribunals.

Article 26. A protest against a judgment, decision, ruling, or decree of a court may be revoked by the procurator who lodged the protest or by a superior procurator, prior to the consideration of the protest by a court.

Article 27. The Procurator General of the USSR and his deputies shall have the right to suspend execution of a protested judgment, decision, ruling, or decree of any court of the USSR or of a union or autonomous republic, prior to resolution of the case by way of supervision.

The procurator of a union republic shall have the right to suspend execution of a protested judgment, decision, ruling, or decree of any court of the union republic or of autonomous republics which form part of it, prior to resolution of the case, by way of supervision.

Article 28. Participation of the Procurator General of the USSR in sessions of the Plenum of the Supreme Court of the USSR shall be obligatory.

Article 29. In the event that the Procurator General of the USSR discovers that a decree of the Plenum of the Supreme Court of the USSR does not conform to law, he shall be obliged to make a recommendation to the Presidium of the Supreme Soviet of the USSR with respect to such matter.

Article 30. The Procurator General of the USSR shall have the right to submit recommendations for consideration by the Plenum of the Supreme Court of the USSR concerning guiding explanations to be given to judicial agencies on questions of judicial practice.

Article 31. Procurators of union and autonomous republics, territories, regions, and autonomous regions shall participate in consideration of criminal and civil cases by Presidiums of Supreme Courts of union or autonomous republics, territorial or regional courts, or courts of autonomous regions.

CHAPTER V

Supervision over Observance of Legality in Places of Deprivation of Freedom

Article 32. The Procurator General of the USSR and procurators subordinate to him, within the limits of their competence, shall be obliged to exercise supervision to the end that only persons confined under guard with the sanction of a procurator or by decree of a court should be kept in places of deprivation of freedom, as well as [supervision]over observance of the rules established by law for the keeping of confined persons.

Agencies of the procuracy shall be charged with responsibility for observance of socialist legality in places of deprivation of freedom.

Article 33. A procurator shall be obliged to visit regularly places of deprivation of freedom to familiarize himself at first hand with the operation of their administration, to suspend execution of orders or regulations of the administration of places of deprivation of freedom which contradict the law and to protest them in the established procedure, as well as to take measures to bring to criminal or disciplinary responsibility persons guilty of violation of legality in places of deprivation of freedom.

Article 34. A procurator shall be obliged to free from under guard, without delay, anyone who has been unlawfully subjected to arrest or unlawfully kept under guard in places of deprivation of freedom.

Article 35. In exercising supervision over the legality of the keeping of persons confined in places of deprivation of freedom, the Procurator General of the USSR and procurators subordinate to him, within the limits of their competence, shall have the right:

(1) with the aim of verifying observance of the procedure established by law for the keeping of persons confined under guard, to visit places of deprivation of freedom at any time, with unobstructed access to all buildings;

(2) to familiarize himself with documents on the basis of which persons have been subjected to deprivation of freedom;

(3) personally to question confined persons;

(4) to verify conformity to law of orders and regulations of the administration of places of deprivation of freedom which determine the conditions and regime for the keeping of confined persons;

(5) to require personal explanations of representatives of the administration of places of deprivation of freedom concerning violations of the legality of keeping of confined persons.

Article 36. The administration of a place of deprivation of freedom shall be obliged within twenty-four hours to send to a procurator a complaint addressed to him or a petition of a confined person.

A procurator who has received a complaint or petition of a confined person shall be obliged to consider it within the time periods established by law, to take necessary measures, and to inform the complainant of his decision.

A procurator shall be obliged to see that complaints and petitions of confined persons are dispatched without delay by the administration of places of deprivation of freedom to those agencies or those officials to whom they are addressed.

Article 37. The administration of a place of deprivation of freedom shall be obliged to carry out proposals of a procurator regarding observance of the rules established by law for the keeping of confined persons.

CHAPTER VI

Structure of Agencies of the Procuracy, Procedure for Appointment and Service of Procuracy Personnel

Article 38. The Procuracy of the USSR shall be headed by the Procurator General of the USSR.

The Procurator General of the USSR, in accordance with Article 114 of the Constitution of the USSR, shall be appointed for a term of seven years by the Supreme Soviet of the USSR.

Article 39. The Procurator General of the USSR shall direct the activity of agencies of the procuracy and shall exercise supervision over the work of the procurators subordinate to him.

In the Procuracy of the USSR there shall be formed a Collegium, composed of the Procurator General of the USSR (as president) and leading personnel of the procuracy.

The members of the Collegium shall be appointed by the Presidium of the Supreme Soviet of the USSR upon recommendation of the Procurator General of the USSR.

At its sessions the Collegium shall consider, with the participation in necessary instances of personnel of local agencies of the procuracy, the most important questions of carrying out procuratorial supervision for legality in practice, verifying execution, and selecting and preparing procuratorial and investigatorial cadres,[shall consider]drafts of major orders and instructions, and shall hear reports of chiefs of administrations and sections of the Procuracy of the USSR, of procurators of union republics, and of other procuracy personnel.

Decisions of the Collegium shall be carried out by orders of the Procurator General of the USSR. In the event of disagreement between the Procurator General of the USSR and the Collegium, the Procurator General of the USSR shall carry out his own decision,reporting to the Presidium of the Supreme Soviet of the USSR concerning the disagreements which arose. Members of the Collegium may also contact the Presidium of the Supreme Soviet of the USSR.

Article 40. The Procurator General of the USSR shall have deputies, who shall be appointed upon his recommendation by the Presidium of the Supreme Soviet of the USSR.

Article 41. Within the Procuracy of the USSR there shall be formed administrations and sections, as well as a Chief Military Procuracy .

Chiefs of administrations and sections of the Procuracy of the USSR shall be senior assistants and assistants to the Procurator General of the USSR.

Within administrations and sections there shall be procurators of the administrations and sections.

The Chief Military Procuracy shall be headed by a Chief Military Procurator. Sections may be created within the Chief Military Procuracy.

Article 42. The table of organization of the central staff of the USSR Procuracy shall be confirmed by the Presidium of the Supreme Soviet of the USSR.

Article 43. Procuracies shall be formed in union republics, in autonomous republics, in territories, in regions, in autonomous regions, in national areas, in cities of republican, territorial, and regional rank, and in districts.

By decision of the Procurator General of the USSR a single procuracy may be created for several administrative districts.

Article 44. Military procuracies of military areas, fleets, formations, and garrisons shall be formed in the Soviet Army and Navy.

Article 45. In rail and water transportation, independent procuracies may be created in necessary instances by decision of the Procurator General of the USSR, with the rights of district procuracies and subordinate to the appropriate territorial procuracies.

Article 46. Procuracies of union republics shall be headed by procurators of union republics.

Procurators of union republics shall be appointed for a term of five years by the Procurator General of the USSR.

In procuracies of union republics there shall be formed collegia, composed of the procurator of the union republic (as president) and leading personnel of the procuracy of the republic.

The members of a collegium shall be appointed by the Procurator General of the USSR upon recommendation of the procurator of the union republic.

Collegia in procuracies of union republics shall consider in their sessions questions of verifying the organization of execution of orders of the Procurator General of the USSR with respect to the exercise of supervision over legality, shall hear reports of section chiefs, of procurators of ASSR's, territories, and regions, and of other personnel of procuracies of republics, and shall also consider questions of selecting and training procuratorial and investigative cadres, and drafts of major orders and instructions.

Decisions of a collegium shall be carried out by orders of the procurator of the union republic. In the event of disagreement between the procurator of the union republic and the collegium, the procurator of the union republic shall carry out his own decision, reporting to the Procurator General of the USSR concerning disagreements which arose. Members of the collegium may also contact the Procurator General of the USSR.

Procurators of union republics shall have deputies, senior assistants, and assistants.

In procuracies of union republics there shall be formed sections, whose chiefs shall be senior assistants or assistants of procurators of union republics.

Article 47. Procuracies of autonomous republics shall be headed by procurators of autonomous republics.

Procurators of autonomous republics shall be appointed for a term of five years by the Procurator General of the USSR.

Procurators of autonomous republics shall have deputies, senior assistants, and assistants.

In procuracies of autonomous republics there may be formed sections, whose chiefs shall be senior assistants or assistants of procurators of autonomous republics.

Article 48. Procuracies of territories, regions, and autonomous regions shall be headed by procurators of territories, regions, or autonomous regions.

Procurators of territories, regions, and autonomous regions shall be appointed for a term of five years by the Procurator General of the USSR.

Procurators of territories, regions, and autonomous regions shall have deputies, senior assistants, and assistants.

In procuracies of territories and regions there may be formed sections, whose chiefs shall be senior assistants or assistants of procurators of territories, regions, or autonomous regions.

Article 49. Procuracies of areas, districts, and cities shall be headed by procurators of areas, districts, or cities.

Procurators of areas, districts, and cities shall be appointed for a term of five years by procurators of union republics with confirmation by the Procurator General of the USSR.

Procurators of areas, districts, and cities shall have deputies and assistants.

Article 50. Investigators shall be attached to the Procurator General of the USSR, to procurators of union republics, and to the Chief Military Procurator, for especially important cases.

In procuracies of autonomous republics, territories, regions, and autonomous regions, there shall be senior investigators.

In procuracies of areas, cities, and districts, there shall be senior investigators and investigators.

Article 51. The table of organization and size of staffs of agencies of the procuracy shall be established by the Procurator General of the USSR within limits of the number of personnel which has been confirmed and of the wage fund.

Article 52. To the offices of procurator and investigator shall be appointed persons having a higher legal education.

In individual cases, persons who do not have a higher legal education may be appointed to the office of procurator or investigator only with permission of the Procurator General of the USSR.

Persons who have completed institutions of higher legal education shall be appointed to the office of procurator or investigator only after passing a one-year probationary period as investigator of a district (or city) procuracy or assistant to a district (or city) procurator.

Except for scholarly work and teaching, it shall not be permitted to serve in agencies of the procuracy and simultaneously to work in other institutions.

Article 53. Persons not younger than twenty-five years of age may be appointed procurators of territories, regions, autonomous regions, areas, cities, and districts, as well as military procurators.

Article 54. The procedure for appointing personnel to the office of procurator or investigator and for relieving them from such office, except for personnel the procedure for whose appointment is indicated in Articles 40, 46, 47, 48, and 49, shall be established by the Procurator General of the USSR.

Article 55. The procedure for disciplinary responsibility of procurators and investigators shall be established by the Presidium of the Supreme Soviet of the USSR upon recommendation of the Procurator General of the USSR.

Article 56. Established grade ranks shall be conferred on personnel of agencies of the Procuracy of the USSR in accordance with offices occupied by them.

The grade rank of Actual State Councillor of Justice shall be conferred by the Presidium of the Supreme Soviet of the USSR.

The grade ranks of State Councillor of Justice of grades I, II, and III shall be conferred by the Presidium of the Supreme Soviet of the USSR upon recommendation of the Procurator General of the USSR.

Other grade ranks shall be conferred by order of the Procurator General of the USSR, and the grade ranks of jurist of the first, second, and third classes, and of junior jurist [shall be conferred] as well by orders of procurators of union republics.

Article 57. Procuratorial and investigatory personnel holding grade ranks shall wear uniforms and established insignia of distinction when executing service duties.

12. STATUTE ON THE SUPREME COURT

Introductory Note

When it was orginally constituted in 1923, the USSR Supreme Court had the principal function of checking the conformity of federal statutes, decrees, regulations, and actions to the USSR Constitution and, in case of constitutional violation, of proposing to the Presidium of the Central Executive Committee the suspension of the statute, decree, regulation, or action. The Court's judicial functions were limited to hearing protests against decisions of republican supreme courts on grounds of violation of an all-union law or violation of the interests of another union republic and to proposing annulment of such decisions to the Presidium of the Central Executive Committee. The Supreme Court at this period possessed no independent right to overturn judicial decisions of the courts of the union republics.

In the 1930's the Court gradually shed its constitutional functions and acquired greater judicial functions. With the creation of the all-union procuracy (1933), the business of protesting unconstitutional legislative, administrative, and judicial acts was transferred to that agency. In 1934 the Court was for the first time empowered to quash rulings of republican supreme courts without referring the matter to the Presidium of the Central Executive Committee.

Prior to 1957, the activity of the Court was regulated by a chapter of the 1938 Law on Court Organization of the USSR and Union and Autonomous Republics. The 1957 Statute was the product of an effort to transform the USSR Supreme Court into a body which would continue to guide the work of lower courts but which would handle fewer actual cases. Union-republican courts, which had already been strengthened in 1954 by the creation of presidiums in courts above the level of people's court, were now further strengthened by drastically reducing the size of the USSR Supreme Court and dispatching a large number of judges from the high court to union-republican supreme courts. Further, presidents of republican supreme courts were made members of the USSR Supreme Court's plenum ex officio. In addition, the 1957 Statute forbade the USSR Supreme Court to hear a case which had not first passed through the supreme court of the union republic in which it arose.

A 1967 amendment to the Statute on the Supreme Court of the USSR furthered the movement to strengthen republican courts by allowing the president of the USSR Supreme Court, and his deputies, to refer to republican supreme courts protests against decisions of those courts as an alternative to bringing the protests before the USSR Supreme Court itself for consideration.

STATUTE ON THE SUPREME COURT OF THE USSR

(confirmed by a law of the Supreme Soviet of the USSR,
February 12, 1957, and amended by an edict of the Presidium
of the Supreme Soviet of the USSR, September 30, 1967)

Article 1. In accordance with Article 104 of the Constitution of the USSR,
the Supreme Court of the USSR shall be the highest judicial agency of the Union
of Soviet Socialist Republics.

The Supreme Court of the USSR shall be charged with supervision over the
judicial activity of judicial agencies of the USSR, as well as of judicial agencies
of union republics within the limits established by the present Statute. The Supreme Court of the USSR shall verify the application of all-union legislation by
union-republican judicial agencies, as well as the execution[by them]of decrees
of the Plenum of the Supreme Court of the USSR.

The Supreme Court of the USSR, in instances and in the procedure provided
by law, shall decide questions arising from legal assistance treaties concluded
by the USSR with other states.

The Supreme Court of the USSR shall have the right of legislative initiative.

Article 2. The Supreme Court of the USSR shall be responsible to the Supreme
Soviet of the USSR and, in the interval between sessions of the Supreme Soviet of
the USSR, to the Presidium of the Supreme Soviet of the USSR.

In administering justice members of the Supreme Court of the USSR and people's assessors of the Supreme Court of the USSR shall be independent and subordinate only to law.

Article 3.   The Supreme Court of the USSR shall consist of a President of
the Supreme Court of the USSR, Vice-Presidents of the Supreme Court of the
USSR, members of the Supreme Court of the USSR, and people's assessors, [all]
elected by the Supreme Soviet of the USSR, as well as of the presidents of the
Supreme Courts of the union republics, who shall be members of the Supreme
Court of the USSR ex officio.

The numerical composition of the Supreme Court of the USSR shall be established by the Supreme Soviet of the USSR at the time of election of the Supreme Court of the USSR.

Article 4. In accordance with Article 105 of the Constitution of the USSR, the Supreme Court of the USSR shall be elected for a term of five years.

Article 5. The Supreme Court of the USSR shall be governed in its activity by all-union laws as well as by the laws of union republics.

Article 6. The Supreme Court of the USSR shall include:

(a)   a Plenum of the Supreme Court of the USSR;

(b)   a Judicial Division for Civil Cases;

(c)   a Judicial Division for Criminal Cases;

(d)   a Military Division.

Article 7. The Plenum of the Supreme Court of the USSR shall consist of the President of the Supreme Court of the USSR, the Vice-Presidents of the Supreme Court of the USSR, and the members of the Supreme Court of the USSR.

Participation of the Procurator General of the USSR in sessions of the Plenum shall be obligatory.

Article 8.   The Plenum of the Supreme Court of the USSR shall be convoked by the President of the Supreme Court of the USSR at least once every three months.

A session of the Plenum shall be considered authorized [to act] if not less than 2/3 of its membership is present.

Decrees of the Plenums shall be adopted by a simple majority of the votes of the members of the Plenum of the Supreme Court of the USSR participating in the session.

Article 9.   The Plenum of the Supreme Court of the USSR shall:

(a)   consider protests of the President of the Supreme Court of the USSR and of the Procurator General of the USSR against decisions, judgments, and rulings of divisions of the Supreme Court of the USSR;

(b)   consider protests of the President of the Supreme Court of the USSR and of the Procurator General of the USSR against decrees of the Supreme Courts of union republics in the event that such decrees contradict all-union legislation or violate the interests of other union republics;

(c)   consider judicial statistics and materials summarzing judicial practice, and give guiding explanations to courts, in connection with the consideration of judicial cases, concerning questions of application of legislation;

(d) make recommendations to the Presidium of the Supreme Soviet of the USSR concerning questions which are subject to resolution by legislation and concerning questions of interpretation of USSR laws;

(e) resolve conflicts between judicial agencies of union republics;

(f) hear reports of presidents of judicial divisions of the Supreme Court concerning the activity of the divisions and reports of presidents of the Supreme Courts of union republics concerning judicial practice in the application of all-union legislation, as well as of decrees of the Plenum of the Supreme Court of the USSR.

Article 10. Judicial divisions shall be appointed by the Plenum of the Supreme Court of the USSR from among the members of the Supreme Court of the USSR.

The President of the Supreme Court of the USSR shall be granted the right to make changes in necessary instances in the composition of divisions, with subsequent submission for confirmation by the Plenum of the Supreme Court of the USSR.

Members of military tribunals of branches of the Armed Forces, areas, military groups, and fleets may be allowed, in case of necessity, to serve as reserve judges for consideration of judicial cases in the Military Division of the Supreme Court of the USSR.

Article 11. The Judicial Division for Civil Cases and the Judicial Division for Criminal Cases of the Supreme Court of the USSR shall:

(a) consider as a court of first instance civil and criminal cases, respectively, of exceptional importance referred by law to their jurisdiction;

(b) consider by way of judicial supervision protests of the President of the Supreme Court of the USSR, the Procurator General of the USSR, and their deputies against decisions and judgments of the Supreme Courts of union republics in civil and criminal cases in the event that such decisions or judgments contradict all-union legislation or violate the interests of other union republics.

Article 12. The Military Division of the Supreme Court of the USSR shall:

(a) consider as a court of first instance criminal cases of exceptional importance referred by law to its jurisdiction;

(b) consider appeals and interlocutory appeals and protests against judgments, decisions, and rulings of military tribunals of branches of the Armed Forces, areas, military groups, fleets, and separate armies in instances provided by law;

(c) consider by way of judicial supervision protests of the President of the Supreme Court of the USSR, the Procurator General of the USSR, and their deputies, as well as protests of the President of the Military Division of the Supreme Court of the USSR and the Chief Military Procurator against judgments, decisions, and rulings of military tribunals of branches of the Armed Forces, areas, military groups, fleets, and separate armies.

Article 13. In considering cases as a court of first instance, divisions of the Supreme Court of the USSR shall include a member of the Supreme Court of the USSR as the presiding judge and two people's assessors.

Divisions shall consider cassational appeals and protests, as well as protests by way of judicial supervision, in benches of three members of the court.

Article 14. Decisions of the Judicial Division for Civil Cases and judgments of the Judicial Division for Criminal Cases and the Military Division of the Supreme Court of the USSR shall be rendered in the name of the Union of Soviet Socialist Republics.

Article 15. The President of the Supreme Court of the USSR shall:

(a) submit to the Supreme Court of the USSR, in accordance with the present Statute, protests against decisions, judgments, and rulings of judicial divisions of the Supreme Court of the USSR, against decisions, judgments, and decrees of Supreme Courts of union republics, and against judgments, decisions, and rulings of military tribunals of branches of the Armed Forces, areas, military groups, fleets, and separate armies;

submit to presidiums and plenums of the Supreme Courts of union republics, in accordance with the competence of presidiums and plenums determined by the legislation of the union republics, protests against decisions, judgments, and decrees of the Supreme Courts of union republics in the event that they contradict all-union legislation or violate the interests of other union republics;

(b) preside at sessions of the Plenum of the Supreme Court of the USSR and, if he wishes, assume the presidency at judicial sessions of divisions of the Supreme Court of the USSR during the consideration of any case;

(c) exercise general organizational direction of the work of the divisions of the Supreme Court of the USSR;

(d) secure the preparation of materials on questions subject to consideration at a Plenum of the Supreme Court of the USSR;

(e) organize the work of keeping all-union judicial statistics;

(f) direct the work of the staff of the Supreme Court of the USSR.

In the absence of the President of the Supreme Court of the USSR, the Vice-President of the Supreme Court of the USSR shall exercise all his rights and duties.

Article 15[1]. Vice-Presidents of the Supreme Court of the USSR shall:

(a) submit to the Supreme Court of the USSR, in accordance with the present Statute, protests against decisions and judgments of the Supreme Courts of union republics, as well as protests against judgments, decisions, and rulings of military tribunals of branches of the Armed Forces, areas, military groups, fleets, and separate armies;

(b) submit to presidiums and plenums of the Supreme Courts of union republics, in accordance with the competence of presidiums and plenums determined by the legislation of the union republics, protests against decisions, judgments, and decrees of the Supreme Courts of union republics in the event that they contradict all-union legislation or violate the interests of other union republics;

(c) assume, if he wishes, the presidency at judicial sessions of divisions of the Supreme Court of the USSR during the consideration of cases.

Article 16. Presidents of divisions of the Supreme Court of the USSR shall:

(a) exercise direction of the work of the respective divisions;

(b) preside at preparatory and judicial sessions of divisions;

(c) form benches for judicial sessions of divisions from among the members of the respective divisions and the people's assessors;

(d) present to the Plenum of the Supreme Court of the USSR reports on the activity of the divisions.

The President of the Military Division shall also be charged with the organizational direction of military tribunals.

Article 17. The President, Vice-President, and members of the Supreme Court of the USSR, as well as people's assessors of the Supreme Court of the USSR, may not be brought to responsibility in court or arrested without the consent of the Supreme Soviet of the USSR and, in the interval between sessions, without the consent of the Presidium of the Supreme Soviet of the USSR.

Article 18. The President, Vice-President, and members of the Supreme Court of the USSR, as well as people's assessors of the Supreme Court of the USSR, may be relieved of their duties before expiration of their term of office only by decree of the Supreme Soviet of the USSR and, in the period between sessions, by decree of the Presidium of the Supreme Soviet of the USSR with subsequent confirmation by the Supreme Soviet of the USSR.

Article 19. The table of organization of the staff of the Supreme Court of the USSR shall be confirmed by the Presidium of the Supreme Soviet of the USSR.

Article 20. The Supreme Court of the USSR shall publish a Bulletin of the Supreme Court of the USSR.

13. STATUTE ON MILITARY TRIBUNALS

Introductory Note

Military tribunals form the only hierarchy of federal courts in the Soviet Union, being subordinate not to republican supreme courts but directly to the Military Division of the Supreme Court of the USSR. Similarly, the military procuracy and military criminal investigators are not subject to control by procurators of the union republics but are immediately subordinate to the Chief Military Procuracy of the federal procuracy office.

The 1958 Statute superseded the provisions on military tribunals contained in the often amended 1926 USSR Statute on Military Tribunals and the Military Procuracy. The military procuracy continued to be regulated by the 1926 statute until adoption of a new Statute on the Military Procuracy in 1966. In addition, the 1955 Statute on Procuracy Supervision (See Document 11) regulates certain basic aspects of the military procuracy's activities.

The Statute limits the jurisdiction of military tribunals to crimes committed by military personnel and to cases of espionage (by whomever committed). Prior to the 1958 Statute, military tribunals had jurisdiction not only over cases of espionage but also over many other types of crimes against the state committed by civilians. The 1958 Statute also abolished the previous system of appointment of people's assessors by regional or territorial soviets, replacing it with election of assessors at general meetings of military personnel.

The prisoner escort guards referred to in Articles 9 (c) and 28 are now under the Ministry of the Protection of Public Order of the USSR, which is the successor of the Ministry of Internal Affairs of the USSR (MVD).

STATUTE ON MILITARY TRIBUNALS

(confirmed by a law of the Supreme Soviet of the USSR,
December 25, 1958, amended by a decree of the Presidium of the
Supreme Soviet of the USSR, February 21, 1968)

CHAPTER I

General Provisions

Article 1.　In accordance with Article 102 of the Constitution of the USSR,
military tribunals shall be courts of the USSR and shall be part of the unitary
judicial system of the USSR.

Judgments and decisions rendered by military tribunals shall be proclaimed
in the name of the Union of Soviet Socialist Republics.

Article 2.　In carrying out the tasks of socialist justice, military tribunals
shall be called upon to wage a struggle against infringements on the security of
the USSR, the fighting capacity of its Armed Forces, military discipline, and
the established procedure for performing military service in the Armed Forces
of the USSR.

Article 3.　Cases in military tribunals shall be considered collegially.

In considering cases as a court of first instance, military tribunals shall include the president, or the vice-president, or a member of the tribunal as the
presiding judge, and two people's assessors.

Cases on appeals and interlocutory appeals and protests, as well as cases on
protests by way of judicial supervision, shall be considered by a bench of three
members of the military tribunal.

Article 4.　Citizens of the USSR who are in the active military service and
who have attained the age of 25 years by election day may be elected as presidents, vice-presidents, and members of military tribunals.

Presidents, vice-presidents, and members of military tribunals shall be elected by the Presidium of the Supreme Soviet of the USSR for a term of five years.

Article 5. Every citizen of the USSR who is in the active military service may be elected as people's assessor of a military tribunal.

People's assessors of military tribunals shall be elected by open ballot at general meetings of military personnel of a military unit (or institution) for a term of two years.

During discharge of their duties in court people's assessors shall have all the rights of a judge.

Article 6. In administering justice, presidents, vice-presidents, and members of military tribunals, as well as people's assessors of military tribunals, shall be independent and subordinate only to law.

Article 7. Military tribunals shall be governed in their activity by the legislation of the USSR and the legislation of union republics.

Article 8. Military tribunals shall be organized in, and shall function in, areas, military groups, fleets, armies, flotillas, military formations, and garrisons. When necessary, military tribunals of branches of the Armed Forces of the USSR may be created as well.

CHAPTER II

Jurisdiction of Military Tribunals

Article 9. Military tribunals shall have jurisdiction over:

(a) cases of all crimes committed by military personnel, as well as by persons under military obligation during their training periods;

(b) cases of all crimes committed by officers, noncommissioned officers, and enlisted personnel of agencies of state security;

(c) cases of crimes against the established procedure for performing service committed by persons of the commanding staff of corrective-labor institutions, as well as by noncommissioned officers and enlisted men called up to serve in the escort guard of the MVD of the USSR;

(d) all cases of espionage;

(e) cases of crimes committed by persons with respect to whom there is a special reference in the legislation of the USSR.

Article 10. In areas where, because of exceptional circumstances, ordinary courts do not function, military tribunals shall consider all criminal and civil cases.

Article 11. In connection with criminal cases, military tribunals shall consider civil suits of military units (and institutions), state and social enterprises, institutions, and organizations, as well as by individual citizens, for compensation for material damage caused them by crimes.

Article 12. In the prosecution of one person or of a group of persons for the commission of several crimes, if the case of at least one of the crimes is subject to the jurisdiction of a military tribunal, but the case of the others [is subject to the jurisdiction] of any other court, the case of all the crimes shall be considered by the military tribunal.

In the prosecution of a group of persons for the commission of one or several crimes, if the case of at least one of the accused is subject to the jurisdiction of a military tribunal, but the case of the rest [is subject to the jurisdiction] of any other court, the case of all the accused shall be considered by the military tribunal.

Article 13. Cases of crimes committed by persons specified in sections "a," "b," and "c" of Article 9 of the present Statute during the period of their service but who are discharged by the time the case is considered in court shall be considered by military tribunals.

Cases of crimes committed by persons prior to being called to military service or prior to starting service in agencies of state security, but who by the time the case is considered are in military service or in service in agencies of state security, shall be considered by ordinary courts.

Article 14. Military tribunals of armies, flotillas, military formations, and garrisons shall have jurisdiction over cases of crimes of persons holding military ranks up to lieutenant-colonel or second captain inclusive, as well as over all civil cases in instances provided by Article 10 of the present Statute.

Article 15. Military tribunals of branches of the Armed Forces, of areas, of military groups, of fleets, and of individual armies shall have jurisdiction over:

(a) cases of crimes of persons holding the military ranks of colonel and first captain;

(b) cases of crimes of persons occupying offices of commander of a regiment, second ship commander, and higher, and of persons equal to them in service status;

(c) cases of all crimes for which in peacetime the death penalty is provided by law.

Article 16. The Military Division of the Supreme Court of the USSR shall have jurisdiction over criminal cases of exceptional importance, cases of crimes of military personnel holding the military rank of general (or admiral), as well as of military personnel occupying the office of commander of a formation and higher, and their equals.

Article 17. The question of the transfer of cases from military tribunals of one branch of the Armed Forces, area, military group, fleet, or separate army to the military tribunal of another branch of the Armed Forces, area, military group, fleet, or separate army shall be decided by the president of the Military Division of the Supreme Court of the USSR.

Within the limits of a branch of the Armed Forces, area, military group, or fleet, the question of transfer of a case from one military tribunal to another shall be decided by the president of the military tribunal of the branch of the Armed Forces, area, military group, or fleet.

Article 18. A higher military tribunal and the Military Division of the Supreme Court of the USSR shall have the right to take jurisdiction as a court of first instance over any case subject to the jurisdiction of a lower military tribunal.

CHAPTER III

Supervision over the Judicial Activity of Military Tribunals

Article 19. The Supreme Court of the USSR shall exercise supervision over the judicial activity of military tribunals.

Article 20. The Military Division of the Supreme Court of the USSR shall:

(a) consider cases on appeals and interlocutory appeals and on protests against judgments, decisions, and rulings of military tribunals of branches of the Armed Forces, areas, military groups, fleets, and separate armies;

(b) consider by way of judicial supervision cases on protests of the President of the Supreme Court of the USSR and Procurator General of the USSR and their deputies, of the President of the Military Division of the Supreme Court of the USSR, and of the Chief Military Procurator against judgments, decisions, and rulings of military tribunals of branches of the Armed Forces, areas, military groups, fleets, and separate armies.

Article 21. Military tribunals of branches of the Armed Forces, areas, military groups, and fleets shall:

(a) consider cases on appeals and interlocutory appeals and on protests against judgments, decisions, and rulings of military tribunals of armies, flotillas, military formations, and garrisons;

(b) consider by way of judicial supervision cases on protests of the President of the Supreme Court of the USSR and the Procurator General of the USSR and their deputies, of the President of the Military Division of the Supreme Court of the USSR, of the Chief Military Procurator, and of the presidents of military tribunals and military procurators of branches of the Armed Forces, areas, military groups, and fleets against judgments, decisions, and rulings of military tribunals of armies, flotillas, military formations, and garrisons.

CHAPTER IV

Organizational Direction of Military Tribunals

Article 22. The table of organization and staff size of military tribunals shall be determined by the President of the Military Division of the Supreme Court of the USSR jointly with the USSR Ministry of Defense.

The personnel of military tribunals and of the Military Division of the Supreme Court of the USSR shall be part of the staff of the Armed Forces of the USSR and shall be provided with all forms of allowances on equal terms with the personnel of military units and institutions of the USSR Ministry of Defense.

A list of staff offices for the officers of military tribunals and the Military Division of the Supreme Court of the USSR and [a list] of military ranks corresponding to such offices shall be confirmed by the Presidium of the Supreme Soviet of the USSR on the joint recommendation of the President of the Supreme Court of the USSR and the USSR Minister of Defense.

Article 23.   Officers and noncommissioned officers of military tribunals and of the Military Division of the Supreme Court of the USSR shall be in the active military service, and statutes on performance of military service, troop rules, and orders of the USSR Ministry of Defense determining the procedure for performing service shall extend to them.

The conferring of the military ranks of junior and senior officers on military personnel of the Military Division of the Supreme Court of the USSR and military tribunals shall be done on the recommendations of the president of the Military Division and presidents of military tribunals of branches of the Armed Forces, areas, military groups, and fleets in a procedure established by the Council of Ministers of the USSR.

The military ranks of generals shall be conferred by the Council of Ministers of the USSR on the joint recommendation of the President of the Supreme Court of the USSR and the USSR Minister of Defense.

Article 24.   The President of the Military Division of the Supreme Court of the USSR shall:

(a) organize verification of the activity of military tribunals;

(b) direct study of the judicial practice of military tribunals and the keeping of judicial statistics;

(c) prepare jointly with the USSR Ministry of Defense proposals on questions of the organization of military tribunals;

(d) publish orders concerning the organization of the work of military tribunals.

Article 25.   The presidents of military tribunals of branches of the Armed Forces, areas, military groups, and fleets shall:

(a) organize verification of the activity of inferior military tribunals;

(b) direct study of the judicial practice of inferior military tribunals and the keeping of judicial statistics;

(c) give instructions concerning the organization of the work of inferior military tribunals;

(d) determine by agreement with the appropriate military councils the number of people's assessors for military tribunals of branches of the Armed Forces, areas, military groups, fleets, and lower military tribunals.

Article 26. Appointment and dismissal from office of employees of military tribunals shall be done by the president of the respective military tribunal.

Article 27. The President of the Military Division of the Supreme Court of the USSR shall inform the USSR Minister of Defense and the head of the Chief Political Administration of the Soviet Army and Navy about questions which arise in the activity of military tribunals.

Presidents of military tribunals of branches of the Armed Forces, areas, military groups, fleets, armies, and flotillas shall inform the appropriate military councils about questions which arise in the activity of military tribunals, and presidents of military tribunals of troop formations and garrisons [shall so inform] the appropriate military command and political agencies.

Article 28. Material and technical supply, financing, providing transportation and means of communication, and keeping the archives of military tribunals shall be carried out by appropriate institutions of the USSR Ministry of Defense.

Protection of the buildings of military tribunals shall be provided by military units of those formations and garrisons for which the military tribunals function.

Escorting persons arrested to military tribunals and guarding them shall be done by military units of those formations and garrisons for which the military tribunals function, as well as by units of the escort guard of the MVD of the USSR.

CHAPTER V

Responsibility of Members of Military Tribunals

Article 29. Presidents, vice-presidents, and members of military tribunals shall bear disciplinary responsibility for violation   of military discipline and for service offenses in the procedure established by the legislation of the USSR on disciplinary responsibility of judges.

Article 30. Presidents, vice-presidents, and members of military tribunals may not be brought to criminal responsibility, removed from office, or subjected to arrest without the consent of the Presidium of the Supreme Soviet of the USSR.

14. LAW ON COURT ORGANIZATION

Introductory Note

In 1924 the Central Executive Committee of the USSR adopted the "Fundamental Principles of Court Organization of the USSR and Union Republics." These Fundamental Principles prescribed only the most important postulates of court organization; on the basis of the Fundamental Principles each of the union republics adopted its own comprehensive legislation on court organization.

In 1938, as part of a movement to centralize the administration of justice, the USSR Supreme Soviet enacted a law "On Court Organization of the USSR and of Union and Autonomous Republics," which replaced the republican legislation on court organization and provided uniform regulation of court organization for the entire Soviet Union. The 1938 law abolished the plenums (or presidiums) which had existed in union-republican supreme courts, autonomous republic supreme courts, and regional and territorial courts, and it removed from courts below the level of union-republic supreme court the right to hear protests by way of supervision (that is, protests against court decisions which have already taken legal effect).

In 1957, as part of the same movement toward decentralization which brought important changes in the Statute on the Supreme Court of the USSR (see Document 12), the union republics were once again given the right to enact laws on court organization, and the all-union authority was once again restricted to the enactment of fundamental principles. Consequently, the Supreme Soviet in 1958 adopted the "Fundamental Principles of Legislation on Court Organization of the USSR and of Union and Autonomous Republics," on the basis of which the union republics later enacted their own laws. There are no major differences among the various republican laws on court organization.

The 1960 RSFSR law (like that of the other union republics) provides for presidiums in the RSFSR Supreme Court, autonomous republic supreme courts, and regional and territorial courts, with the right to hear protests by way of supervision. In fact these presidiums had already been established and given the right to hear supervisory protests by an all-union law of 1954.

LAW ON COURT ORGANIZATION OF THE RSFSR

(adopted by the Supreme Soviet of the RSFSR, October 27, 1960, and
amended by edicts of the Presidium of the Supreme Soviet of the RSFSR,
June 29, 1961, October 13, 1961, October 11 1962, February 20, 1964, and
September 9, 1968)

CHAPTER I

General Provisions

Article 1. Judicial system. In accordance with Article 107 of the Constitution of the RSFSR, justice in the RSFSR shall be administered by the Supreme Court of the RSFSR, by Supreme Courts of autonomous republics, by territorial, regional, and city courts, by courts of autonomous regions, by courts of national areas, and by district (or city) people's courts.

Article 2. Goals of justice. Justice in the RSFSR in called upon to protect from any infringements:

(a) the social and state system secured by the USSR Constitution, by the RSFSR Constitution, and by constitutions of autonomous republics, the socialist system of economy, and socialist ownership;

(b) political, labor, housing, and other personal and property rights and interests of citizens guaranteed by the USSR Constitution, by the RSFSR Constitution, and by constitutions of autonomous republics;

(c) rights and legally protected interests of state enterprises, institutions, collective farms, cooperative and other social organizations.

Justice in the RSFSR has as its task the securing of the strict and undeviating execution of the laws by all institutions, organizations, officials, and citizens.

Article 3. Tasks of courts. By all its activity a court shall educate citizens in the spirit of loyalty to the Motherland and to the cause of communism, and in the spirit of strict and undeviating execution of Soviet laws, of an attitude of care toward socialist ownership, of observance of labor discipline, of an honorable attitude toward state and social duty, and of respect for the rights, honor, and dignity of citizens and for rules of socialist community living.

In applying measures of criminal punishment a court not only chastises criminals but also has as its purpose their correction and re-education.

Article 4.   Administration of justice through judicial consideration of civil and criminal cases.   Justice in the RSFSR shall be administered through:

(a)   consideration and resolution in judicial sessions of civil cases concerning disputes affecting the rights and legal interests of citizens, state enterprises, institutions, collective farms, and cooperative and other social organizations;

(b)   consideration in judicial sessions of criminal cases and either the application of measures of punishment established by law to persons guilty of committing a crime or the acquittal of the innocent.

Article 5.   Equality of citizens before the law and the courts.   Justice in the RSFSR shall be administered on the basis of equality of citizens before the law and the courts, without regard to their social, property, or occupational status, nationality, race, or religious confession.

Article 6.   Administration of justice in strict accordance with law.   Justice in the RSFSR shall be administered in strict accordance with legislation of the USSR, the RSFSR, and autonomous republics.

Article 7.   Independence of judges and their subordination only to law.   In accordance with Article 116 of the Constitution of the RSFSR, judges and people's assessors in administering justice shall be independent and subordinate only to law.

Article 8.   Formation of all courts on basis of election.   In accordance with Articles 110-113 of the Constitution of the RSFSR, all courts in the RSFSR shall be formed on the basis of election.

Article 9.   Requirements for candidates for judge and people's assessor.   Every citizen of the USSR who possesses the right to vote and has attained the age of 25 years by election day may be elected a judge or a people's assessor.

Article 10.   Collegial consideration of cases in all courts.   Cases in courts shall be considered collegially.

Consideration of cases in all courts of first instance shall be by a judge and two people's assessors.

Cases on appeals or on protests shall be considered in judicial divisions of higher courts by benches of three members of the particular court.

Cases on protests against decisions, judgments, rulings, or decrees of courts which have taken legal effect shall be considered in judicial divisions of the Supreme Court of the RSFSR in benches of three members of the court.

Presidiums of courts shall consider cases with a majority of the members of the presidium present.

Article 11.   Equal rights of people's assessors and judges in the administration of justice.   During discharge of their duties in court people's assessors shall exercise all the rights of a judge.

Article 12.   Open examination of cases in all courts.   In accordance with Article 115 of the Constitution of the RSFSR, examination of cases in all courts of the RSFSR shall be open, insofar as an exception is not provided by law.

Article 13.   Guaranteeing an accused the right to defense.   In accordance with Article 115 of the Constitution of the RSFSR, an accused shall be guaranteed the right to defense.

Article 14.   Language in which judicial proceedings shall be conducted. In accordance with Article 114 of the Constitution of the RSFSR, judicial proceedings in the RSFSR shall be conducted in the Russian language or in the language of the autonomous republic or autonomous region or national area, but in instances provided by constitutions of autonomous republics [they shall be conducted] in the language of the majority of the population of the district, persons not having command of that language being secured full acquaintance with materials of the case through an interpreter as well as the right to speak in court in their native language.

Article 15.   Period for which people's assessors shall be called upon for discharge of duties in court.   People's assessors shall be called upon for discharge of their duties in courts in turn, according to a list, for not more than two weeks a year, except in instances when extension of this period is necessitated to complete the consideration of a case commenced with their participation.

Article 16.   Retention of average wages for people's assessors during discharge of their duties in court.   People's assessors who are workers, employees, or collective farmers shall receive their average wages at their place of work for the time during which they discharge their duties in court.

People's assessors who are not workers, employees, or collective farmers shall be conpensated for expenses connected with discharge of their duties in court.

The manner and amounts of reimbursement shall be established by the Presidium of the Supreme Soviet of the RSFSR.

Article 17.   Reports of people's judges to the voters.   People's judges shall systematically report to the voters on their work and the work of the people's court.

Article 18.   Accountability of courts to the agencies which elected them. Territorial, regional, and city courts, courts of autonomous regions, and courts of national areas shall be accountable to the respective Soviets of Working People's Deputies.

Supreme courts of autonomous republics shall be accountable to Supreme Soviets of autonomous republics or, in the interval between sessions, to presidiums of Supreme Soviets of autonomous republics.

The Supreme Court of the RSFSR shall be accountable to the Supreme Soviet of the RSFSR or, in the interval between sessions, to the Presidium of the Supreme Soviet of the RSFSR.

Article 19.   Early recall of judges and people's assessors.   Judges and people's assessors may be prematurely deprived of their powers only by recall of the voters or agency which elected them or by reason of a court judgment passed on them.

Procedure for early recall of judges and people's assessors shall be established by the Statute on Early Recall of Judges and People's Assessors confirmed by the Presidium of the Supreme Soviet of the RSFSR.

Article 20.   Relief of judges from office.   Judges may be relieved from office before expiration of the term of office in connection with lengthy illness or transfer to other work, as well as upon their request if there exist valid reasons.

Early relief of people's judges shall be carried out by a decision of the executive committee of the Soviet of Working People's Deputies of the national area, autonomous region, city, region, or territory, by preliminary agreement with the Supreme Court of the RSFSR or, in an autonomous republic, by decree of the Presidium of the Supreme Soviet of the autonomous republic, as well as by preliminary agreement with the Supreme Court of the RSFSR.

Early relief of presidents, vice-presidents, and members of territorial, regional, and city courts, courts of autonomous regions, and courts of national areas shall be carried out by decision of the Soviet of Working People's Deputies of the territory, region, city, autonomous region, or national area, respectively.

Early relief from office of a president, vice-presidents, or members of Supreme Courts of autonomous republics, as well as of the Supreme Court of the RSFSR, shall be carried out by a decree of the Presidium of the Supreme Soviet of the autonomous republic or the Presidium of the Supreme Soviet of the RSFSR, respectively, with subsequent submission for confirmation by the Supreme Soviet of the autonomous republic [or] the Supreme Soviet of the RSFSR.

Article 21. Procedure for elections of people's judges to replace those who have departed before expiration of the term of office. In the event of departure of a people's judge before the expiration of his term of office, the election of a people's judge to replace him for the remainder of his term of office shall be organized by the Presidium of the Supreme Soviet of the autonomous republic, or by the executive committee of the territorial, regional, or city Soviet of Working People's Deputies, of the Soviet of Working People's Deputies of the autonomous region, or of the Soviet of Working People's Deputies of the national area, in accordance with the Statute on Elections of District (or City) People's Courts of the RSFSR.

Article 22. Procedure for elections of a president, vice-presidents, and members of courts to replace those who have departed before expiration of the term of office. In the event of departure before expiration of the term of office of a president, vice-presidents, or members of courts of national areas, courts of autonomous regions, city, regional, or territorial courts, Supreme Courts of autonomous republics, or the Supreme Court of the RSFSR, elections of a new president, vice-presidents, or members of courts for the remainder of the term of office shall be conducted at a regular session of the Soviets of Working People's Deputies of the national area, autonomous region, city, region, territory, Supreme Soviets of autonomous republics, or the Supreme Soviet of the RSFSR, respectively.

Article 23. College of advocates. Colleges of advocates shall operate for the purpose of providing defense at the preliminary investigation and in court, and also for rendering other legal aid to citizens, enterprises, institutions, and organizations.

Colleges of advocates shall be voluntary societies of persons engaged in advocacy, and they shall operate on the basis of a Statute confirmed by the Supreme Soviet of the RSFSR.

Article 24. <u>Participation of a procurator in court.</u> The Procurator General of the USSR, the Procurator of the RSFSR, and procurators subordinate to them, on the basis of and in accordance with the procedure established by law, shall participate in administrative sessions and in judicial sessions during consideration of criminal and civil cases, shall support the state accusation in court, shall present and support suits in court, and shall exercise supervision over the legality and validity of judgments, decisions, rulings, and decrees rendered by courts, as well as over the execution of judgments.

Article 25. <u>Social accusers and social defense counsel.</u> Social accusation and defense in court may be carried out by representatives of social organizations in the procedure established by law.

In instances provided for by legislation, victims of a crime may also support an accusation.

Article 26. <u>Direction and supervision of the activity of RSFSR courts.</u> The Supreme Court of the RSFSR shall exercise direction and supervision of the activity of all courts of the RSFSR.

Supreme Courts of autonomous republics, territorial, regional, and city courts, courts of autonomous regions, and courts of national areas shall exercise direction and supervision of the activity of the district (or city) people's courts of autonomous republics, territories, regions, cities, autonomous regions, and national areas, respectively.

CHAPTER II
District (or City) People's Courts

Article 27. <u>Formation of district (or city) people's courts.</u> District (or city) people's courts shall operate in each district or in a city not divided into districts.

The Council of Ministers of the RSFSR, upon the recommendation of the Supreme Court of the RSFSR, may form one people's court for a district and city, or for a district and cities and settlements situated in the territory of the district, or for a city and part of a rural district.

Article 28. <u>Procedure for election of district (or city) people's courts.</u> People's judges of district (or city) people's courts shall be elected by citizens of the district (or city) on the basis of universal, equal, and direct suffrage by secret ballot for a term of five years.

People's assessors of district (or city) people's courts shall be elected by open ballot at general meetings of workers, employees, and peasants at their place of work or residence, and at general meetings of military personnel in their military units, for a term of two years.

Procedure for elections of district (or city) people's courts shall be established by the Statute on Elections of District (or City) People's Courts of the RSFSR confirmed by the Presidium of the Supreme Soviet of the RSFSR.

Article 29. Number of people's judges and people's assessors. The number of people's judges and people's assessors for each district (or city) people's court shall be established by the executive committee of the territorial, regional, or city Soviet of Working People's Deputies, the Soviet of Working People's Deputies of the autonomous region, or the Soviet of Working People's Deputies of the national area, upon the recommendation of the president of the territorial, regional, or city court, court of the autonomous region, or court of the national area, respectively.

The number of people's judges and people's assessors for each district (or city) people's court in an autonomous republic shall be established by the Presidium of the Supreme Soviet of the autonomous republic upon recommendation of the president of the Supreme Court of the autonomous republic.

Article 30. Competence of district (or city) people's courts. District (or city) people's courts shall consider all criminal and civil cases with the exception of cases referred by law to the juristiction of other courts.

Article 31. Presidents of district (or city) people's courts. In a district where several people's judges are elected, the district Soviet of Working People's Deputies, and in a city not divided into districts, the city Soviet of Working People's Deputies, upon the recommendation of the president of the Supreme Court of the autonomous republic, territorial, regional, or city court, court of the autonomous region, or court of the national area, respectively, shall appoint a president of the district (or city) people's court from among the elected people's judges.

The president of a district (or city) court shall:

(a)   preside at judicial sessions or assign people's judges to do so;

(b)   direct study of the judicial practice of the court;

(c) direct the work of the court's secretarial office;

(d) appoint sheriffs and direct their work;

(e) exercise general organizational direction of the work of the court.

Article 32. Replacement of temporarily absent presidents of district (or city) people's courts or people's judges. In the event of the temporary absence (illness, vacation, etc.) of the president of a district (or city) people's court, discharge of his duties shall be entrusted to one of the people's judges by the executive committee of the district (or city) Soviet of Working People's Deputies.

In the event of the temporary absence of a people's judge, discharge of his duties shall be entrusted to a people's judge of the same district or to a people's judge of another district by the president of the Supreme Court of the autonomous republic, territorial, regional, or city court, court of the autonomous region, or court of the national area, respectively, or to one of the people's assessors by the executive committee of the district (or city) Soviet of Working People's Deputies.

CHAPTER III

Territorial, Regional, and City Courts, Courts of Autonomous Regions, and Courts of National Areas

Article 33. Procedure for election of territorial, regional, and city courts, courts of autonomous regions, and courts of national areas. In accordance with Article 112 of the Constitution of the RSFSR, territorial, regional, and city courts, courts of autonomous regions, and courts of national areas shall be elected by territorial, regional, or city Soviets of Working People's Deputies, Soviets of Working People's Deputies of autonomous regions, or Soviets of Working People's Deputies of national areas, respectively, for a term of five years.

The numerical composition of territorial, regional, and city courts, courts of autonomous regions, and courts of national areas shall be established by the territorial, regional or city Soviet of Working People's Deputies, Soviet of Working People's Deputies of the autonomous region, or Soviet of Working People's Deputies of the national area, respectively, at the time of election of the court.

Article 34. Competence of territorial, regional, city courts, courts of autonomous regions, and courts of national areas. Territorial, regional, and city courts, courts of autonomous regions, and courts of national areas shall consider:

(a) civil and criminal cases of first instance referred by law to their juris-diction;

(b) cases on appeals and on protests against decisions, judgments, and rulings of district (or city) people's courts which have not taken legal effect;

(c) cases on protests against decisions, judgments, and rulings of district (or city) people's courts which have taken legal effect and against decrees of people's judges to bring to trial.

Territorial, regional, and city courts, courts of autonomous regions, and courts of national areas shall check the work of district (or city) people's courts, shall render practical help in their work, shall exercise direction and supervision of their activity, and shall organize the study and summarizing of judicial practice.

Article 35. Composition of territorial, regional, city courts, courts of auton-omous regions, and courts of national areas. Territorial, regional, and city courts, courts of autonomous regions, and courts of national areas shall consist of a president, vice-president, members of the court, and people's assessors, and shall include:

(a) a judicial division for civil cases;

(b) a judicial division for criminal cases;

(c) a presidium of the court.

Article 36. Judicial divisions of territorial, regional, and city courts, courts of autonomous regions, and courts of national areas. The judicial division for civil cases and the judicial division for criminal cases of a territorial, regional, or city court, court of an autonomous regions, or court of a national area shall consider, respectively, civil and criminal cases of first instance referred by law to the jurisdiction of such courts, as well as cases on appeals and on protests against decisions, judgments, and rulings of district (or city) people's courts which have not taken legal effect.

Orgainizational direction of the work of judicial divisions shall be carried out by the presidents of the judicial divisions.

Presidents of judicial divisions shall be appointed by the executive committee of the appropriate Soviet of Working People's Deputies, upon the recommendation of the president of the territorial, regional, or city court, court of the autonomous region, or court of the national area, from among the vice-presidents and mem-bers of the court.

224

Article 37.   Presidiums of territorial, regional, and city courts, courts of autonomous regions, and courts of national areas.   The presidium of a territorial, regional, or city court, court of an autonomous region, or court of a national area shall consist of a president, vice-presidents, and members of the court in a number determined by the executive committee of the Soviet of Working People's Deputies of the territory, region, city, autonomous region, or national area, respectively.

The membership of the Presidium shall be appointed by the executive committee of the respective Soviet of Working People's Deputies upon the recommendation of the president of the territorial, regional, or city court, court of the autonomous region, or court of the national area.

Participation of the procurator of the territory, region, city, autonomous region, or national area in a session of the presidium shall be obligatory during the consideration of judicial cases.

Article 38.   Competence of presidiums of territorial, regional, and city courts, courts of autonomous regions, and courts of national areas.   The presidium of a territorial, regional, or city court, court of an autonomous region, or court of a national area shall consider cases on protests against decisions, judgments, and rulings of district (or city) people's courts which have taken legal effect, [on protests] against decrees of people's judges to bring to trial, as well as [on protests] against rulings of judicial divisions of the territorial, regional, or city court, court of an autonomous region, or court of a national area rendered with respect to appeals or protests.

The presidium of a territorial, regional, or city court, court of an autonomous region, or court of a national area shall consider questions concerning the work of judicial divisions, materials of verifications of the work of district (or city) people's courts, judicial statistics, and materials summarizing judicial practice, and questions of work with cadres.

Article 39.   Presidents of territorial, regional, and city courts, courts of autonomous regions, and courts of national areas.   The president of a territorial, regional, or city court, court of an autonomous region, or court of a national area shall:

(a)   preside at judicial sessions of divisions or assign his deputy, the president of a judicial division, or a member of the court to do so;

(b)   bring protests, in the procedure established by law, against decisions, judgments, and rulings of district (or city) people's courts which have taken legal effect, against decrees of people's judges to bring to trial, as well as against rulings of judicial divisions rendered with respect to appeals or protests;

(c)   convoke the presidium of the court and preside at its sessions; submit for consideration by the presidium questions requiring its decision;

(d)   assign members of the court to judicial divisions;

(e)   organize the work of summarizing judicial practice and keeping judicial statistics;

(f)   entrust discharge of the duties of a people's judge, in the event of his temp - orary absence, to a people's judge of the same district or to a people's judge of another district;

(g)   appoint sheriffs for district (or city) people's courts;

(h)   exercise general organizational direction of the work of the court.

In the absence of the president of the court, the vice-president of the court shall exercise his rights and duties.

CHAPTER IV

Supreme Courts of Autonomous Republics

Article 40.   Supreme Courts of ASSR's—the highest judicial agencies of autonomous republics.   The Supreme Court of an autonomous republic shall be the highest judicial agency of the autonomous republic.

The Supreme Court of an autonomous republic shall be charged with supervision of the judicial activity of all courts of the autonomous republic.

The Supreme Court of an autonomous republic shall have the right of legislative intiative.

Article 41.   Procedure for election of Supreme Courts of autonomous republics.   In accordance with Article 111 of the Constitution of the RSFSR, the Supreme Court of an autonomous republic shall be elected by the Supreme Soviet of the autonomous republic for a term of five years.

The numerical composition of the Supreme Court of an autonomous republic shall be established by the Supreme Soviet of the autonomous republic   at the time of election of the court.

Article 42. Competence of Supreme Courts of autonomous republics. The Supreme Court of an autonomous republic shall consider:

(a) civil and criminal cases of first instance referred by law to its jurisdiction;

(b) cases on appeals and on protests against decisions, judgments, and rulings of district (or city) people's courts which have not taken legal effect;

(c) cases on protests against decisions, judgments, and rulings of district (or city) people's courts which have taken legal effect and against decrees of people's judges to bring to trial.

The Supreme Court of an autonomous republic shall check the work of district (or city) people's courts, shall render practical help in their work, shall exercise direction and supervision of their activity, and shall organize the study and summarizing of judicial practice.

Article 43. Composition of Supreme Courts of autonomous republics. The Supreme Court of an autonomous republic shall consist of a president, vice-presidents, members of the court, and people's assessors, and shall include:

(a) a judicial division for civil cases;

(b) a judicial division for criminal cases;

(c) a presidium of the court.

Article 44. Judicial divisions of Supreme Courts of autonomous republics. The judicial division for civil cases and the judicial division for criminal cases of the Supreme Court of an autonomous republic shall consider, respectively, civil and criminal cases of first instance referred by law to the juristiction of such a court, as well as cases on appeals and on protests against decisions, judgments, and rulings of district (or city) people's courts which have not taken legal effect.

Organizational direction of the work of judicial divisions shall be carried out by the presidents of the judicial divisions.

Presidents of judicial divisions shall be appointed by the Presidium of the Supreme Soviet of the autonomous republic upon the recommendation of the president of the Supreme Court of the autonomous republic from among the vice-presidents or members of the court.

Article 45. Presidiums of Supreme Courts of autonomous republics. The

227

Presidium of the Supreme Court of an autonomous republic shall consist of the president, vice-presidents, and members of the Supreme Court in a number determined by the Presidium of the Supreme Soviet of the autonomous republic.

The members of the Presidium of the Supreme Court shall be appointed by the Presidium of the Supreme Soviet of the autonomous republic upon the recommendation of the president of the Supreme Court of the autonomous republic.

Participation of the procurator of the autonomous republic in a session of the presidium of the court during the consideration of judicial cases shall be obligatory.

Article 46. Competence of Presidiums of Supreme Courts of autonomous republics. The Presidium of the Supreme Court of an autonomous republic shall consider cases on protests against decisions, judgments, and rulings of district (or city) people's courts which have taken legal effect, against decrees of people's judges to bring to trial, as well as against rulings of judicial divisions of the Supreme Court of the autonomous republic rendered with respect to appeals or protests.

The Presidium of the Supreme Court of an autonomous republic shall consider questions concerning the work of judicial divisions, materials of verifications of the work of district (or city) people's courts, judicial statistics and materials summarizing judicial practice, and questions of work with cadres.

Article 47. Presidents of Supreme Courts of autonomous republics. The president of the Supreme Court of an autonomous republic shall:

(a) preside at judicial sessions of divisions or assign his deputy, the president of a judicial division, or a member of the court to do so;

(b) bring protests, in the procedure established by law, against decisions, judgments, and rulings of district (or city) people's courts which have taken legal effect, against decrees of people's judges to bring to trial, as well as against rulings of judicial divisions rendered with respect to appeals or protests;

(c) convoke the presidium of the court and preside at its sessions; submit for consideration by the presidium questions requiring its decision;

(d) assign members of the court to judicial divisions;

(e) organize the work of summarizing judicial practice and keeping judicial statistics;

(f) entrust discharge of the duties of a people's judge, in the event of his temporary absence, to a people's judge of the same district or to a people's judge of another district;

(g) appoint sheriffs for district (or city) people's courts;

(h) exercise general organizational direction of the work of the court.

In the absence of the president of the Supreme Court of an autonomous republic, the vice-president of the court shall exercise his rights and duties.

CHAPTER V

The Supreme Court of the RSFSR

Article 48. The Supreme Court of the RSFSR--the highest judicial agency of the RSFSR. In accordance with Article 109 of the Constitution of the RSFSR, the Supreme Court of the RSFSR shall be the highest judicial agency of the RSFSR.

The Supreme Court of the RSFSR shall be charged with supervision of the judicial activity of all judicial agencies of the RSFSR.

The Supreme Court of the RSFSR shall have the right of legislative initiative.

Article 49. Procedure for election of the Supreme Court of the RSFSR. In accordance with Article 110 of the Constitution of the RSFSR, the Supreme Court of the RSFSR shall be elected by the Supreme Soviet of the RSFSR for a term of five years.

The numerical composition of the Supreme Court of the RSFSR shall be established by the Supreme Soviet of the RSFSR at the time of election of the Court.

Article 50. Competence of the Supreme Court of the RSFSR. The Supreme Court of the RSFSR shall consider:

(a) civil and criminal cases of first instance referred by law to its jurisdiction;

(b) cases on appeals and on protests against decisions, judgments, and rulings of Supreme Courts of autonomous republics, of territorial, regional, and city courts, courts of autonomous regions, and courts of national areas, which have not taken legal effect;

(c) cases on protests against decisions, judgments, rulings, and decrees of all courts of the RSFSR which have taken legal effect.

The Supreme Court of the RSFSR shall give guiding explanations to courts on application of RSFSR legislation.

The Supreme Court of the RSFSR shall perform verifications of the work of Supreme Courts of autonomous republics, territorial, regional, and city courts, courts of autonomous regions, courts of national areas, and district (or city) people's courts, shall render practical help in their work, shall exercise direction and control of their activity, shall study and summarize judicial practice, and shall keep judicial statistics for the republic.

Article 51. Composition of the Supreme Court of the RSFSR. The Supreme Court of the RSFSR shall consist of a President, Vice-Presidents, members of the Supreme Court of the RSFSR, and people's assessors, and shall include:

(a) a judicial division for civil cases;

(b) a judicial division for criminal cases;

(c) a Presidium of the Supreme Court of the RSFSR;

(d) a Plenum of the Supreme Court of the RSFSR.

Article 52. Judicial divisions of the Supreme Court of the RSFSR. The judicial division for civil cases and the judicial division for criminal cases of the Supreme Court of the RSFSR shall consider:

(a) civil and criminal cases of first instance referred by law to the jurisdiction of the Supreme Court of the RSFSR, as well as cases on appeals and on protests against decisions, judgments, and rulings rendered by the Supreme Courts of autonomous republics, by territorial, regional, and city courts, by courts of autonomous regions, and by courts of national areas, which have not taken legal effect;

(b) cases on protests against decisions, judgments, and rulings rendered by all courts of the republic which have taken legal effect and against decrees to bring to trial of judges of the Supreme Courts of autonomous republics, territorial, regional, and city courts, courts of autonomous regions, and courts of national areas, if the decisions, judgments, rulings, or decrees have not been the subject of consideration on appeal in the Supreme Court of the RSFSR, as well as cases on protests against decrees of presidiums of Supreme Courts of autonomous republics, territorial, regional, and city courts, courts of autonomous regions, and courts of national areas.

Article 53. Presidents of judicial divisions of the Supreme Court of the RSFSR.

Presidents of judicial divisions of the Supreme Court of the RSFSR shall be appointed by the Presidium of the Supreme Soviet of the RSFSR upon the recommendation of the President of the Supreme Court of the RSFSR from among the Vice-Presidents or members of the Court.

Presidents of judicial divisions shall:

(a) exercise organizational direction of the work of the respective divisions;

(b) present reports on the activity of the division to the plenum of the Supreme Court of the RSFSR.

Article 54. The Presidium of the Supreme Court of the RSFSR. The Presidium of the Supreme Court of the RSFSR shall consist of the President of the Court, his Vice-Presidents, and members of the Court in a number determined by the Presidium of the Supreme Soviet of the RSFSR.

The membership of the Presidium of the Supreme Court of the RSFSR shall be appointed by the Presidium of the Supreme Soviet of the RSFSR upon the recommendation of the President of the Supreme Court of the RSFSR.

Participation of the Procurator of the RSFSR or his deputy in a session of the Presidium of the Supreme Court of the RSFSR during the consideration of judicial cases shall be obligatory.

Article 55. Competence of the Presidium of the Supreme Court of the RSFSR. The Presidium of the Supreme Court of the RSFSR shall consider:

(a) cases on protests against decisions, judgments, and rulings of judicial divisions of the Supreme Court of the RSFSR, as well as against decrees to bring to trial of judges of the Supreme Court of the RSFSR;

(b) materials of verifications of the work of courts, judicial statistics, and materials summarizing judicial practice;

(c) questions of work with cadres;

(d) questions of the work of judicial divisions and of sections of the Supreme Court of the RSFSR.

The Presidium of the Supreme Court of the RSFSR shall issue instructions and methodological directives concerning questions of the work of courts.

Decrees of the Presidium of the Supreme Court of the RSFSR shall be adopted by a simple majority of the votes.

Article 56. The Plenum of the Supreme Court of the RSFSR. The Plenum of the Supreme Court of the RSFSR shall consist of the President, Vice-Presidents, and all members of the Supreme Court of the RSFSR.

Participation of the Procurator of the RSFSR in a session of the Plenum shall be obligatory.

The Plenum of the Supreme Court of the RSFSR shall be convoked at least once every three months.

A session of the Plenum shall be considered authorized [to act] if not less than 2/3 of its membership is present.

Decrees of the Plenum shall be adopted by a simple majority of the votes of the members of the Plenum of the Supreme Court of the RSFSR participating in the session.

Article 57.   Competence of the Plenum of the Supreme Court of the RSFSR. The Plenum of the Supreme Court of the RSFSR shall:

(a) give courts guiding explanations concerning questions of application of RSFSR legislation during consideration of civil and criminal cases on the basis of summaries of judicial practice, judicial statistics, and decisions adopted in cases considered by the Supreme Court of the RSFSR, as well as on the recommendations of the Procurator of the RSFSR;

(b) make recommendations to the Presidium of the Supreme Soviet of the RSFSR on questions which are subject to resolution by legislation and on questions of interpretation of RSFSR laws;

(c) hear reports of the presidents of judicial divisions of the Supreme Court of the RSFSR on the activity of the divisions;

(d) assign the members of judicial divisions of the Supreme Court of the RSFSR from among the members of the Supreme Court of the RSFSR;

(e) hear questions concerning the work of the Presidium of the Supreme Court of the RSFSR.

Article 58.   The President of the Supreme Court of the RSFSR.   The President of the Supreme Court of the RSFSR shall:

(a) preside at judicial sessions of divisions or assign his deputy, the president of a judicial division, or a member of the Court to do so;

(b) bring protests, in the procedure established by law, against decisions, judgments, rulings, and decrees of all courts of the RSFSR, as well as against decrees of judges to bring to trial;

(c) suspend execution of a protested decision, judgment, ruling, or decree of any court of the RSFSR;

(d) convoke the Presidium and Plenum of the Supreme Court of the RSFSR and preside at their sessions;

(e) submit for consideration by the Presidium and Plenum of the Supreme Court of the RSFSR questions requiring their decision;

(f) exercise general organizational direction of the work of the Supreme Court of the RSFSR;

(g) organize the work of verifying the activity of the courts, of rendering practical help to them, of studying and summarizing judicial practice, and of keeping judicial statistics;

(h) organize the work of selecting and training cadres of judicial agencies.

In the absence of the President of the Supreme Court of the RSFSR, the Vice-President of the Supreme Court of the RSFSR shall exercise his rights and duties.

Article 59. Procedure for approving the table of organization of the Supreme Court of the RSFSR. The table of organization of the Supreme Court of the RSFSR shall be issued by the Presidium of the Supreme Soviet of the RSFSR.

Article 60. Bulletin of the Supreme Court of the RSFSR. The Supreme Court of the RSFSR shall publish the Bulletin of the Supreme Court of the RSFSR.

CHAPTER VI

Sheriffs

Article 61. Procedure for appointing sheriffs. There shall be sheriffs for district (or city) people's courts.

Sheriffs shall be appointed by the president of the district (or city) people's court or by a people's judge and shall be confirmed in office by the president of the Supreme Court of the autonomous republic, of the territorial, regional, or city court, of the court of the autonomous region, or of the court of the national area.

Article 62. Competence of sheriffs. Sheriffs shall be charged with the execution of decisions, rulings, and decrees in civil cases, as well as with the execution of judgments, rulings, and decrees in criminal cases to the extent that they involve property exactions.

Requirements imposed by sheriffs for execution of court decisions, judgments, rulings, and decrees shall be binding upon all officials and citizens.

CHAPTER VII

Responsibility of Judges

Article 63. Procedure for bringing judges and people's assessors to criminal responsibility. Judges may not be brought to criminal responsibility, removed in such connection from their posts, or subjected to arrest:

(a) with respect to people's judges, presidents, vice-presidents, and members of territorial, regional, and city courts, courts of autonomous regions, courts of national areas, and Supreme Courts of autonomous republics, without the consent of the Presidium of the Supreme Soviet of the RSFSR;

(b) with respect to the President, Vice-Presidents, and members of the Supreme Court of the RSFSR, as well as people's assessors of that Court, without the consent of the Supreme Soviet of the RSFSR and, in the interval between sessions, of the Presidium of the Supreme Soviet of the RSFSR.

Article 64. Disciplinary responsibility of judges. For dereliction of duty and unworthy acts undermining the authority of justice, judges shall bear disciplinary responsibility.

Procedure for disciplinary responsibility of judges shall be established by the Statute on Disciplinary Responsibility of Judges of Courts of the RSFSR, confirmed by the Presidium of the Supreme Soviet of the RSFSR.

15. STATUTE ON ELECTIONS OF PEOPLE'S COURTS

Introductory Note

The term "people's courts" was introduced shortly after the Revolution to designate the new regime's courts of original jurisdiction. The term was intended to stress the popular character of decision-making in the new courts and the simplicity of their procedures. For many years courts of original jurisdiction continued to be called simply "people's courts." Under the Fundamental Principles of the Legislation on Court Organization of the USSR and Union and Autonomous Republics of 1958 (cf. Document 14), people's courts are formed either for an entire district or for an entire city (in the case of a city not divided into districts), and are called "district people's courts" or "city people's courts."

The 1936 Constitution established for the first time the principle that people's judges should be elected directly by the people, though elections were in fact not organized until 1948-49. Prior to 1936 people's judges were elected by the executive committee of provincial congresses of soviets. (Judges of higher courts, who are not called people's judges, have never been elected directly by the people but are elected by soviets at the corresponding level of government.)

An all-union law of 1958 extended the term of people's judges from three to five years, thus making their terms equal to those for judges of higher courts. Under a reform adopted in 1965, the district (or city) is divided into a number of electoral areas corresponding to the number of judges to be elected to the court. Each electoral area nominates a candidate to be elected by the citizens of that area. Formerly all candidates were nominated for the district (or city) as a whole and each was elected by citizens of the entire district (or city).

While pre-Revolutionary Russian courts had employed juries to hear criminal cases, the earliest Soviet decree on the courts replaced the jury with a system under which a single professional judge hears both criminal and civil cases of first instance together with two lay judges, called "people's assessors." Since 1958, people's assessors of people's courts have been elected by general meetings at factories, institutions, and other organizations; formerly, they were elected in the same manner as people's judges. (People's assessors of higher courts-- who sit only when those courts are acting as courts of first instance— are not elected by the people but rather by the soviet at the corresponding level of government.)

In the translation which follows, Chapter 4 (Procedure for Voting) and Chapter 5 (Determination of the Results of the Voting) of Section II have been omitted, since these chapters are virtually identical with the corresponding sections (Articles 71 to 107) of the Statute on Elections to the Supreme Soviet of the USSR, supra, pp. 112-117.

STATUTE ON ELECTIONS OF DISTRICT (OR CITY)
PEOPLE'S COURTS OF THE UKRAINIAN SSR

(confirmed by an edict of the Presidium of the Supreme Soviet of the
Ukrainian SSR, November 2, 1960, and amended by an edict of the Presidium
of the Supreme Soviet of the Ukrainian SSR, October 14, 1965)

SECTION I

The Electoral System

Article 1.   On the basis of Article 89 of the Constitution of the Ukrainian SSR
and Article 21 of the Law on Court Organization of the Ukrainian SSR, district (or
city) people's courts shall be elected [as follows]:

people's judges, by the citizens of the district [or] city on the basis of universal, equal, and direct suffrage by secret ballot for a term of five years;

people's assessors, at general meetings of workers, of employees, and of peasants at their place of work or residence and of military personnel by military
units for a term of two years by open ballot.

Article 2.   Every citizen of the Ukrainian SSR who has attained the age of
25 years by election day may be elected people's judge or people's assessor of
a district (or city) people's court.

Article 3.   On the basis of Article 17 of the Constitution of the Ukrainian SSR,
citizens of all other union republics shall enjoy in the territory of the Ukrainian
SSR the right to elect and to be elected people's judge or people's assessor on
equal terms with citizens of the Ukrainian SSR.

Article 4.   Expenses connected with the holding of elections of people's courts
of the Ukrainian SSR shall be borne by the state.

SECTION II

Elections of People's Judges

CHAPTER 1

Lists of Voters

Article 5. Lists of voters for elections of people's judges shall be compiled [as follows]: in cities not divided into districts, by executive committees of city Soviets of Working People's Deputies; in cities divided into districts, by executive committees of district Soviets; in settlements, by executive committees of settlement Soviets; and in rural areas, by executive committees of rural Soviets of Working People's Deputies.

Article 6. All Soviet citizens who reside at the time the lists are compiled in the territory of the given Soviet and who have attained the age of 18 years by election day shall be included in the lists of voters, regardless of race or nationality, sex, religious confession, educational qualifications, domicile, social origin, property status, or past activities.

Article 7. Persons adjudged insane in the procedure established by law shall not be entered in the lists of voters.

Article 8. Lists of voters shall be compiled by each electoral sector in accordance with a form established by the Presidium of the Supreme Soviet of the Ukrainian SSR, in alphabetical order, indicating last name, first name, patronymic, age, and place of residence of the voter, and shall be signed by the president and secretary of the executive committee of the Soviet of Working People's Deputies.

Article 9. Lists of voters who are in military units or troop formations shall be compiled over the signature of the commanding officer. All other military personnel shall be entered in lists of voters at their place of residence by the appropriate executive committees of Soviets of Working People's Deputies.

Article 10. Twenty days before the elections the executive committee of a

238

Soviet of Working People's Deputies shall post the lists of voters for public familiarization or shall ensure voters the opportunity to familiarize themselves with such lists in the building of the Soviet or of the electoral sector by other means.

Article 11. Petitions concerning irregularities in the list of voters (non-inclusion in the list, exculsion from the list, distortion of a last name, first name, or patronymic) shall be submitted to the executive committee of the Soviet of Working People's Deputies which published the list.

Article 12. The executive committee of a Soviet of Working People's Deputies shall be obliged to consider within three days every petition concerning irregularities in the list of voters and to enter the necessary corrections in the list of voters or to issue to the petitioner a written statement of the grounds for rejecting his petition. In the event that he disagrees with the decision of an executive committee of a Soviet of Working People's Deputies, the petitioner may submit a complaint to the executive committee of the superior Soviet of Working People's Deputies whose decision shall be final.

CHAPTER 2

Organization of Elections

Article 13. Elections of people's judges of district (and city) people's courts shall be held in the course of a single day, which shall be the same throughout the Ukrainian SSR.

A day for elections shall be established by the Presidium of the Supreme Soviet of the Ukrainian SSR not later than 30 days before the elections. Elections shall be held on a non-work day.

Article 14. Elections of people's judges shall be organized by executive committees of regional [or] city (for cities of republican rank) Soviets of Working People's Deputies through executive committees of district [or] city Soviets of Working People's Deputies. Executive committees of regional [or] city (for cities of republican rank) Soviets of Working People's Deputies shall oversee throughout the territory of the region or city the execution of the present Statute in the

239

course of the elections and shall resolve complaints against improper actions of executive committees of district [or] city Soviets of Working People's Deputies.

Article 15. Executive committees of district [or] city (for cities not divided into districts) Soviets of Working People's Deputies shall be charged with:

(a) formation, in the territory of the district or city, of electoral areas and electoral sectors for conducting elections of people's judges, and confirmation of Sector Electoral Commissions;

(b) registration of candidates for people's judge nominated in accordance with the requirements of the Constitution of the Ukrainian SSR, the Law on Court Organization of the Ukrainian SSR, and the present Statute;

(c) supplying electoral sectors with ballots in a form established by the Presidium of the Supreme Soviet of the Ukrainian SSR;

(d) establishment of the results of elections of people's judges for the district [or] city;

(e) issuance of certifications of election to people's judges who have been elected;

(f) consideration of complaints against improper actions of Sector Electoral Commissions.

Article 16. In accordance with Article 20 of the Law on Court Organization of the Ukrainian SSR, one district (or city) people's court shall be elected in every district [and] in every city of regional rank not divided into districts.

Article 17. One or several people's judges shall be elected to each district (or city) people's court.

The number of people's judges of district (or city) people's courts to be elected to each people's court shall be established by the Presidium of the Supreme Soviet of the Ukrainian SSR upon the recommendation of the President of the Supreme Court of the Ukrainian SSR.

Elections of people's judges shall be carried out by electoral areas formed in the territory of a district [or] city according to the number of people's judges to be elected to the given district (or city) people's court.

One people's judge shall be elected from each electoral area.

Article 18. Lists of district (or city) people's courts, with an indication of the number of people's judges to be elected for each court, shall be published by the executive committee of the regional [or] city (for cities of republican rank)

Soviet of Working People's Deputies not later than 28 days before the elections.

In accordance with the specified list, the executive committee of the district [or] city (for cities not divided into districts) Soviet of Working People's Deputies shall determine the boundaries of electoral areas for elections of people's judges with an indication of the numbers of the electoral sectors included in such areas. Lists of electoral areas shall be published not later than 25 days before the elections.

Article 19. For the receipt of ballots and the counting of votes in the territory of the district [or] city, electoral sectors for elections of people's judges shall be formed.

Article 20. Electoral sectors shall be formed [as follows]: in cities not divided into districts, by executive committees of city Soviets of Working People's Deputies; in cities divided into districts and in rural areas, by executive committees of district Soviets of Working People's Deputies.

Electoral sectors shall be formed not later than 25 days before the elections.

Article 21. Electoral sectors shall be formed on the basis of one electoral sector for a population of 500 to 3000 people.

Article 22. In a rural settlement or group of rural settlements containing less than 500 but not less than 100 people, separate electoral sectors may be formed.

Article 23. In districts where small rural settlements predominate, electoral sectors may be formed with a population of less than 100 people but not under 50 people.

Article 24. In military units and troop formations, separate electoral sectors shall be formed numbering not less than 50 and not more than 3000 voters.

Article 25. In every electoral sector a Sector Electoral Commission shall be formed.

Sector Electoral Commissions shall consist of representatives from professional organizations of workers and employees, cooperative organizations, communist party organizations, youth organizations, [and] from cultural, technical, and scholarly societies and other social organizations and societies of the working people registered in the procedure established by law, as well as [representatives] from meetings of workers and employees at enterprises and institutions, military personnel in military units, meetings of peasants in collective farms and rural localities, and state farm workers and employees in state farms.

Article 26. Sector Electoral Commissions shall include a president, vice-president, secretary, and 2 to 8 members of the commission and shall be confirmed by the executive committee of the district or city Soviet of Working People's Deputies not later than 20 days before the elections.

The president or secretary of a Sector Electoral Commission shall be freed from his usual work 10 days before the elections with pay at his usual place of work.

Article 27. A Sector Electoral Commission shall:

(a) accept petitions concerning irregularities in the lists of voters and submit them for consideration by the executive committee of the Soviet of Working People's Deputies which compiled the list;

(b) receive ballots for the electoral sector;

(c) count the votes for each candidate for people's judge;

(d) transfer a protocol of the voting to the executive committee of the district [or] city Soviet of Working People's Deputies;

(e) turn a record of election proceedings over for safekeeping to the executive committee of the district [or] city Soviet of Working People's Deputies.

Article 28. A session of a Sector Electoral Commission shall be considered valid if more than half the total membership of the commission participates in it.

All questions in an electoral commission shall be decided by a simple majority of the votes; if the votes are evenly divided, the vote of the president shall be decisive.

Article 29. For the counting of votes cast in a district or city for each candidate for people's judge, executive committees of district [or] city Soviets of Working People's Deputies shall form counting commissions consisting of 5 to 7 persons.

CHAPTER 3

Procedure for Nominating Candidates for People's Judge

Article 30. The right of nominating candidates for people's judge shall be guaranteed to social organizations and societies of the working people—communist party organizations, trade unions, cooperative organizations, youth organizations, and cultural societies, as represented by their central, republican, regional, district, and city agencies—and also to general meetings of workers and employees at enterprises and institutions and of military personnel in military units, and to general meetings of peasants in collective farms and rural localities and of state farm workers and employees in state farms.

Article 31. Not later than 15 days before the elections, all social organizations or societies of the working people which have nominated candidates for people's judge shall be obliged to register such candidates in the executive committee of the district [or] city Soviet of Working People's Deputies.

The executive committee of the district [or] city Soviet of Working People's Deputies shall be obliged to register all candidates for people's judge nominated by social organizations and societies of the working people in accordance with the requirements of the Constitution of the Ukrainian SSR, the Law on Court Organization of the Ukrainian SSR, and the present Statute.

Article 32. A social organization or society of the working people which has nominated a candidate for people's judge shall be obliged to present the following documents to the executive committee of the district [or] city Soviet for registration of the candidate:

(a) a protocol of the meeting or session at which the candidate for people's judge was nominated, signed by the members of the presidium and indicating their place of residence; the protocol must indicate the name of the organization which nominated the candidate, the place, time, and number of participants of the meeting or session, the last name, first name, and patronymic of the candidate for people's judge, his age, nationality, party membership or non-membership, education, occupation, and place of residence;

(b) a declaration of the candidate for people's judge of his agreement to be voted on in the given district (or city) people's court in the given electoral area from the organization which nominated him.

Article 33. A candidate for people's judge may be voted on for only one people's court and in one electoral area.

Candidates for people's judge may not be members of Sector Electoral Commissions in those districts or cities where they are being voted on.

Article 34. The refusal of the executive committee of a district [or] city

Soviet of Working People's Deputies to register a candidate for people's judge may be appealed within two days to the executive committee of the regional [or] city (for cities of republican rank) Soviet of Working People's Deputies, whose decision shall be final.

Article 35. The last name, first name, patronymic, age, nationality, party membership or non-membership, education, and occupation of every registered candidate for people's judge, the number of the electoral area, and the name of the social organization which nominated the candidate shall be published by the executive committee of the district [or] city Soviet of Working People's Deputies not later than 12 days before the elections.

Article 36. All registered candidates for people's judge must be included on the ballot.

Article 37. The executive committee of a district [or] city Soviet of Working People's Deputies shall be obliged to send ballots to all electoral sectors not later than 5 days before the elections.

Article 38. Ballots shall be printed in the languages of the population of the relevant electoral area and in a number sufficient for all the voters.

Article 39. Every organization which has nominated a candidate for people's judge registered in the executive committee of a district [or] city Soviet of Working People's Deputies, and also every citizen, shall be guaranteed the right of unrestricted campaigning [literally, agitation] for such candidate at meetings, in the press, and by other methods.

CHAPTER 4

Procedure for Voting
[omitted]

CHAPTER 5

Determination of the Results of Elections
[omitted]

CHAPTER 6

Procedure for Elections of a People's
Judge to Replace One Who Has Departed

Article 67. In the event of the departure of a people's judge before expiration of his term of office, new elections of a people's judge shall be organized by the executive committee of the regional [or] city (for cities of republican rank) Soviet of Working People's Deputies through executive committees of district [or] city Soviets of Working People's Deputies not later than two months from the day of departure of the people's judge.

Article 68. A day for elections to replace a people's judge who has departed shall be established by the executive committee of the regional [or] city (for cities of republican rank) Soviet of Working People's Deputies not later than 15 days before the elections. Elections shall be held on a non-work day.

In accordance with this:

(a) electoral sectors shall be formed and Sector Electoral Commissions confirmed not later than 12 days before the elections;

(b) lists of voters shall be posted for public inspection by the appropriate executive committees of Soviets of Working People's Deputies 10 days before the elections;

(c) candidates for people's judge shall be registered by executive committees of district [or] city Soviets of Working People's Deputies not later than 7 days before the elections; information about candidates who have been registered and the names of social organizations which have nominated candidates shall be published not later than 5 days before the elections.

Article 69. Elections of a people's judge to replace one who has departed before expiration of his term of office shall be organized and conducted in accordance with the present Statute.

SECTION III

Elections of People's Assessors

Article 70. Elections of people's assessors of district (or city) people's courts shall be ordered by the Presidium of the Supreme Soviet of the Ukrainian SSR not later than 30 days before expiration of the term of office of the people's assessors elected in the previous elections and shall be held at general meetings of workers and employees at enterprises, institutions, and organizations, of peasants in collective farms and rural localities, of state farm workers and employees in state farms and of military personnel in military units, or at meetings of voters at their place of residence.

Article 71. The number of people's assessors to be elected to each district (or city) people's court shall be established by the executive committee of the regional [or] city (for cities of republican rank) Soviet of Working People's Deputies upon the recommendation of the president of the regional court.

Article 72. The executive committee of a district [or] city (for cities of regional rank not divided into districts) Soviet of Working People's Deputies shall establish the number of people's assessors of a district (or city) people's court to be elected at the general meeting of each collective and shall notify the collectives of enterprises, institutions, and organizations as well as of settlement and rural Soviets and of military units.

Article 73. General meetings of voters for elections of people's assessors at enterprises, institutions, and organizations shall be convoked by social organizations and societies of the working people—communist party organizations, trade unions, cooperative organizations, youth organizations, and cultural societies. Meetings of voters at their place of residence in cities and settlements by blocks, streets, or apartment-house administrations shall be convoked by executive committees of district, city, [or] settlement Soviets, and in rural localities by executive committees of rural Soviets of Working People's Deputies.

Voters shall be notified about the time and place of general meetings for elections of people's assessors not later than three days before the meetings.

Article 74. All voters who have come to a general meeting shall be registered prior to the start of the meeting.

Article 75. General meetings for elections of people's assessors of district (or city) people's courts shall be considered authorized [to act] if a majority of the voters at their place of work or place of residence takes part in them.

Article 76. Citizens who have attained the age of 18 years by election day shall participate in election of people's assessors of district (or city) people's courts, with the exception of persons who have been adjudged insane in the procedure established by law.

Article 77. Persons for whom a majority of the votes were cast, provided also [that the number of such votes constituted] more than half the votes of the voters who took part in the meetings, shall be considered elected to be people's assessors of the district (or city) people's court.

Article 78. The results of voting for elections of people's assessors of district (or city) people's courts shall be entered in a protocol. The protocol shall indicate: the name of the enterprise. institution. organization. settlement.or rural locality where the meetings of voters took place; the date the meeting was held; the total number of voters in the given collective; the total number of voters who were present at the meeting; the number of votes cast "for" and "against" each candidate separately; the last name. first name. and patronymic of the people's assessors elected by the general meeting. The protocol shall be drawn up in   two copies and signed by all the   members of the presidium of the meeting.

One copy of the protocol shall be sent to the executive committee of the district [or] city Soviet of Working People's Deputies, [and] the second preserved in the files of the enterprise, institution, organization, settlement [or] rural Soviet, or military unit.

Article 79. The executive committee of a district [or] city Soviet of Working People's Deputies shall oversee the course of elections of people's assessors and shall also consider complaints against improper actions and violations of the present Statute in the conduct of elections of people's assessors of a district (or city) people's court.

Article 80. The executive committee of a district [or] city Soviet of Working People's Deputies, on the basis of protocols of general meetings, shall verify the legality of the elections and shall compile according to a form established by the Presidium of the Supreme Soviet of the Ukrainian SSR a general list of people's assessors of a district (or city) people's court in two copies. One copy of such list shall be sent to the district (or city) people's court, and the second, together with all the records of proceedings for elections of a people's court, shall remain in the files of the executive committee of the district [or] city Soviet of Working People's Deputies.

247

Article 81.   The executive committee of a district [or] city Soviet of Working People's Deputies shall issue to people's assessors of a district (or city) people's court a certification of election according to a form established by the Presidium of the Supreme Soviet of the Ukrainian SSR, signed by the president and secretary of the executive committee of the Soviet of Working People's Deputies.

SECTION IV

Responsibility for Violation of the Electoral Rights of Citizens

Article 82.   Anyone who through force, deception, threats, or bribery shall obstruct a citizen in the free exercise of his right to elect or to be elected a people's judge or people's assessor, as well as an official who has falsified electoral documents or intentionallly miscounted votes in elections of people's courts, shall be subject to criminal responsibility according to the legislation in force.

16. STATUTE ON STATE ARBITRAZH

Introductory Note

At the beginning of the period of the New Economic Policy (NEP), specialized tribunals were established to resolve disputes between state economic agencies. These tribunals were called "arbitrazh," a word borrowed from the French word for arbitration. However, arbitration, both in the French and the Soviet sense does not mean (as it sometimes means in the United States) mediation or conciliation: for that there is a separate Russian term, "treteiskii sud" (court of conciliation) (see Document 17). Also Soviet "arbitrazh," as applied to disputes between Soviet economic agencies, did not, and does not, have the usual connotation of arbitration that the parties voluntarily submit to the settlement of their disputes by persons chosen by them. That connotation is, on the other hand, reflected in the procedure of the Soviet Foreign Trade Arbitration Commission (Vneshnetorgovaia arbitrazhnaia komissia) and the Soviet Maritime Arbitration Commission (Morskaia arbitrazhnaia komissia), which in fact, though called "arbitrazh," are referred to in Soviet legislation as "courts of conciliation." The main purpose of referring to agencies for settlement of disputes between domestic economic enterprises as "arbitrazh" seems to have been the desire to emphasize that such disputes should be settled not according to strict law but according to the economic interests of the State, and not by professional jurists but by economists. These two ideas became especially prominent in the period of the First Five-Year Plan.

Since the mid-1930's , however, there has been a great emphasis upon the obligation of arbitrazh to decide disputes according to law, and professional jurists have played an increasingly important role in arbitrazh practice. Arbitrazh remains outside the hierarchy of the regular courts and is subordinate to administrative agencies (ultimately to the Council of Ministers of the USSR), but it is best understood as an economic court.

In addition to hearing ordinary commercial disputes between state economic agencies (called "property disputes" in the Statute), arbitrazhes also hear disputes arising in the course of contract negotiations. Settlement of these "pre-contract disputes" does involve something like mediation, in that the arbiter is supposed to strive, together with the parties, to work out a lawful contract based on a full discussion of all the circumstances. Also they may commence cases on their own initiative. In addition, arbiters are required to inform the appropriate agencies if they find that certain of the more important delivery plans have not been fulfilled properly and (like the regular courts) to inform the procuracy if they discover activity punishable criminally.

Two types of arbitrazhes function in the USSR. "Departmental arbitrazhes" (typically in a ministry) hear disputes arising between organizations of the particular "department." "State arbitrazhes " hear disputes between organizations which are not subordinate to the same department.

The State Arbitrazh of the USSR Council of Ministers is the highest of the state arbitrazhes. State arbitrazhes also function under the councils of ministers of each of the union republics, and in the larger republics state arbitrazhes operate under the councils of minister of autonomous republics and under the executive committees of soviets of territories, regions, and cities (Moscow and Leningrad only).

In 1959 the competence of the state arbitrazhes was broadened to include all disputes arising between state, cooperative, and social organizations (with the single exception of cases in which a collective farm is a party); at the same time the jurisdiction of the State Arbitrazh of the USSR Council of Ministers was reduced, giving more cases to the lower state arbitrazhes, and freeing State Arbitrazh of the USSR Council of Ministers to fulfill certain new legislative and organizational tasks—the issuance of "special conditions of delivery," the issuance of instructions on acceptance of goods by buyers, and the issuance of explanations concerning the application of legislation on delivery of goods. These reforms were incorporated into the 1960 Statute.

Ruble amounts in the Statute are given in pre-1961 rubles. These amounts should be divided by ten for conversion to present rubles.

The "economic councils," to which the Statute frequently refers, were abolished in 1965. In that year the ministerial system of organization of the economy, which had been used until 1957, was restored, and ministries were re-instituted to replace the regionally organized economic councils.

STATUTE ON STATE ARBITRAZH OF THE USSR COUNCIL OF MINISTERS

(confirmed by a decree of the USSR Council of Ministers, August 17, 1960, and amended by a decree of the USSR Council of Ministers, October 29, 1962)

1. State Arbitrazh of the USSR Council of Ministers shall be an agency for the resolution of the biggest and most important economic disputes among state, co-operative, and other social enterprises, organizations, and institutions.

2. The basic tasks of State Arbitrazh of the USSR Council of Ministers shall be:

(a) to ensure protection of the property rights and legal interests of enterpri-ses, organizations, and institutions in the resolution of economic disputes;

(b) to strengthen and develop collaboration among enterprises, organizations, and institutions for fulfillment of the national-economic plan; to struggle against manifestations of localist and narrow departmental tendencies;

(c) to give active assistance in the resolution of economic disputes to enter-prises, organizations, and institutions so as to facilitate the execution by them of laws, as well as of the decrees and regulations of the Government of the USSR, in matters of economic construction, with the application of material sanctions for nonfulfillment of plans and assignments for deliveries of products, for deliveries of poor-quality and incomplete products, and for other violations of state discip-line and of contractual obligations;

(d) to cooperate in the fulfillment of plans and assignments for deliveries of products and of other obligations, as well as in the elimination of inadequacies in the economic activity of enterprises, organizations, and institutions exposed by Arbitrazh in the course of the consideration of economic disputes.

3. State Arbitrazh of the USSR Council of Ministers shall resolve disputes in which enterprises, organizations, or institutions of different union republics, or

enterprises, organizations, or institutions of union rank, participate, namely:

(a) disputes arising in the conclusion of contracts for an amount exceeding 10 million rubles, including contracts for the delivery of products not distributed on a planned basis;

(b) disputes arising in the conclusion of contracts for use of non-public railroad sidings in freight shipments of over 100 cars per day;

(c) disputes arising in the performance of contracts and on other grounds, when the amount of the suit exceeds 100,000 rubles;

(d) disputes transferred by the USSR Council of Ministers for consideration by Arbitrazh;

(e) disputes accepted by Arbitrazh at the request of Councils of Ministers of union republics.

State Arbitrazh of the USSR Council of Ministers may assign to state arbitrazhes in the union republics the consideration of disputes specified in subsections "a" and "c" of the present section if the parties are situated in the territory of the same union republic.

4. Individual economic disputes may, by mutual consent of the parties, be transferred for resolution by a court of conciliation chosen by the parties to consider the given case.

5. State Arbitrazh of the USSR Council of Ministers shall:

(a) issue Special Conditions of Delivery of individual types of producer products and Special Conditions of Delivery of individual types of consumer goods, as well as instructions on the procedure for accepting products and goods in terms of quantity and quality;

(b) give to enterprises, organizations, and institutions explanations:

on the application of the Statute on Delivery of Producer Products and the Statute on Delivery of Consumer Goods;

on the application of the Conditions of Delivery of Goods for Export, by agreement with the Ministry of Foreign Trade and the USSR Council of Ministers' State Committee for Foreign Economic Relations;

on the application of the Conditions for Fulfillment by Import Combines of Orders of Soviet Organizations, by agreement with the Ministry of Foreign Trade;

(c) declare invalid in their entirety or in specific part contracts that contradict laws, or decrees or regulations of the Government of the USSR, or state plans or assignments, and require the parties to introduce necessary modifications into contracts already concluded;

(d) for the purpose of ensuring necessary uniformity in the resolution of disputes, study and summarize the work experience of state arbitrazhes and arbitrazhes of economic councils, ministries, and departments, instruct them on matters of practice in the application of the statutes on deliveries of products and other all-union normative acts regulating economic relations, and also instruct state arbitrazhes on matters of keeping statistical accounts;

(e) report to the USSR Council of Ministers on the most serious violations of state discipline and of legislation on the quality and completeness of products released, as well as on manifestations of localist tendencies and other violations of socialist legality in the economic activity of enterprises, organizations, and institutions;

(f) issue, by agreement with the Councils of Ministers of union republics, Rules on the Procedure for Consideration of Disputes by State Arbitrazhes.

6. State Arbitrazh of the USSR Council of Ministers shall consider disputes upon petitions of interested enterprises, organizations, and institutions or upon petitions of their superior agencies.

State Arbitrazh of the USSR Council of Ministers shall be granted the right to initiate cases if there is information on violations by an enterprise, organization, or institution of plan or contract discipline or of the requirements of economic accountability. The forfeits and fines provided by the legislation in force which are exacted in such instances shall go either into the union budget or for the benefit of the enterprise, organization or institution in whose interests the case was initiated.

State Arbitrazh of the USSR Council of Ministers shall be granted the right, in resolving disputes on exaction from enterprises and organizations of a forfeit, daily penalty, or fine for nonfulfillment or improper fulfillment of planning or contractual obligations, to forward sums exacted from the defendant to the union budget in full or in part in those instances when the plaintiff has committed violations of legislation which do not lessen the responsibility of the defendant.

7. Upon receipt of a petition to sue, State Arbitrazh of the USSR Council of Ministers shall verify whether, prior to filing suit in Arbitrazh, the plaintiff took measures to settle the dispute directly with the defendant. If evidence that such measures were taken is not presented, the petition to sue shall not be accepted for consideration and shall be returned to the plaintiff.

8. In resolving economic disputes, State Arbitrazh of the USSR Council of Ministers shall be governed by laws of the USSR and of union and autonomous republics and by decrees and regulations of the USSR Council of Ministers and Councils of Ministers of union and autonomous republics, as well as by decrees and regulations of economic councils, orders and instructions of ministries and departments, and decisions of local agencies of state power issued within the limits of their established competence.

9. State Arbitrazh of the USSR Council of Ministers shall be granted the right:

(a) for clarification of the circumstances of a case under consideration, to summon officials of the disputing enterprises, organizations, and institutions and of their superior agencies, as well as of enterprises, organizations, and institutions which are not parties to the case but whose representatives' explanations are necessary for the resolution of the dispute;

(b) to require from enterprises, organizations, and institutions the presentation of documents, information, and conclusions necessary for the resolution of the dispute;

(c) to order expert examinations;

(d) in necessary instances, to verify directly at enterprises, organizations, or institutions the materials and circumstances of a case being considered.

10. Enterprises, organizations, and institutions brought in as defendants or co-defendants in disputes being considered in State Arbitrazh of the USSR Council of Ministers shall be obliged, upon receipt of a copy of the petition to sue, to send to Arbitrazh an answer to the suit [and] all documents necessary for resolution of the dispute, and also to send a responsible representative to participate in the session of Arbitrazh.

If a responsible representative of the defendant or co-defendant fails to appear at the session or if a written answer to the suit or other documents necessary for resolution of the dispute are not presented on time without valid reasons, the State Arbiter may consider the case in the absence of a responsible representative of the defendant or co-defendant, if the materials on hand are sufficient for adopting a decision.

The nonappearance of a responsible representative of the plaintiff at the session, or the failure of the plaintiff to present, without valid reasons, documents demanded by Arbitrazh, shall give the State Arbiter the right to terminate proceedings in the case.

11. Disputes in State Arbitrazh of the USSR Council of Ministers shall be considered by a State Arbiter and by responsible representatives of the parties. Decisions shall be adopted on the basis of discussion of all the circumstances of the dispute at the Arbitrazh session.

If the parties come to an agreement, it shall be entered in the protocol and shall acquire the force of a decision.

In the event of disagreement between the parties, a decision on the dispute shall be adopted by the State Arbiter.

When disputes are considered by State Arbitrazh of the USSR Council of Ministers, the responsible representatives of the parties shall be directors of enterprises, organizations, or institutions, chiefs of administrations and of sections of economic councils, ministries, and departments, or their deputies and, when necessary, other leading personnel as authorized in each individual instance by directors of enterprises, organizations, or institutions.

12. Decisions of State Arbitrazh of the USSR Council of Ministers shall be final and shall be executed by the parties themselves within the time period specified in the decision.

If, within the established time period, an order is not presented to the bank to transfer sums subject to exaction under the decision, or if the decision in a suit not involving a sum of money is not executed on time, Arbitrazh may issue to the interested party an order for compulsory execution of the decision and may simultaneously exact from the party who has failed to execute the decision on time a fine up to 1% of the unpaid sum or, in suits not involving a sum of money, up to 1000 rubles, to be paid into the union budget.

Should it be necessary for the decision to be executed at once an order for compulsory execution shall be issued by State Arbitrazh of the USSR Council of Ministers simultaneously with the decision.

13. Orders of State Arbitrazh of the USSR Council of Ministers shall have the force of documents of execution, shall be carried into execution in the established procedure through the bank, financial agencies, or sheriffs, and may be presented for execution six months after the end of the time period set by Arbitrazh.

In the event that it is impossible for an order to be executed by a bank, financial agency, or sheriff, and as a consequence it is returned to the petitioner, a new six-month period for execution of the decision shall be calculated from the date of return of the order.

14. State Arbitrazh of the USSR Council of Min isters, if it exposes significant inadequacies in the work of enterprises, organizations, or institutions,
shall inform their directors or superior agencies, as well as social organizations,
so that appropriate measures may be taken.

Directors of enterprises, organizations, and institutions shall be obliged to
inform State Arbitrazh of the USSR Council of Ministers of the measures they
have adopted to eliminate the inadequacies specified.

If it exposes facts of nonfulfillment without valid reasons of plans or assignments for deliveries of products to other economic administrative regions or
union republics or for all-union needs, State Arbitrazh of the USSR Council of
Ministers shall inform the appropriate agencies so that disciplinary sanctions
or monetary deductions may be imposed on offenders and in the event of
repeated nonfulfillment without valid reasons of the said plans or assignments,
or in the event of delivery of poor-quality or incomplete products, shall refer
the materials to the procuracy for resolution of the question of bringing the
offenders to criminal responsibility.

15. The following shall not be subject to resolution in State Arbitrazh of the
USSR Council of Ministers:

(a) disputes between enterprises, organizations, or institutions of a single
USSR ministry or department, or system of cooperatives;

(b) disputes of collective farms with each other as well as with state
enterprises or institutions or with cooperative or other social organizations;

(c) disputes over taxes and non-tax payments exacted for the state budget
under the Statute on Exaction of Taxes and Non-Tax Payments;

(d) disputes concerning the operations of banks connected with exercise
by them of functions of financial supervision over proper utilization of capital
investment funds by enterprises, organizations, and institutions;

(e) disputes arising in reaching agreement on technical specifications for
manufacture of products and on guarantee periods for service of delivered products;

(f) disputes over the establishment of prices for products subject to
delivery, as well as over establishment of rates for services rendered, if such
prices or rates, according to the legislation in force, may not be established
by agreement of the parties;

(g) other disputes whose resolution is referred to the competence of
other agencies by laws, or by decrees or regulations of the Government of the

USSR.

16. State Arbitrazh of the USSR Council of Ministers shall be headed by a Chief Arbiter.

The Chief Arbiter and Deputy Chief Arbiters shall be appointed to office and removed from office by the USSR Council of Ministers.

17. The Chief Arbiter of State Arbitrazh of the USSR Council of Ministers shall direct the work of the Arbitrazh and shall, within the limits of his competence and on the basis of and in execution of laws, as well as of decrees and regulations of the Government of the USSR, issue orders, instructions, and decrees and shall verify their execution, shall issue statutes on sections, and shall appoint to office and remove from office personnel of the staff.

18. The Chief Arbiter of State Arbitrazh of the USSR Council of Ministers and Deputy Chief Arbiters, on petitions of interested organizations or on their on initiative, shall verify the correctness of decisions adopted by:

(a) State Arbitrazh of the USSR Council of Ministers;

(b) state arbitrazhes in union republics in disputes considered by them in accordance with section 3 of the present statute.

The Chief Arbiter and Deputy Chief Arbiters may, on the basis of verification of the said decisions, modify or vacate the decision, adopt a different decision for the case, transfer the case for new consideration, terminate proceedings in the case, refuse to reconsider the decision, or suspend execution of the decision.

Review of the said decisions shall, in necessary instances, be conducted with participation of responsible representatives of the parties.

19. Petitions for reconsideration of decisions of State Arbitrazh of the USSR Council of Ministers and decisions of state arbitrazhes in union republics in disputes specified in section 18, subsection "b," of the present Statute may be submitted by the directors of interested enterprises, organizations, or institutions to the Chief Arbiter of State Arbitrazh of the USSR Council of Ministers within one month from the day the decision is rendered. Submission of a petition for reconsideration of a decision shall not suspend execution of the decision.

20. The Chief Arbiter of State Arbitrazh of the USSR Council of Ministers and Deputy Chief Arbiters may suspend execution of decisions adopted by state arbirazhes in union republics which contradict general state interests or violate the legal interests of union republics, and may raise the question of reconsideration

257

of such decisions in the established procedure.

Petitions to suspend execution of the said decisions may be submitted by economic councils, ministries, or departments of the USSR and of union republics, by Councils of Ministers of autonomous republics, and by executive committees of territorial, regional, and city (for cities of republican rank) Soviets of Working People's Deputies, within a month from the day the decision is rendered.

21. A collegium shall be established in State Arbitrazh of the USSR Council of Ministers, composed of the Chief Arbiter (as president), the Deputy Chief Arbiters, and leading personnel of Arbitrazh.

The membership of the collegium shall be appointed by the USSR Council of Ministers upon the recommendation of the Chief Arbiter.

The Collegium of State Arbitrazh of the USSR Council of Ministers shall, at its sessions, consider questions pertaining to execution of decrees and regulations of the USSR Government on deliveries, quality, and completeness of products; questions of strengthening the struggle against manifestations of localist and narrow departmental tendencies and against other violations of socialst legality in the economic activity of enterprises, organizations, and institutions; shall consider drafts of special conditions of delivery of individual types of products and goods, and drafts of explanations concerning application of the Statutes on deliveries of products and goods, as well as major questions of organization of the work of Arbitrazh; shall hear reports of state arbiters of State Arbitrazh of the USSR Council of Ministers on their work in the resolution of disputes.

Decisions of the Collegium shall be carried out by orders of the Chief Arbiter of State Arbitrazh of the USSR Council of Ministers.

22. The structure of State Arbitrazh of the USSR Council of Ministers shall be confirmed by the USSR Council of Ministers.

23. State Arbitrazh of the USSR Council of Ministers shall have a seal with a depiction of the State Seal of the USSR and its own name.

17. TEMPORARY RULES FOR COURTS OF CONCILIATION

Introductory Note

Courts of conciliation (treteiskie sudy), with judges chosen for each individual dispute by the parties involved, have been used to settle civil disputes between citizens since 1917. While courts of conciliation have not been frequently employed in disputes between citizens, they have assumed importance in recent years in disputes between state economic agencies under a 1959 decree of the USSR Council of Ministers. The Temporary Rules, translated below, were enacted in 1960 on the basis of the 1959 decree. The Rules originally restricted courts of conciliation to hearing "large and complex" cases, but in 1962 this requirement was eliminated.

Use of courts of conciliation has been strongly encouraged by State Arbitrazh of the USSR Council of Ministers as a means of drawing the public into participating in resolution of economic disputes. Conciliation judges are private individuals rather than official arbiters, and cases are often heard in factory auditoriums with the workers in attendance.

TEMPORARY RULES FOR CONSIDERATION OF ECONOMIC DISPUTES BY A COURT OF CONCILIATION

(issued by the State Arbitrazh of the USSR Council of Ministers,
August 31, 1960, and amended by a decree of State Arbitrazh of the USSR
Council of Ministers, May 17, 1962)

1. For the purpose of strengthening democratic forms of resolution of economic disputes among enterprises, organizations, and institutions, individual economic disputes may, by mutual consent of the parties, be transferred for resolution by a court of conciliation chosen by them to consider the concrete case.

A dispute may be transferred to a court of conciliation with the consent of all parties to the dispute after the parties have taken the necessary measures for direct settlement of the dispute.

A court of conciliation shall consider disputes that are within the competence of agencies of arbitrazh regardless of the subordination or domicile of the parties to the dispute.

2. A court of conciliation shall be elected by the directors of the economic organizations that are parties to the case from among managers of enterprises, directors of organizations and institutions, engineering and technical personnel, personnel of research and social organizations, and other persons competent to resolve the dispute that has arisen.

3. A court of conciliation shall include one or several judges. When a court of conciliation consists of three or more members, they shall elect a president.

4. A party that deems necessary the consideration of a dispute in a court of conciliation shall notify the other party to that effect and shall indicate the person it has elected as a conciliation judge. The consent of the person elected as conciliation judge shall be required.

260

A party which has received a proposal to have a dispute considered in a court of conciliation must within ten days make known (orally or in writing) its consent to or rejection of such proposal. If within the stated time period a notice of non-consent to the proposal is not received, the proposal to consider the dispute in a court of conciliation shall be considered to be adopted.

5. When agreement has been reached concerning consideration of a dispute in a court of conciliation and concerning the composition of the court, the interested party shall be obliged to formalize his demands in the form of a written petition which shall be transferred to one of the conciliation judges.

The petition must indicate:

(a) the names of the parties and their domicile;

(b) the demands of the petitioner, with a statement of the circumstances constituting the basis of such demands and an indication of the evidence supporting the demands.

Documents necessary for consideration of the dispute must be appended to the petition.

The second party shall be obliged to present to the court of conciliation an explanation of the reasons for his rejection of the petitioner's demand and documents upon which he relies as a basis of his objections.

6. The right to transfer a dispute to a court of conciliation shall be extinguished upon expiration of the time period specified in the law (period of limitations).

Transfer of the dispute for consideration by a court of conciliation shall interrupt the period of limitations.

The petition shall be considered to be submitted to a court of conciliation on the day it is transferred to a conciliation judge. If the petition is sent by post, the day of submission of the application shall be the day it is turned over to the post office.

7. Disputes shall be considered at the place where one of the parties is situated or, at the discretion of the court of conciliation, at any other place where the court deems it expedient, in terms of the interests of the cases, to consider the dispute.

The court of conciliation shall inform the parties of the day of consideration of the dispute. The dispute shall be subject to consideration by the court of conciliation within a period of not more than a month.

The court of conciliation shall have the right to demand from organizations participating in the case the materials needed to resolve the dispute, and to order expert examination.

If the court of conciliation deems it necessary to receive materials from an organization not participating in the case, such materials must be demanded by the appropriate party and presented to the court of conciliation in the established procedure.

8. In resolving economic disputes, conciliation judges shall not be bound by the demands of the parties which put them forward, and must be governed by the laws of the USSR, the laws of the union and autonomous republics, and other normative acts pertaining to the given dispute.

9. A court of conciliation shall consider disputes with the participation of the directors or other authorized responsible personnel of the economic organizations that appear as parties in the case.

10. If for proper resolution of a dispute a co-defendant must be brought into the case, a court of concilation shall bring the co-defendant with his consent, to the consideration of the case in the court of conciliation.

11. A court of conciliation shall render a decision in a dispute on the basis of investigation of all circumstances of the case.

In the consideration of a dispute by a court of conciliation consisting of two conciliation judges, a unamimous decision shall be rendered. In the event of disagreement between the judges, they shall choose a third judge from among the persons specified in section 2 of the present Rules.

In such an instance, as in all other instances when the court consists of three or more judges, the decision shall be rendered by a majority of the votes.

12. The decision of a court of conciliation shall be set forth in written form and signed by all the members of the court.

The decision must indicate the substance of the decision, the circumstances of the case, and the reasons constituting the basis for the decision, the time period and procedure for its execution, the place of consideration of the dispute, the date the decision was rendered, the composition of the court of conciliation, the names of the organizations participating in the dispute, and the last names and offices of the representatives of the parties. The decision shall also indicate on which party and in what measure shall be imposed the travel and work expenses of the conciliation judges, the costs of expert examination, and other costs which the court of conciliation deems it expedient to impose upon the parties. The decision must be announced at the session of the court and sent to the parties within 5 days.

13. The decision of a court of conciliation shall be binding upon the parties and shall not be subject to appeal. The parties shall be obliged to fulfill the decision of a court of conciliation precisely and within the time period established in the decision.

14. The file of a case considered by a court of conciliation shall be turned over for safekeeping to the state arbitrazh located in the place where the case was considered, within 5 days from the day the decision was rendered.

15. In the event of nonexecution of a decision by the defendant within the time period established by the court of conciliation, the plaintiff shall have the right to resort to the state arbitrazh where the file of the case is kept with a petition to issue an order for compulsory execution of the decision.

An order for compulsory execution of a decision shall be issued by state arbitrazh in the same procedure as that in which orders for execution of decisions of state arbitrazh are issued.

A party that considers that a decision rendered by a court of conciliation contradicts the law shall have the right within one month from the day the decision is rendered to resort to the chief arbiter of the state arbitrazh where the file of the case is kept with an application to verify the correctness of the decision of the court of conciliation.

If upon consideration of an application for verification of the correctness of a decision or of an application to issue an order, the chief arbiter deems the decision of the court of conciliation to be in contradiction of law, he shall render a reasoned decree to vacate the given decision. The case shall then be subject to transfer to the appropriate arbitrazh having juristiction.

A case transferred to arbitrazh shall be assigned for hearing and considered in the usual manner.

16. In those instances when a court of conciliation, in considering disputes, exposes serious inadequacies in the work of enterprises, organizations, or institutions, the court of conciliation shall so indicate in the decision or shall render a special ruling, which shall be forwarded to the directors of the appropriate institutions in order that proper measures may be taken.

17. In cases conducted in courts of conciliation, a state fee shall not be exacted.

18. STATUTE ON COMRADES' COURTS

Introductory Note

Comrades' courts first appeared in Soviet Russia in military units of the Petrograd military district in December 1917. By mid-1918 Trotsky, as Commissar of War, had extended their operation to the entire Red Army, and in 1919 Lenin signed a decree instituting "disciplinary comrades' courts" in factories. After a relative decline during the years of the NEP, comrades' courts again flourished in the late 1920's and early 1930's, not only in factories and other state and social institutions but also, for the first time, in apartment houses and rural villages. Though comrades' courts were used extensively in the 1930's, they practically ceased to function in the closing years of the decade.

Federal legislation of 1951 revived comrades' courts in factories to handle violations of labor discipline, and in 1959 the Commissions of Legislative Proposals of the Soviet of the Union and of the Soviet of Nationalities of the USSR Supreme Soviet worked out a draft model statute on comrades' courts. During the discussion which followed publication of the draft, it was decided to permit each of the union republics to adopt its own statute rather than to pass a federal statute on comrades' courts.

In 1961 and 1962, each of the fifteen union republics adopted a statute on comrades' courts. While all fifteen statutes follow the same basic pattern, they differ with regard to the question of where comrades' courts may be formed, the number of judges to be elected to the court, competence over cases, jurisdiction with respect to persons, and other matters. The Estonian statute, unlike that of the RSFSR, permits comrades' courts to order that a chronic alcoholic's wages or pension be paid directly to his spouse.

STATUTE ON COMRADES' COURTS

(confirmed by an edict of the Presidium of the Supreme Soviet of
the RSFSR, July 3, 1961, and amended by edicts of the Presidium of the
Supreme Soviet of the RSFSR, March 3,1962, October 23, 1963, and
Janauary 16, 1965)

Article 1. Comrades' courts are elective social agencies called upon actively to foster the education of citizens in the spirit of a communist attitude toward
labor [and] socialist ownership and the observance of the rules of socialist community life, and the development among Soviet people of a sense of collectivism
and comradely mutual assistance and of respect for the dignity and honor of citizens. The most important aspect of the work of comrades' courts shall be the
prevention of violations of law and misconduct that cause harm to society, the
education of people through persuasion and social pressure, and the creation of
conditions of intolerance toward any antisocial acts. Comrades' courts shall be
invested with the trust of the collective, shall express its will, and shall be responsible to it.

Article 2. Comrades' courts at enterprises and in institutions, organizations,and higher and specialized secondary educational institutions shall be created by decision of a general meeting of the workers and employees or of the students.

Comrades' courts in collective farms and in dwelling houses served by housing operations offices or housing managements or united in street committees,
as well as those in rural population centers and settlements, shall be created
by a decision of a general meeting of collective farm members, dwelling house
residents, or citizens of the village or settlement, with the consent of the appropriate executive committees of Soviets of Working People's Deputies.

In large collectives comrades' courts may be created in enterprise shops, collective farm brigades, etc.

Comrades' courts may be created in collectives numbering not less than 50 persons.

In individual instances, with the consent of the superior trade union agency or executive committee of the appropriate local Soviet of Working People's Deputies comrades' courts may be created in collectives numbering fewer than 50 persons.

Article 3. Comrades' courts shall be elected by open ballot at general meetings of working people's collectives for a term of two years. Meetings to elect comrades' courts shall be convoked, as appropriate, by factory, plant, or local trade union committees, by collective farm boards, or by executive committees of local Soviets of Working People's Deputies.

Persons who have received a majority of the votes with respect to the other candidates and more than half the votes of those present at the meeting shall be considered elected as members of the court.

The number of members of the court shall be established by the general meeting. Members of the court shall elect from among themselves by open ballot a president of the comrades' court, his vice-presidents, and a secretary of the court.

Article 4. Comrades' courts shall report at least once a year on their activity to general meetings of working people's collectives.

Members of a comrades' court who fail to justify the trust placed in them may be recalled prematurely by a general meeting. Election of new members of a comrades' court to replace those who have been recalled or have dropped out for other reasons shall be held in the procedure provided by Articles 2 and 3 of the present Statute.

Cases Considered by Comrades' Courts

Article 5. Comrades' courts shall consider cases concerning:

(1) violations of labor discipline, including: absence without valid reasons, late arrival at work or departure from work before the end of a working day; poor quality of performance of work, or time wasted as result of a worker's unconscientious attitude toward his duties; failure to observe rules of technical safety or other rules of labor protection, except instances entailing criminal responsibility; destruction, loss, or damage of inventory, instruments, materials,

or other state or social property because of the unconscientious attitude of a person toward his duties, not resulting in significant damage:

(1a) the unwarranted use for personal purposes of means of transportation, agricultural equipment, machine-tools, instruments, raw materials, or other property belonging to a state enterprise, institution, or organization, or to a collective farm or any other cooperative or social organization, if such actions did not cause significant damage to the specified enterprises, institutions, or organizations.

(1b) petty stealing of state or social property; petty hooliganism and petty speculation, if committed for the first time, as well as theft of inexpensive articles of comsumption in everyday life found in the personal ownership of citizens, if committed for the first time, and when the guilty person and the victim are members of a single collective.

Note. Cases enumerated in this section shall be referred to comrades' courts by agencies of the police or procuracy or by a court, and cases of petty stealing of state or social property by the administration of enterprises, institutions, or organizations, and collective farm boards as well, with notification to the procurator. In the event that there is no comrades' court at the place of work or residence of an offender, and also if information concerning the offender's personality or the circumstances of the case testify to the inappropriateness of considering it in a comrades' court, the case shall be considered in a district (or city) people's court in the procedure established by law. Cases of persons who have already been brought to a comrades' court twice for petty stealing shall not be subject to consideration in a comrades' court.

(2) appearance in an intoxicated condition or unworthy conduct in public places or at work; the making of home-brewed liquor or other strong alcoholic beverages, committed for the first time, without the purpose of sale and in a small quantity;

(3) an unworthy attitude toward women, failure to fulfill duties of rearing children, an unworthy attitude toward parents;

(4) insults, circulation of false rumors shaming a member of the collective, beatings, or light bodily injuries not resulting in impairment of health, if such acts are first offenses; foul language;

(5) the damaging of trees or other greenery;

(6) the damaging of dwelling or other buildings or of communal equipment,

when the damage caused is not substantial; failure to observe the rules of fire safety;

(7) violations of apartment or dormitory regulations; disputes between residents concerning the use of auxiliary premises, house outbuildings, payment for communal services, payment of expenses for current repairs of places of common use, or concerning establishment of a procedure for the use of land plots by co-owners of house property;

(8) property disputes between citizens involving sums up to 50 rubles, if the parties to the dispute agree to consideration of the case in a comrades' court;

(8a) disputes over the procedure for using buildings that are in the common ownership of two or several citizens, over the division of property of a collective-farm household or the allotment of a share of the collective-farm household, over the division of property between spouses, when the disputing parties agree to consideration of the case in a comrades' court;

(9) other antisocial acts not entailing criminal responsibility;

(10) administrative violations of law, if agencies or officials to whom the right of imposing a fine in administrative procedure is granted consider it necessary to transfer such a case for consideration by a comrades' court;

unwarranted exercise of rights, failure to render aid to a sick person, illegal practice of medicine, acquisition of property known to have been obtained by criminal means, and other criminal acts, if they do not represent a great social danger, and [if] agencies of the police or procuracy or a court consider it necessary to transfer such cases for consideration by a comrades' court.

Article 6.   Consideration of a case in a comrades' court shall be carried out at the offender's place of work or place of residence.

Article 7.   Comrades' courts shall not have the right to consider cases of violations of law or of civil disputes in which [criminal] judgments or [civil] decisions have already been rendered [by a court].

A disciplinary penalty imposed by the administration [of an enterprise, etc.] shall not exclude the possibility of considering the same offense in a comrades' court on the intiative of a social organization or of the comrades' court itself.

Procedure for Consideration of Cases in Comrades' Courts

Article 8.   Comrades' courts shall consider cases:

(1)   on the recommendation of factory, plant, or local trade union committees, of voluntary people's patrols for the protection of public order, of street, house, sector, and block committees, and other social organizations, and of citizens' meetings;

(2)   on the recommendation of executive committees of local Soviets of Working People's Deputies, of administrative commissions attached to executive committees of district [or} city Soviets of Working People's Deputies, or of permanent commissions of Soviets;

(3)   upon reports of state agencies, directors of enterprises, institutions, or organizations, or collective farm boards;

(4)   upon materials transferred by a court or procurator, or by a [police] inquiry agency with the consent of a procurator;

(5)   upon citizens' petitions;

(6)   on the initiative of the comrades' court itself.

Article 9. A comrades' court shall consider cases within 15 days from the time they are received. Cases of petty hooliganism and petty speculation shall be considered by comrades' courts within 7 days of the time they are received. The time and place for considering a case shall be determined by the president of the comrades' court and shall be widely publicized among the citizens.

Article 10. Prior to consideration of a case in a comrades' court, the materials which have been received must, in necessary instances, be checked.

Directors of enterprises, institutions, or organizations, as well as other officials or citizens, shall be obliged, upon demand of a comrades' court, to present information and documents necessary for a case.

The president of the court or his vice-president shall acquaint the person brought before the court with the materials on hand and, if there are grounds for considering the case in the comrades' court, shall establish who must be summoned as witnesses to the session of the court. The person brought before the court shall have the right to ask [the court] to request and obtain additional documents and to summon witnesses.

When considering a case at the offender's place of residence, a comrades' court shall in necessary instances take measures that insure participation in the session of the comrades' court of representatives of the collective in which the offender works.

Appearance of citizens upon summons of a comrades' court shall be mandatory.

Article 11. Sessions of a comrades' court and performance by members of the court of commissions connected with the consideration of a case shall be carried out during non-work hours. Cases shall be considered publicly by not fewer than three members of the comrades' court.

A person brought before a comrades' court, the victim, and parties to a dispute may challenge the presiding officer and members of the comrades' court if they have grounds to suppose that the presiding officer or a member of the comrades' court may have a personal interest in the outcome of the case.

The question of satisfying a challenge or rejecting it shall be decided by the full comrades' court that is considering the given case.

A comrades' court shall consider the materials on hand and hear explanations by the person brought before the comrades' court, victim, and witnesses. Those attending the session may, with the permission of the comrades' court, ask questions or speak on the substance of the case being considered.

A comrades' court shall keep a protocol of the session.

Article 12. If a person being brought to a comrades' court fails to appear at the session, the court must postpone consideration of the case, ascertain the reasons for the failure to appear and, depending on the circumstances established, order a second hearing for the case. In the event of the repeated nonappearance of such person without valid reasons, the comrades' court may consider the case in his absence.

With respect to a person brought to a comrades' court on the basis of materials received from the procuracy, a district (or city) people's court, or an inquiry agency, and who evades appearance in the comrades' court, the materials shall be returned to the specified agencies for adoption of necessary measures.

Article 13. The decision of a comrades' court shall be adopted by a majority of the votes of the members of the court participating in the consideration of the given case. The decision shall indicate the substance of the violation and the measure of pressure set by the court. The decision of the comrades' court shall be signed by those who participate in rendering it—the presiding officer and members of the court—and shall be announced publicly and brought to general notice. If the case was considered at the offender's place of residence, the comrades' court may in addition bring its decision to the notice of social organizations at such person's place of work.

Measures of Social Pressure Applied by Comrades' Courts

Article 14.   In considering a case and adopting a decision, a comrades' court shall be governed by the legislation in force, the present Statute, and consciousness of its social duty.

Article 15.   A comrades' court may apply the following measures of pressure to an offender:

(1)   oblige [him] to apologize publicly to the victim or the collective;

(2)   announce a comradely warning;

(3)   announce a social censure;

(4)   announce a social reprimand, with or without publication in the press;

(5)   impose a money fine up to 10 rubles if the offense is not connected with a violation of labor discipline, and a fine up to 30 rubles for cases of petty stealing of state or social property, and up to 50 rubles for repeated petty stealing;

(6)   place before the director of the enterprise, institution, or organization the question of applying one of the following measures in accordance with the labor legislation in force: transferring the offender to lower-paying work or demoting him;

(6a)   place before the director of the enterprise, institution, or organization the question of dismissing, in the established procedure, a person who performs work connected with the education of minors or youth, or work connected with the disposition or keeping of valuable items,   if the comrades' court, taking into account the character of the offenses committed by such person, considers it impossible to entrust such work to him in the future;

(6b)   place before the director of the enterprise, institution, or organization the question of assigning persons who have committed petty hooliganism, petty speculation, petty stealing of state or social property, theft of inexpensive articles of personal comsumption or everyday use, beatings, or light bodily injuries, to unskilled physical labor in the same enterprise, institution, or organization for a period of up to 15 days with pay for the work fulfilled;

(7)   raise the question of evicting the offender from the apartment he occupies if it is impossible to live with him or if he has a predatory attitude toward housing resources;

(8) a comrades' court may, in addition to applying the measures of pressure provided by sections 1-7 of the present article, oblige the offender to make compensation, in an amount not exceeding 50 rubles, for damage caused by his illegal acts. When considering cases of petty speculation, a comrades' court shall adopt a decision to transfer the articles of petty speculation to the income of the state. In cases of stealing of state or social property, the comrades' court in all instances must oblige the offender to make full compensation for material damage that has been caused.

Article 16.   A comrades' court may confine itself to public consideration of a case and not apply the measures of social pressure specified in Article 15 if the offender, having sincerely repented, publicly apologizes to the collective or the victim and voluntarily compensates for damage.

If there are no grounds for condemnation, a comrades' court shall acquit the person brought before it.

In considering property or other civil law disputes, a comrades' court shall satisfy the claim fully or in part, or reject it, or terminate the case if there has been a reconciliation of the parties to the dispute.

A comrades' court shall inform social organizations and officials of the reasons and conditions exposed by it that facilitated commission of the violation of law or other offense.

Article 17.   If a comrades' court, in considering a case, becomes convinced of the necessity of bringing the offender to criminal or administrative responsibility, it shall adopt a decision to transfer the materials to the appropriate agencies.

If a comrades' court, in considering a property or other civil law dispute, comes to the conclusion that it cannot resolve the case because of its complexity, it shall transfer the case to a district (or city) people's court.

Article 18.   The decision of a comrades' court shall be final. If a decision adopted for a case is contrary to the circumstances of the case or to the legislation in force, the appropriate factory, plant, or local trade union committee or executive committee of a local Soviet of Working People's Deputies shall have the right to propose that the comrades' courts reconsider the case.

Article 19.   A decision of a comrades' court awarding compensation for dam-

age   caused or imposing a fine or other property sanction must be executed
within the time period specified in the decision. If the decision is not executed
within the established time period, as well as for executing the decision of a
comrades' court to transfer the articles of petty speculation to the income of
the state, the president of the comrades' court shall refer the case to a people's
judge, who after checking the materials presented and the legality of the decision
shall issue a writ of execution to be executed by a sheriff.

In the event of the illegality of the comrades' court's decision, the people's
judge, by a decree indicating the grounds therefor, shall refuse to issue a writ of
execution and shall inform the comrades' court and the appropriate trade union
committee or executive committee of the Soviet of Working People's Deputies, so
that it may decide whether the case should be reconsidered.

Amounts exacted from persons subjected to a fine shall go into the state budget
in the procedure established by law.

The decision of a comrades' court imposing a fine which is not executed within three months from the day it is rendered shall not be subject to execution.

Article 20.   The decision of a comrades' court to announce a comradely warning, social censure, or social reprimand shall remain in force for one year. If
the person with respect to whom the decision was rendered does not commit a
new violation of the law within this period, the sanction shall be considered removed.

Upon the motion of a social organization, director of an enterprise or institution, collective farm board, or upon petition of the person who was brought to
the comrades' court, or on its own intiative, a comrades' court shall have the
right to remove the aforementioned sanctions before expiration of the one-year
period. Decisions to this effect shall be brought to general notice.

Direction of Comrades' Courts

Article 21.   Direction of comrades' courts in enterprises, institutions, organizations, and higher and specialized secondary educational institutions shall
be exercised by factory, plant, or local trade union committees. Comrades' courts
in collective farms and in dwelling houses served by housing operations offices or
housing managements or united in street committees, as well as in rural population centers and settlements, shall work under the direction of executive committees of local Soviets of Working People's Deputies.

Article 22.   The administration of enterprises, institutions, organizations, housing operations offices and housing managements, collective farm boards, and executive committees of rural and settlement Soviets of Working People's Deputies shall be charged with technical servicing of comrades' courts.

STATUTE ON ADMINISTRATIVE COMMISSIONS

Introductory Note

In addition to the criminal penalties contained in criminal codes, Soviet law, like the law of many other European countries, provides so-called "administrative sanctions" for a variety of minor offenses. The sanctions imposed are normally mild (typically a small money fine), and imposition of the sanction does not give the offender a criminal record.

Administrative sanctions are imposed by people's courts, by state agencies and officials, and by administrative commissions attached to the executive committees of district or city soviets. Persons on whom these sanctions are imposed are not represented by counsel (see Document 20, Article 3), but a procurator participates in sessions of an administrative commission.

While formerly administrative sanctions were imposed by a large number of officials for a wide variety of offenses, the trend in recent legislation has been to limit their application. An edict of the Presidium of the USSR Supreme Soviet of 1961, entitled "On the Further Limitation of Application of Fines Imposed by Administrative Procedure," stated the necessity of "curtailing the circle of state agencies authorized to establish fines and the circle of agencies and officials having the power to imposed fines of limiting the list of offenses for which fines may be imposed, of reducing the amount of fines for individual types of offenses, and of strengthening legality and the principle of collegiality in the activity of agencies imposing fines."

As a continuation of this process, the permanent commissions of legislative proposals of the two chambers of the USSR Supreme Soviet have recently prepared a draft fundamental principles of legislation on administrative responsibility. These fundamental principles will regulate both the procedure for establishing administrative sanctions and the procedure for their imposition. If the fundamental principles are adopted, each of the union republics will adopt a comprehensive code on administrative offenses. One notable feature of the draft fundamental principles is the strict delineation of the competence of the all-union and union-republican authorities in establishing administrative sanctions for given types of offenses. Another major change involves extending the right of appealing to a people's court from administrative sanctions imposed by state agencies and officials and by administrative commissions. While under present law an appeal may be taken only when the sanction imposed is a money fine, the draft fundamental principles provide for appeal to a people's court of any administrative sanction.

STATUTE ON ADMINISTRATIVE COMMISSIONS OF EXECUTIVE
COMMITTEES OF DISTRICT AND CITY SOVIETS OF WORKING
PEOPLE'S DEPUTIES OF THE RSFSR AND ON THE PROCEDURE
FOR CASES OF ADMINISTRATIVE VIOLATIONS

(confirmed by an edict of the Presidium of the Supreme Soviet
of the RSFSR, March 30, 1962, and amended by an edict of the
Presidium of the Supreme Soviet of the RSFSR, September 22, 1965)

I. Tasks of Administrative Commissions and the Procedure for their Organization

Article 1. Administrative commissions shall be attached to executive committees of district [or] city (in cities not divided into districts) Soviets of Working People's Deputies and shall be formed by the respective Soviets of Working
People's Deputies from among deputies of the Soviets and representatives of social organizations to include a president (who shall be a vice-president or member of the executive committee of the corresponding Soviet), a vice-president, a
secretary, and not fewer than 4 members of the commission.

Administrative commissions shall rely in their activity on large numbers of
activists from the population.

In the event of the formation of several administrative commissions attached
to a single executive committee of a district Soviet of Working People's Deputies,
they may be headed by deputies of the respective district Soviet.

Article 2. The main task of administrative commissions shall be the education of citizens in a spirit of strict and undeviating execution of Soviet laws, of an
attitude of care toward socialist ownership, of an honorable attitude toward state
and social duty, of respect for the rights, honor, and dignity of citizens, and of
observance of the rules of socialist community living.

Article 3. Administrative commissions shall consider cases of administrative offenses responsibility for which is directly provided by acts of the highest

agencies of state power and state administration of the USSR, the highest agencies of state power and state administration of the RSFSR, and the highest agencies of state power and state administration of autonomous republics, and by decisions of local Soviets of Working People's Deputies and their executive committees.

Article 4. Administrative commissions may apply one of the following sanctions to a person who has committed an administrative offense:

(a) a warning;

(b) a fine;

(c) another sanction provided by the act establishing responsibility for the given type of offense.

Article 5. A warning shall be applied either as an independent administrative sanction, if it is provided for by the act establishing responsibility for the given type of offense, or instead of imposing a fine on the offender.

Article 6. The size of a fine shall be determined within the limits provided by the act establishing responsibility for the given type of offense, taking into consideration the seriousness of the offense committed and the personality and the financial position of the offender.

Article 7. As a rule, an administrative commission shall inform the offender's collective at his place of work, study, or residence that an administrative sanction has been imposed.

Article 8. The decree of an administrative commission imposing an administrative sanction may be annulled or modified by the administrative commission itself, as well as by the executive committee of the district or city Soviet of Working People's Deputies to which the commission is attached.

Article 9. An administrative commission shall have the right, instead of imposing an administrative sanction, to transfer the materials concerning an offender to a comrades' court or to social organizations at the offender's place or work, study, or residence for application of measures of social pressure.

Article 10. An administrative commission shall have the right to demand necessary documents from institutions, enterprises, and organizations, as well as to call in officials and citizens in order to obtain information on questions being considered by the commission.

Article 11. If during consideration of a case of an administrative offense it is established that the offense by its nature bears the indicia of a crime, the administrative commission shall refer the materials concerning the offender to agencies of the police or to the procuracy.

Article 12. Administrative commissions may consider cases of administrative offenses at the offender's place of work, study, or residence.

Article 13. Direction and supervision of the activity of administrative commissions shall be exercised by executive committees of district [or] city Soviets of Working People's Deputies.

Article 14. Administrative commissions in all their activity shall be responsible to the respective Soviets of Working People's Deputies and their executive committees.

Article 15. Executive committees of district or city Soviets of Working People's Deputies shall be charged with secretarial and technical servicing of administrative commissions.

II. Procedure for Cases of Administrative Offenses

Article 16. The tasks of the proceedings in cases of administrative offenses shall be to establish who are guilty and to ensure proper application of legislation in order that just types of administrative pressure may be applied to each person who has committed an administrative offense.

Article 17. A case of an administrative offense shall not be commenced, an administrative sanction shall not be imposed, a sanction [already] imposed shall not be executed, and a case shall be terminated:

(a) if by the time of the commencement or the consideration of a case of administrative responsibility more than one month has passed since the day the administrative offense was committed;

(b) if the three-month limitation period established for execution of a decree imposing an administrative sanction has run;

(c) if by the time of the commencement or the consideration of a case of administrative responsibility the act establishing such responsibility has been repealed;

(d) if the person who committed the administrative offense had not attained 16 years of age at the time he committed the offense.

Article 18. If a person who has been subjected to an administrative sanction does not commit a new administrative offense within one year, then such a person shall be considered not to have been subjected to an administrative sanction, except in instances where other time periods are provided by legislation of the RSFSR.

Article 19. The commission of an administrative offense shall be established by the appropriate officials [or] representatives of social organizations (social controllers or inspectors, members of voluntary people's patrols, or others) to whom such right has been granted by legislation of the USSR or by legislation of the RSFSR.

Officials and representatives of social organizations must have appropriate documents or badges of established form, which shall be produced upon the demand of a person who has committed an administrative offense.

Article 20. A protocol (or act) conforming to an established form must be drawn up for every administrative offense, except in instances when, under legislation in force, a fine shall be exacted on the spot.

The protocol (or act) of an administrative offense must indicate: the date and place the protocol is drawn up; the office, last name, first name, and patronymic of the person who drew up the protocol; the last name, first name, patronymic, age, type of occupation (and for persons who work, the amount of wages), place of residence, and family status of the offender, a document certifying the identity of the offender, the time, place, and nature of the administrative offense; the name of the act providing responsibility for the given type of violation; the last names and addresses of witnesses (eyewitnesses) and of the victim, if there are such.

If the offender does not have documents which certify his identity, and there are no witnesses who can communicate the necessary data concerning him, he may be taken to a police station, to the executive committee of the rural or settlement Soviet, or to the headquarters of the voluntary people's patrol for ascertainment of identity and the drawing up of a protocol (or act).

Article 21. The protocol (or act) must be signed by the official, or representative of a social organization, who drew it up and by the person who committed the administrative offense.

If there are witnesses or a victim, the protocol (or act) may be signed by those persons as well.

In the event that the offender refuses to sign the protocol (or act), a special note, certified by witnesses of investigative actions, shall be made in it to such effect.

A person who has committed an administrative offense may enter in the protocol (or act), in his own hand an explanation or comments directed at the substance of the content of the protocol (or act) or the grounds for his refusal to sign it, etc.

Article 22. The protocol (or act) shall be sent to the appropriate administrative commission or other agency or official to which the right of imposing an administrative sanction has been granted.

If the offense is accompanied by infliction of damage (cutting of trees, illegal fishing, illegal hunting, or others), the protocol (or act) shall be drawn up in 2 copies, one of which shall be attached to the plaintiff's petition to sue.

Article 23. The protocol (or act) of an administrative offense committed by a serviceman or by an enlisted man or officer of agencies of the MVD involving imposition of a fine by administrative procedure shall be sent to the commander of the appropriate military unit or chief of the [appropriate] institution.

Article 24. When a fine is exacted at the place of the offense, a protocol (or act) shall not be drawn up. For payment of a fine there shall be issued a receipt conforming to an established model, for which personnel of the police and other officials to whom the right of exacting a fine of the spot has been granted shall be supplied with special receipt booklets with numbered pages as receipts.

Article 25. In the event of refusal to pay a fine at the place of the offense, an offender shall be obliged to indicate his address and to sign his name in the receipt booklet for imposition of the fine and to submit the fine within three days to the police station or other agency whose official imposed the fine.

In the event of refusal to pay the fine on the spot or to sign his name in the receipt booklet and to indicate his address, or when doubt arises whether the offender has correctly indicated his address or last name, and when there are no witnesses present who can communicate the necessary information about the offender, he may be taken to the police station, executive committee of the rural or settlement Soviet, or headquarters of the voluntary people's guard for ascertainment of identity and the drawing up of a protocol (or act).

III. Procedure for Consideration by Administrative Commissions of Cases of Administrative Offenses

Article 26. The basis for consideration of a case of administrative responsibility shall be a protocol (or act) of an administrative offense drawn up by an official or by a representative of a social organization.

Article 27. A case of an administrative offense shall be considered by an administrative commission at the place of residence of the offender within 10 days from the day of receipt of the protocol (or act).

Cases of offenses committed by officials of enterprises, institutions, or organizations in connection with their employment shall be considered within the same time period by the administrative commission at the place where such enterprises, institutions, or organizations are located.

Article 28. An administrative commission shall consider cases in an open session, which should take place, as a rule, during non-work hours. The procurator shall be notified of the day of the session of the commission.

A session of the commission shall be considered authorized [to act] if not less than half the membership of the commission participates in it.

Article 29. A case shall be considered with the participation of the person being brought to administrative responsibility; he shall be ensured the right to familiarize himself with the act on the basis of which the case has been   commenced and with other materials related to the case, as well as the right to give explanations concerning the substance of the offense and to submit petitions.

In case of necessity, before the consideration of the case an administrative commission shall assign a member of the commission or representative of the public to verify the substance of the case.

Consideration of a case in the absence of the offender may take place only when there are on hand data concerning the notification of the offender of the day and place of the session of the commission.

In case of necessity, witnesses, as well as representatives of state agencies or social organizations, may be called to a session of the commission.

Article 30. The summons of the offender, witnesses, and other persons to a session of the commission shall be carried out not later than 3 days before the session of the commission.

Article 31. Whether a person is guilty of committing an administrative offense shall be established on the basis of data indicated in the protocol (or act) of the commission of the offense and data received during the consideration of the case at the session of the commission.

Article 32. The protocol of a session of an administrative commission shall indicate: the date of the session, the last names of persons participating in the session of the commission, the content of the case being considered, and the decision of the commission.

Article 33. The decree of a commission in a case shall be rendered and announced without delay upon conclusion of its consideration. Rendering of the decree shall be obligatory even when the person brought to responsibility has been found not guilty of committing the administrative offense or when a sanction is not imposed.

Article 34. The decree of a commission imposing a sanction must indicate:

(a) the year, month, date, and place the decision is rendered;

(b) the name of the commission which considered the case;

(c) the last name, first name, patronymic, age, place of work (or study), and place of residence of the offender;

(d) the time, place, and substance of the offense;

(e) the type of administrative sanction and, when a money fine is imposed, its amount and the time period and procedure for payment;

(f) the time period and procedure for appealing the decree.

Article 35. The decree of a commission shall be adopted by a simple majority of the votes and shall be signed by the president and the members of the commission who participated in the consideration of the case.

Article 36. The decree of a commission imposing a sanction must be handed to the offender, with receipt acknowledged in writing, not later than 5 days from the day it is rendered.

IV. Procedure for Consideration by Other Agencies and Officials of Cases of Administrative Offenses

Article 37. In considering cases of administrative offenses and imposition of sanctions, agencies and officials which have been granted the right to impose administrative sanctions must be governed by the rules established for the consideration of cases and imposition of sanctions by administrative commissions (Articles 3 to 7, 9 to 12, 26, 27, 31, 33, 34, and 36 of the present statute), with the following exceptions:

(a) cases shall be considered by the respective agency or official at the place the offense is committed;

(b) notification of the person who committed the administrative offense of the day of consideration of the case shall be made only in case of the necessity of receiving personal explanations from him.

Article 38. Agencies or officials to which the right of imposing an administrative sanction has been granted may transfer materials concerning the offender to administrative commissions for imposition of an administrative sanction.

V. Procedure for Appealing Decrees Imposing Administrative Sanctions

Article 39. The decree of an administrative commission or other agency or official having the right to impose administrative sanctions may be appealed by the offender within 10 days from the day such decree is handed to him.

Article 40. An appeal against a decree imposing a fine shall be submitted to the district (or city) people's court at the place of residence of the offender.

An appeal against a decree of an administrative commission imposing any other sanction shall be submitted to the appropriate executive committee of a district or city Soviet of Working People's Deputies.

An appeal against a decree of another agency or official imposing any other sanction (not a fine) shall be submitted to the superior agency or official.

VI. Procedure for Executing Decrees Imposing Administrative Sanctions

Article 41.　A decree imposing a fine must be executed by the offender within 15 days from the day the decree is handed to him.

A fine shall be submitted to institutions of the State Bank of the USSR. A receipt for payment of the fine shall be presented to the administrative commission or to the agency which imposed the fine.

Article 42.　In the event of non-payment of a fine within the 15-day period, the decree imposing the fine shall be sent to the place of work of the person fined for withholding of the amount of the fine by uncontested procedure from his wages.

In the event the person fined has no wages, the decree imposing a fine shall be sent to the sheriff at the fined person's place of residence for satisfaction of the sanction from his property.

Article 43.　Decrees imposing other administrative sanctions shall be executed by the procedure determined by the normative act establishing responsibility for the given type of offense.

20. STATUTE ON THE STATE NOTARIAT

Introductory Note

State notaries in the Soviet Union are officials who verify the legality of certain types of legal documents (wills, contracts, etc.), distribute property being transferred under a will or by intestacy, issue certificates for various purposes, and perform a variety of other acts having legal consequences. They are quasi-judicial officers, and their decisions may be appealed to the courts. The "state notariat" is the agency in which notaries function.

The basic legislation regulating the state notariat is the all-union "Fundamental Principles of the Organization of the State Notariat" of 1926. On the basis of these federal principles, each of the union republics has enacted a statute on the state notariat, which provides detailed regulation of state notarial offices within the republic.

The 1965 RSFSR Statute on the State Notariat, which replaced the 1947 RSFSR statute, made changes required by adoption in 1964 of new codes of civil law and of civil procedure. In addition, the 1965 statute for the first time required state notaries to report violations of law to the agency involved (Article 8) and established the rule that, except in special cases, notaries must have a higher legal education (Article 13).

The statute also provided for the first time regulation of notarial acts which are performed on behalf of foreigners or involve other legal problems with a foreign element (Chapter XVI).

Under the 1947 statute, state notarial offices in the RSFSR were subordinate to the republican ministry of justice. When that ministry was abolished in 1963, notarial offices were transferred to the supervision of the Supreme Court of the RSFSR.

STATUTE ON THE STATE NOTARIAT OF THE RSFSR

(confirmed by an edict of the Presidium of the
Supreme Soviet of the RSFSR, September 30, 1965)

CHAPTER I
General Provisions

Article 1.   The tasks of the state notariat of the RSFSR shall be the strengthening of socialist legality, the prevention of violations of the law, the protection
of the rights and legal interests of eitizens, as well as of state institutions and
enterprises, collective farms, and other cooperative and social organizations,
through certification of transactions and performance of other notarial acts.

Article 2.   For the performance of notarial acts, state notarial offices shall
be organized.

In population centers where there are no state notarial offices, the notarial
acts indicated in Article 4 of the present Statute shall be performed by executive
committees of district, city, settlement, or rural Soviets of Working People's
Deputies.

Article 3.   State notarial offices shall perform the following notarial acts:
(1) certify transactions;
(2) adopt measures for the protection of inherited property;
(3) issue certificates of the right to an inheritance;
(4) issue certificates of the right of ownership with respect to a share in the
common property of spouses;
(5) impose prohibitions against alienating a residence;
(6) witness the accuracy of copies of documents and extracts from them;
(7) witness the authenticity of a signature on documents;
(8) witness the accuracy of the translation of documents from one language to
another;

287

(9) ceritfy the fact that a citizen is alive;

(10) certify the fact that a citizen is in a certain place;

(11) certify that a citizen is the same person as one depicted in a photograph;

(12) certify the time at which documents are produced;

(13) safeguard evidence;

(14) carry out maritime protests;

(15) transfer petitions of citizens and organizations to other citizens and organizations;

(16) accept for deposit sums of money and commercial paper;

(17) endorse documents of execution;

(18) protest promissory notes;

(19) present checks for payment and certify non-payment of checks;

(20) accept documents for safekeeping.

Article 4. Executive committees of district, city, settlement, and rural Soviets of Working People's Deputies in population centers where there are no state notarial offices shall perform the following notarial acts:

(1) certify transactions, except powers of attorney for performance of acts abroad;

(2) adopt measures for the protection of inherited property;

(3) impose prohibitions against alienating a residence;

(4) witness the accuracy of copies of documents and extracts from them;

(5) witness the authenticity of a signature on documents;

(6) carry out maritime protests;

(7) endorse documents of execution.

Article 5. Notarial acts in state notarial offices shall be performed by a senior state notary, deputy senior state notaries, and state notaries.

Notarial acts in executive committees of district, city, settlement, and rural Soviets of Working People's Deputies shall be performed by the president, secretary, or a member of the executive committee who has been charged with fulfillment of notarial functions by decision of the executive committee of the respective Soviet.

Article 6. A state notary in performing notarial acts shall be governed by laws of the USSR and of union and autonomous republics, by Edicts of the Presidium of the Supreme Soviet of the USSR and the Presidiums of the Supreme Soviets of union and autonomous republics, by decrees of the highest agencies of state administration of the USSR and union and autonomous republics, by acts published by other agencies of state power and state administration within the limits of the competence granted to them, and by the present Statute.

In the performance of notarial acts a state notary shall be independent and subordinate only to law.

Note: In the present and subsequent articles the term "state notary" is used to mean, in addition, senior state notaries, deputy senior state notaries, and officials of executive committees of district, city, settlement, and rural Soviets of Working People's Deputies who perform notarial acts.

Article 7. A state notary shall be obliged to render assistance to citizens and organizations in guarding their rights and legal interests so that lack of legal knowledge and similar circumstances cannot be used to their detriment.

Article 8. A state notary who, in performing notarial acts, has exposed violations of legality or of the rules of socialist community life by individual officials or by citizens or fundamental inadequacies in the work of state institutions, enterprises, collective farms, or other cooperative or social organizations, shall inform the respective institutions, organizations, officials, or collectives of working people of such violations or inadequacies so that necessary steps may be taken to eliminate them.

Article 9. Direction of the activity of state notarial offices shall be exercised by the Supreme Courts of autonomous republics, by territorial and regional courts, by courts of autonomous regions, by courts of national areas, and by the Moscow and Leningrad city courts.

General direction of state notarial offices of the RSFSR shall be exercised by the Supreme Court of the RSFSR.

Article 10. The network of state notarial offices shall be confirmed by the Supreme Court of the RSFSR.

In every republican, territorial, and regional center and in the cities of Moscow and Leningrad, one of the state notarial offices shall be instituted as the first state notarial office.

Article 11. The table of organization of state notarial offices shall be confirmed by the president of the Supreme Court of the autonomous republic, of the territorial or regional court, court of the autonomous region, court of the national area, or the Moscow or Leningrad city court within the limits of the staff size established for state notarial offices.

Article 12. Senior state notaries of first state notarial offices shall be appointed to office and removed from office by the President of the Supreme Court of the RSFSR.

Deputy senior state notaries and state notaries of first state notarial offices, as well as senior state notaries and state notaries of notarial offices, shall be appointed to office and removed from office by the president of the Supreme Court of the autonomous republic, of the territorial or regional court, court of the autonomous region, court of the national area, or the Moscow or Leningrad city court.

Article 13. Senior state notaries, deputy senior state notaries, and state notaries of notarial offices shall be appointed from among citizens of the USSR who have a higher legal education.

In individual cases persons who do not have a higher legal education may be appointed to the said offices, provided that they worked not less than three years as a judge, procurator, state notary, jurisconsult, or advocate.

Appointment to the said offices shall be made, as a rule, after a probationary period. The procedure for passing through the probationary period shall be established by the Supreme Court of the RSFSR.

Article 14. State notaries of notarial offices may not serve in other institutions or organizations or at enterprises. Exceptions may be made only for persons engaged in teaching or scholarly work.

Article 15. State notarial offices shall have a seal with a depiction of the State Coat of Arms of the RSFSR and with their own name.

Article 16. State notarial offices shall be supported by the republican budget under the budget of the Supreme Court of the RSFSR.

CHAPTER II

Procedure for Performance of Notarial Acts

Article 17. The form and procedure for performance of notarial acts shall be determined by the legislation of the USSR and RSFSR and by the present Statute.

Article 18. Notarial acts may be performed in any state notarial office of the RSFSR, except in instances when according to the law or to the present Statute a notarial act must be performed in a specific notarial office.

Article 19. Notarial acts shall be performed in the building of the state notarial office or of the executive committee of the district, city, settlement, or rural Soviet of Working People's Deputies.

In individual cases a state notary may perform notarial acts outside the said buildings if the citizens for whom they are being performed cannot, for valid reasons (sickness, if the citizen is diabled, etc.), come to the building of the notarial office or of the executive committee of the district, city, settlement, or rural Soviet of Working People's Deputies.

Article 20. In performing notarial acts a state notary shall establish the identity and verify the authenticity of the signature of the parties to a transaction or other persons who have requested performance of notarial acts.

Notarially certified transactions and other documents shall be signed in the presence of the state notary. If the signature was written in the absence of the state notary, then the person who signed must affirm personally that the document was signed by him.

A state notary may forego demanding the personal appearance of officials of state institutions or enterprises, collective farms, or other cooperative or social organizations whom he knows, if he has no doubt about the authenticity of their signature.

Article 21. A state notary shall not accept for performance of notarial acts documents which contradict the law or contain information discrediting the honor or dignity of a citizen.

Article 22. Notarial acts shall be performed on the day all documents necessary for such purpose are presented and the state fee is paid.

Performance of notarial acts may be postponed only in instances when necessary information or documents are being demanded from institutions, organizations, or officials or when documents are being sent for expert examination (Articles 26 and 56 of the present Statute).

Article 23.   The text of transactions to be notarially certified and documents to be witnessed must be written clearly and plainly, numbers and time periods contained in a document must be indicated at least once in words, and names of legal persons must be given without abbreviation and must indicate the addresses of their agencies.

Article 24.   If persons who have requested performance of a notarial act do not know the language in which the given document is set forth, the text of the document must be translated to them by a state notary who knows that language or by a translator whom the state notary knows.

Article 25.   In the event of a refusal to perform a notarial act, a state notary shall be obliged to explain the procedure for appealing a refusal and, at the request of the person who was refused performance of the notarial act, to set forth in writing the reasons for the refusal.

Article 26.   A state notary shall have the right to demand information and documents necessary for performance of notarial acts from state institutions and enterprises, collective farms, and other cooperative and social organizations and officials.

Article 27.   State notaries, as well as personnel of notarial offices and executive committees of district, city, settlement, and rural Soviets of Working People's Deputies, shall be obliged to observe secrecy of notarial acts which have been performed.

Information concerning notarial acts which have been performed and documents shall be given out only to persons on whose instructions or in regard to whom notarial acts were performed, or on the demand of the procuracy, court, or investigative agencies in connection with criminal or civil cases they are handling.

Information concerning wills shall be given out by notarial agencies only after the death of the testator.

Article 28.   A state notary shall not have the right to perform notarial acts which affect him or are in his own behalf, which affect or are in behalf of his spouse or his spouse's or his own relatives, or which affect or are in behalf of personnel of the given state notarial office or the given executive committee of a district, city, settlement, or rural Soviet of Working People's Deputies.

Article 29.   State notarial offices and executive committees of district, city, settlement, and rural Soviets of Working People's Deputies shall, at the request of persons seeking performance of notarial acts, draw up drafts of transactions or petitions [and] prepare copies and extracts of documents.

Article 30. In the event of the loss of a document certified by state notary or issued by him, a duplicate of the lost document shall be issued upon a written petition of an interested person.

Article 31. For performance of notarial acts, as well as for the drawing up of drafts of transactions and petitions, for the preparation of copies of documents and extracts from them, and for the issuance of duplicates, a state fee shall be exacted from citizens, enterprises, institutions, and organizations.

Article 32. All notarial acts shall be registered in a notarial register. The number under which a notarial act has been registered in the register shall be indicated in the documents issued by a state notary and in the endorsements of documents certified by him.

The procedure for keeping the register and the forms of notarial certifications and endorsements shall be established by the Supreme Court of the RSFSR.

CHAPTER III

Certification of Transactions

Article 33. A state notary shall certify transactions whose conclusion is required by law to be in notarial form. If the parties so desire, other transactions which are not required by law to be in notarial form shall be certified as well.

Article 34. A state notary shall refuse to certify a transaction if it does not correspond to the requirements of the law or is being concluded for a purpose contradictory to the interests of the socialist state and society.

A transaction concluded in the name of a legal person shall not be subject to certification if it contradicts the purposes specified in its charter or statute.

Article 35. In giving notarial certification to a transaction, a state notary shall verify the capacity of the parties to perform legal transactions.

If legal persons are participating in the transaction, a state notary shall verify their legal capacity.

In the event of conclusion of a transaction by a representative, a state notary shall verify his authority.

Article 36. A state notary shall be obliged to explain to the parties the sense and meaning of drafts of transactions presented by them and to verify whether their content corresponds to the actual intentions of the parties.

Article 37. Notarial certification of transactions shall consist of an inscription to such effect on the document itself over the signature of a state notary and the appending of the seal.

Article 38. Transactions subject to notarial certification shall be presented to a state notary in not fewer than two copies, one of which shall remain in the files of the state notarial office or of the executive committee of the district, city, settlement, or rural Soviet of Working People's Deputies.

Article 39. Transactions involving alienation of property on which a tax or duty has been assessed may be certified on condition that proof of payment of the tax or duty is presented or if the appropriate agencies and the person acquiring [the property] agree to the transfer to him of the assessed tax or duty.

Article 40. In giving notarial certification to transactions involving alienation or pledge of a residence (or part of a residence) or of an apartment in a multi-apartment house of a housing-and-construction collective of individual builders, a state notary shall verify that they belong to the person alienating or pledging them and that there exist no prohibitions against alienation.

If there exists a prohibition, a transaction involving alienation of a residence (or of part of a residence or of an apartment) may be certified only if the creditor and the person acquiring [the property] agree to a transfer of the debt to the person acquiring [the property].

Certification of contracts involving alienation or pledging of a residence (or of part of a residence or of an apartment) shall be carried out at the place where the residence is located.

Article 41. A state notary shall certify wills of citizens possessing the capacity to perform legal transactions drawn up in accordance with the requirements of Articles 540 and 542 of the Civil Code of the RSFSR and personally presented by them to the state notary. Certification of wills through representatives shall not be allowed.

CHAPTER IV

Protection of Inherited Property and Issuance of Certificates of the Right to an Inheritance

Article 42. A state notary at the place of the opening of an inheritance shall adopt measures, either upon the notification of citizens or organizations or on his own initiative, for the protection of the inherited property when necessary in the interests of heirs, persons refusing to accept the inheritance, creditors, or the state.

Protection of inherited property shall be continued until acceptance of the inheritance by all the heirs or, if it is not accepted by them, until expiration of the periods for accepting an inheritance established by Article 546 of the Civil Code of the RSFSR.

If property of a testator or part of it is located outside the place of the opening of the inheritance, a state notary at the place of the opening of the inheritance shall send a commission to a state notary at the place the inherited property is located to adopt measures to protect it.

Article 43. For protection of inherited property, a state notary shall make an inventory and transfer it for safekeeping to the heirs or to other persons.

If the inheritance includes property requiring administration, as well as in the event of commencement of a suit by creditors of the testator before acceptance of the inheritance by the heirs, the state notarial office shall appoint a custodian of the property.

In a locality where there is no state notarial office, the executive committee of the district, city, settlement, or rural Soviet of Working People's Deputies shall, in the aforementioned instances, appoint a guardian of the inherited property.

Article 44. The state notary shall warn persons to whom inherited property has been transferred for safekeeping, the custodian or the guardian, concerning criminal responsibility under Article 185 of the Criminal Code of the RSFSR for embezzlement, alienation, or concealment of inherited property and concerning material responsibility for injuries caused.

Article 45. Persons to whom inherited property has been transferred for safekeeping, the custodian or guardian, if they are not heirs, shall have the right to receive compensation for keeping inherited property.

The said persons shall also be compensated for necessary expenses for keeping or administering inherited property, with a deduction for the benefit actually received from the use of such property.

Article 46. A state notary who has received information concerning an inheritance which has been opened shall be obliged to notify those heirs whose place of residence or work is known to him.

A state notary may also summon heirs by posting a public notice or through a notice in the press.

Article 47. Police organizations, as well as organizations and citizens that own residences, shall be obliged to inform state notarial offices or executive committees of local Soviets of Working People's Deputies concerning the existence of property left by dead persons whose heirs are not present and concerning data known to them relating to the place of residence or of work of putative heirs.

Article 48. In necessary instances state notarial offices, prior to acceptance of the inheritance by the heirs or, if it is not accepted, prior to issuance to the state of a certificate of the right to an inheritance, shall issue orders to give out sums of money from the inherited property:

(1) for covering expenses involved in taking care of the testator during his illness, as well as for his funeral;

(2) for support of citizens who were dependents of the testator;

(3) for satisfaction of claims for wages and similar claims;

(4) for expenses involved in summoning heirs, protecting the inherited property, and administering it.

If the inherited property does not include sums of money, an order shall be issued to give out items whose value must not exceed the sums of expenses incurred.

Article 49. At the request of heirs, state notarial offices at the place of the opening of the inheritance shall issue certificates of the right to an inheritance. Certificates shall be issued within the time periods established by Article 558 of the Civil Code of the RSFSR.

A certificate of the right to an inheritance shall indicate the heirs, the composition and location of the inherited property, its value, and the share due each of the heirs, as well as the amount of the state fee paid.

When property is transferred by right of inheritance to the state, a certificate of the right to an inheritance shall be issued to the appropriate financial agency.

CHAPTER V

Issuance of Certificates of the Right of Ownership of a Share in the Common Property of Spouses

Article 50. State notarial offices on joint petition of spouses shall issue to one or both spouses certificates of the right of ownership of a share in common property acquired during marriage.

Article 51. In the event of the death of one of the spouses, a certificate of the right of ownership of a share in the common property of the spouses shall be issued on petition of the surviving spouse to the notarial office at the place of the opening of the inheritance with the consent of all the heirs who have accepted an inheritance.

A certificate of the right of ownership of a share in the common property of spouses may be issued to the surviving spouse for not more than a 1/2 share of the common property.

CHAPTER VI

Imposition of Prohibitions on Alienation of a Residence

Article 52. Upon notification by banking institutions, or by enterprises or organizations which are on the system of economic accountability, of issuance to citizens of loans for construction, capital repair, or purchase of a residence (or part of a residence), or of an apartment in a multi-apartment house of a housing-and-construction collective of individual builders, as well as upon certification of contracts of pledge of a residence (or part of a residence or an apartment), a state notary at the place the residence is located shall impose a prohibition against alienation of the residence (or part of a residence), or of the apartment in a multi-apartment house of a housing-and-construction collective of individual builders.

The state notarial office shall inform the executive committee of the local Soviet of Working People's Deputies of the imposition of the prohibition.

Article 53. Having received a notification of a banking institution, or of an enterprise or organization which is on the system of economic accountability, of the re-payment of the loan or a notification of the termination of the contract of pledge, the state notary shall remove the prohibition against alienation of the residence (or part of the residence) or apartment in a multi-apartment house of a housing-and-construction collective of individual builders.

The state notarial office shall inform the executive committee of the local Soviet of Working People's Deputies of the removal of the prohibition.

CHAPTER VII

Certifying the Accuracy of Copies of and Extracts from Documents, the Authenticity of a Signature, and the Accuracy of a Translation

Article 54. State notarial offices shall certify the accuracy of copies of, and extracts from, documents issued by state institutions [and] enterprises, collective farms, and other cooperative and social organizations, as well as by citizens, on condition that such documents do not contradict the law and have legal significance and that certifying the accuracy of the copies and extracts is not prohibited by law.

Article 55. The accuracy of copies of acts of the highest agencies of state power and state administration of the USSR and of union and autonomous republics affecting the personal rights or interests of a citizen, as well as of copies of documents set forth in a foreign language, shall be certified in first state notarial offices situated in republican, territorial, [and] regional centers, and in the cities of Moscow and Leningrad.

Article 56. A copy or extract from a document being certified shall be collated with the original. The accuracy of a copy of a document which has erasures, additions, words crossed out, or other unstipulated corrections may not be certified.

If the authenticity of a document presented in order that the accuracy of a copy of it may be certified evokes doubt, the state notary shall have the right to detain and send such document for expert examination.

Article 57. The accuracy of a copy of a document issued by a citizen shall be certified by a state notary in those instances in which the authenticity of the signature of the citizen on the document has been certified by a notarial agency or by the organization in which the citizen works or studies, by the administration of the house in which he resides, or by the administration of the hospital institution in which he is undergoing treatment.

Article 58. In population centers where there are no state notarial offices, the accuracy of copies of documents and extracts from them shall be certified by executive committees of city, district, settlement, or rural Soviets of Working People's Deputies according to rules established by the Council of Ministers of the RSFSR.

Article 59. A state notary shall certify the authenticity of a signature on documents whose content does not contradict the law and does not set forth a transaction.

Article 60. State notarial offices shall certify the accuracy of a translation of a document from one language to another if the state notary knows the relevant languages.

If the state notary does not know the relevant languages, the document may be translated by a translator whom he knows, the authenticity of whose signature shall be certified by the state notary.

CHAPTER VIII

Certification of Facts

Article 61. State notarial offices shall certify the fact that a citizen is alive.

The fact that a minor is alive shall be certified at the request of his parents, guardian, or curator.

Article 62. State notarial offices at the request of a citizen shall certify the fact that he is at a certain place. The fact that a minor is at a certain place shall be certified at the request of his parents, guardian, or curator.

Article 63. As confirmation of the circumstances indicated in Articles 61 and 62 of the present Statute, a state notary shall issue a certificate to interested persons.

Article 64. The fact that a citizen is the same person as one depicted in a photograph shall be certified by a state notarial office on the photograph presented by the citizen.

Article 65. State notarial offices shall certify the time of presentation of a document to a state notary. An inscription of certification shall be made to this effect on the document with an indication of the person who presented it.

CHAPTER IX

Safeguarding Evidence

Article 66. At the request of interested persons, state notarial offices shall safeguard evidence necessary in the event a case will arise in judicial or administrative agencies, if there is reason to suppose that production of the evidence will subsequently become impossible or difficult.

By way of safeguarding evidence, the state notary shall interrogate witnesses, inspect written and material evidence, or order an expert examination.

Article 67. In carrying out procedural acts to safeguard evidence, a state notary shall be governed by the relevant rules of the Code of Civil Procedure of the RSFSR.

The state notary shall notify the other party and interested persons of the time and place of the safeguarding of evidence; however, their failure to appear shall not be an impediment to carrying out acts to safeguard evidence.

Safeguarding evidence without notifying the other party and interested persons shall be done only in instances that do not permit delay or when it cannot be determined who will subsequently participate in the case.

Article 68. In the event of failure of a witness or expert to appear in answer to a summons, the state notary shall so inform the people's court at the place of residence of the witness or expert in order that measures provided by Articles 62 and 76 of the Code of Civil Procedure of the RSFSR may be taken.

A state notary shall warn a witness or expert concerning responsibility under Articles 181 and 182 of the Criminal Code of the RSFSR for giving testimony or an opinion which he knows to be false or for refusing or evading to give testimony or an opinion.

Article 69. State notarial offices shall not safeguard evidence for cases which, at the time the interested person comes to the notarial office, are in a Soviet court or administrative agency.

CHAPTER X

Carrying out Maritime Protests

Article 70. A state notary shall accept the declaration of the captain of a vessel concerning an incident which took place when the vessel was under sail or at mooring which may be the basis for presenting financial demands to the owner of the vessel.

Article 71. A state notary shall draw up an act of maritime protest on the basis of the declaration of a captain, data from the vessel's journal, or interrogation of the captain himself and, if possible, not fewer than two witnesses from among the senior personnel of the vessel's crew and two witnesses from among the vessel's officers. A copy of the act shall be issued to the captain or to an authorized person.

CHAPTER XI

Transfer of Petitions of Citizens and Organizations to Other Citizens and Organizations

Article 72. Citizens and, in financial matters, state institutions and enterprises, collective farms, and other cooperative and social organizations, may make petitions to each other through state notarial offices.

State notarial offices shall transfer petitions to the said persons by delivering them by mail with return notification.

At the request of a person who submitted a petition, a state notarial office shall issue a certificate of transfer of the petition.

CHAPTER XII

Acceptance for Deposit for Transfer to a Creditor of Sums of Money and Commercial Paper

Article 73. State notarial offices, in instances provided by Article 185 of the Civil Code of the RSFSR, shall accept from a debtor, on deposit in the notarial office, sums of money and commercial paper for transfer to a creditor.

The state notarial office shall inform the creditor of the receipt of sums of money or commercial paper and upon his demand shall surrender to him the sums of money or commercial paper due him.

Sums of money or commercial paper shall be accepted on deposit by a state notarial office at the place of performance of the obligation.

Article 74. Return of sums of money or commercial paper to the person who deposited them (the debtor) shall be permitted only with the written consent thereto of the person for whose benefit the payment was made (the creditor) or by decree of a court.

CHAPTER XIII

Endorsement of Documents of Execution

Article 75. For exaction of sums of money or demanding property from a debtor, state notaries shall endorse documents of execution establishing the indebtedness.

A list of documents for which indebtedness shall be exacted by uncontested procedure on the basis of the endorsement of notarial agencies shall be established by the Council of Ministers of the RSFSR.

Article 76. An endorsement shall be made on a document of execution:

(1) if the documents presented confirm the indisputability of the indebtedness or of other responsibility of the debtor to the person seeking the exaction;

(2) if not more than three years have passed since the day the right to sue arose or, in relations between state institutions and enterprises, collective farms,

and other cooperative and social organizations, not more than one year.

If for the demand with respect to which the endorsement is being issued there has been established by law any other period of limitations, the endorsement shall be issued within the limits of such period.

Article 77. An endorsement of a document of execution must contain:

(1) the office, last name, and initials of the official making the endorsement;

(2) the name and address of the person seeking the exaction;

(3) the name and address of the debtor;

(4) designation of the time period within which the exaction shall be make;

(5) designation of the sums subject to exaction or the objects subject to demand, including daily penalties and interest, if such are due;

(6) designation of the sum of the state fee paid by the person seeking the exaction or subject to exaction from the debtor;

(7) the date (year, month, and day) the endorsement is made;

(8) the number under which the endorsement has been registered in the register;

(9) the signature of the official who made the endorsement and the coat-of-arms seal of the state notarial office or executive committee of the district, city, settlement, or rural Soviet of Working People's Deputies.

Article 78. Exaction on the basis of an endorsement of a document of execution shall be carried out in the procedure established for execution of judicial decisions.

Article 79. An endorsement of a document of execution may be presented for compulsory execution within three years from the day of its completion if the person seeking the execution or the debtor is a citizen, and within one year for all other demands, if other time periods have not been established by legislation.

CHAPTER XIV

Protest of Promissory Notes, Presentation of Checks for Payment, and Certification of Non-payment of Checks

Article 80. Non-payment or non-acceptance of promissory notes shall be protested by state notarial offices at the place of payment in accordance with the Statute on Negotiable and Non-negotiable Promissory Notes.

Article 81. For certification by a state notarial office of non-payment of a check, the check must be presented to the state notarial office at the place of domicile of the payor within ten days, and a foreign check within six months, from the day of issuance of the check, but not later than 12 o'clock of the day following expiration of this period.

A state notarial office on the same day shall present the check to the bank for payment and in the event of non-payment shall make a notation to such effect in the register and shall make a notation on the check.

When the notation is made on the check, the state notarial office shall send a notification to the drawer of the check of the non-payment of his check by the bank and of the notation on the check.

CHAPTER XV

Acceptance of Documents for Safekeeping

Article 82. State notarial offices shall accept for safekeeping documents, which shall be listed on an inventory, one copy of which list shall remain in the files of the state notarial office.

Documents accepted for safekeeping shall be returned to the person who submitted them for safekeeping or to a legally authorized person either upon presentation of the second copy of the inventory list together with the document in which the state notary acknowledged receipt, or by decree of a court.

CHAPTER XVI

Notarial Acts for Foreigners and Persons without Citizenship. Application of Foreign Law. International Treaties and Agreements. Commissions of Foreign Agencies of Justice

Article 83. Foreign citizens, as well as persons without citizenship residing in the USSR, shall have the right to resort to notarial agencies of the RSFSR on equal terms with Soviet citizens.

Article 84. In accordance with the legislation of the USSR and RSFSR and with international agreements in which the USSR and RSFSR participate, a state notary shall apply norms of foreign law.

A state notary shall accept documents drawn up in accordance with the requirements of foreign law and shall also perform endorsements of certification in the form provided by foreign legislation, insofar as this does not contradict the fundamental principles of the Soviet system.

Article 85. State notarial offices shall execute commissions of foreign agencies of justice, transferred to them in the established procedure, for the performance of individual notarial acts in accordance with the legislation of the USSR and RSFSR and with international agreements in which the USSR and RSFSR participate.

State notarial offices may resort in the established procedure to foreign agencies of justice with commissions for performance of individual notarial acts.

Article 86. Documents drawn up abroad with the participation of foreign [governmental] authorities or issued by them shall be accepted by state notarial offices of the RSFSR on condition that they are legalized by agencies of the Ministry of Foreign Affairs of the USSR.

Such documents shall be accepted by state notarial offices without legalization in those instances provided by the legislation of the USSR and RSFSR and by international agreements in which the USSR and RSFSR participate.

Article 87. If an international agreement in which the USSR or RSFSR participates refers performance of a notarial act to the competence of Soviet notarial agencies, then it must be performed in a notarial office determined according to the rules of the present Statute.

In those instances in which the rules of the present Statute do not establish a definite place of performance for a given notarial act, it may be performed by agreement between the interested persons in any state notarial office of the RSFSR, and in the absence of agreement in the first Moscow state notarial office.

Article 88. Acts connected with protection of property located in the territory of the RSFSR remaining after the death of a foreign citizen or property due to a foreign citizen after the death of a Soviet citizen, as well as conduct of matters concerning the inheritance of such property, shall be carried out by notarial agencies in accordance with the legislation of the USSR and RSFSR and with international agreements in which the USSR and RSFSR participate.

CHAPTER XVII

Appeal of Acts of State Notaries

Article 89. An interested person who considers an act of a state notary or his refusal to carry out a notarial act to be incorrect shall have the right to submit an appeal to such effect to a court in the procedure established by Article 271 of the Code of Civil Procedure of the RSFSR.

Article 90. A demand based on an endorsement of a document of execution by a state notary may be disputed by the debtor only by bringing a suit.

CHAPTER XVIII

Publication of Instructions on the Procedure for Fulfillment of Notarial Acts

Article 91. An instruction on the procedure for fulfillment of notarial acts by state notarial offices of the RSFSR shall be issued by the Supreme Court of the RSFSR.

Article 92. The procedure for fulfillment of notarial acts by executive committees of district, city, settlement, and rural Soviets of Working People's Deputies shall be determined by an instruction confirmed by the Council of Ministers of the RSFSR.

21. STATUTE ON THE ADVOCATES

Introductory Note

There are two types of practicing lawyers in the Soviet Union. The first, the advocate (advokat), is analogous to a general practicioner in the United States, that is, a lawyer who maintains an office and represents clients from the general public in a variety of legal matters. Soviet advocates work in legal consultation offices (iuridicheskie konsul'tatsii), which are creatures of a regional or city "college of advocates." Only a member of the college of advocates may work as an advocate.

The second type of Soviet practicing lawyer, the jurisconsult (iuriskonsul't), like the American "house counsel," is legal advisor to, and an employee of, an economic enterprise or other institution or organization (see Document 22).

In 1939, as part of the movement to centralize the administration of justice (see introductory notes to Documents 11 and 14), the USSR Council of People's Commissars adopted a Statute on the Advocates (Advokatura) of the USSR, applicable throughout the Soviet Union. When in the late 1950's legislation on court organization was returned to the competence of the union republics (see introductory note to Document 14), the right to adopt statutes on the advocates was returned to the union republics as well.

The 1962 RSFSR statute strengthened internal self-management in colleges of advocates (cf. Articles 7, 15-23) and regularized the procedure for imposition by them of disciplinary penalties on advocates (Article 42), though the Minister of Justice retained the right to expel an advocate from the college (Article 13). In addition, the statute stated for the first time the rights and duties of advocates (Articles 26, 28-37).

Colleges of advocates, like state notarial offices, were formerly subordinate to the RSFSR Ministry of Justice. When that ministry was abolished in 1963, the colleges of advocates were placed under the supervision not of the RSFSR Supreme Court (as were the notarial offices) but rather of the Juridical Commission of the

RSFSR Council of Ministers, which was formed at the time the Ministry of Justice was abolished.

Where the Statute reads RSFSR Ministry of Justice one should read Juridical Commission of the RSFSR Council of Ministers, and where the statute reads RSFSR Minister of Justice one should read President of the Juridical Commission of the RSFSR Council of Ministers.

STATUTE ON THE ADVOCATES OF THE RSFSR

(confirmed by a law of the Supreme Soviet of the RSFSR
July 25, 1962)

CHAPTER I

General Provisions

Article 1. In accordance with Article 23 of the Law on Court Organization of the RSFSR, republican (in autonomous republics), territorial, regional, and city (in the cities of Moscow and Leningrad) colleges of advocates shall function for the purpose of providing defense [in criminal cases] at the preliminary investigation and in court and representation in civil cases in court and arbitrazh, and of rendering other legal assistance to citizens, enterprises, institutions, organizations, and collective farms in the RSFSR.

Colleges of advocates shall be voluntary associations of persons engaged in advocates' activity and shall function on the basis of the present Statute.

Article 2. Colleges of advocates shall be called upon to foster the protection of the rights and legal interests of citizens, enterprises, institutions, organizations, and collective farms, the observance and strengthening of socialist legality, and the administration of justice.

Article 3. Colleges of advocates shall carry out the tasks with which they are charged through:

(a) consultations on legal questions, advice, [and] explanations and memoranda concerning legislation;

(b) drawing up petitions, complaints, and other documents of a legal nature at the request of citizens, enterprises, institutions, organizations, and collective farms;

(c) participation of advocates at the preliminary investigation and in the judicial examination as defenders of accused persons [and] as representatives of victims, civil plaintiffs, and civil defendants;

309

(d) participation in the judicial examination of civil cases as representatives of plaintiffs, defendants, and other persons participating in the case.

(e) representation in court and arbitrazh upon commission of enterprises, institutions, organizations, and collective farms, and rendering other legal assistance to them.

Article 4. Only a person who is a member of a college of advocates may engage in advocates' activity.

Article 5. Organization, direction, and supervision of the activity of colleges of advocates shall be exercised by the Councils of Ministers of autonomous republics and by the executive committees of territorial, regional, and the Moscow and Leningrad city Soviets of Working People's Deputies.

General direction of colleges of advocates in the RSFSR and supervision of their activity shall be exercised by the RSFSR Ministry of Justice.

Article 6. The amount of the payment exacted for rendering legal assistance, as well as the procedure for rendering free legal assistance, shall be determined by an instruction of the RSFSR Ministry of Justice confirmed by the RSFSR Council of Ministers.

Article 7. Colleges of advocates shall be relieved of registering in financial agencies their staff structure, salaries for individual offices, wage funds, and budgets of administrative and economic expenses.

Article 8. Colleges of advocates shall enjoy the rights of a legal person.

SECOND CHAPTER

The Membership of Colleges of Advocates

Article 9. Citizens of the USSR who have a higher legal education and work experience as a jurist of not less than two years may be members of a college of advocates.

Persons who have completed institutions of higher legal education who do not have work experience as a jurist, or who have less than two years of such experience, shall be admitted into a college of advocates only after a probation period of not less than six months.

The procedure for the probation period shall be established by the RSFSR Ministry of Justice.

As an exception, with permission of the Council of Ministers of the autonomous republic or of the executive committee of the territorial, regional, or Moscow or Leningrad city Soviet of Working People's Deputies, persons who do not have a higher legal education may be admitted as members of a college if they have not less than 5 years of work experience as a jurist.

Article 10.   Persons who have a criminal record or who do not, by their moral or professional qualifications, measure up to the title of Soviet advocate shall not be admitted as members of a college of advocates.

Article 11.   Admittance to membership in a college of advocates shall be handled by the presidium of the college of advocates.

Applications for admission to membership in a college of advocates shall be considered not later than one month from the time they are received by the presidium of a college of advocates and, as a rule, in the presence of the person who submitted the application.

The presidium of a college of advocates shall within seven days notify the Council of Ministers of the autonomous republic or the executive committee of the territorial, regional, or Moscow or Leningrad city Soviet of Working People's Deputies of every admission to membership in the college of advocates.

The Council of Ministers of the autonomous republic or the executive committee of the territorial , regional, or Moscow or Leningrad city Soviet of Working People's Deputies shall have the right to discharge the newly admitted member within a month from the day of notification of admission of a new member to a college of advocates.

Article 12.   Every member of a college of advocates shall have the right to leave the college of advocates at any time at his own wish.

Advocates who have left a college for elective offices must, at their request, be admitted into the same college of advocates after completion of work in such offices.

Article 13. Expulsion from a college of advocates shall be carried out by the presidium of the college, or by the Council of Ministers of the autonomous republic or the executive committee of the territorial, regional, or Moscow or Leningrad city Soviet of Working People's Deputies, or by the RSFSR Minister of Justice in the event of:

(a) manifest unfitness to discharge the duties of an advocate;

(b) systematic violation of the rules of internal order of the college of advocates or unconscientious fulfillment of his duties;

(c) receipt by an advocate of monetary remuneration except through the legal consultation office;

(d) commission of offenses which discredit the title of Soviet advocate;

(e) commission of a crime.

Article 14. A decree of the presidium of a college of advocates refusing admission to membership in the college or expelling a member from the college may be appealed to the Council of Ministers of the autonomous republic or to the executive committee of the territorial, regional, or Moscow or Leningrad city Soviet of Working People's Deputies within a month from the day it is rendered.

The Council of Ministers of the autonomous republic or the executive committee of the territorial, regional, or Moscow or Leningrad city Soviet of Working People's Deputies may annul the decree of the presidium of a college of advocates refusing admission to membership in the college or expelling a member from the college of advocates.

THIRD CHAPTER

Agencies of a College of Advocates

Article 15. The agencies of a college of advocates shall be:

(a) a general meeting of the members of the college of advocates;

(b) a presidium of the college of advocates;

(c) an inspection commission.

In colleges of advocates numbering more than 300 advocates, conferences of the members of the college may be convoked instead of a general meeting.

Article 16. A general meeting (or conference) of the members of a college of advocates shall be the highest agency of the college of advocates.

A general meeting (or conference) of the members of a college of advocates shall:

(a) elect the presidium of the college of advocates and the inspection commission;

(b) hear and confirm reports on the activity of the presidium and inspection commission and adopt decisions with respect to questions of the work of the college of advocates;

(c) establish the numerical strength, staff structure, and budget of income and expenditures of the college of advocates with subsequent confirmation of them by the Council of Ministers of the autonomous republic or by the executive committee of the territorial, regional, or Moscow or Leningrad city Soviet of Working People's Deputies;

(d) confirm rules of internal order of the college of advocates by agreement with trade union agencies;

(e) consider other questions connected with the activity of the college of advocates.

Article 17. A general meeting (or conference) of the members of a college of advocates shall be convoked at least once a year.

A general meeting shall be considred to be authorized [to act] if not less than two thirds of the members of the college participate in it.

A conference of the members of a college of advocates shall be convoked on the basis of a norm established by the presidium of the college of advocates. A conference shall be considred to be authorized [to act] if not less than two thirds of the delegates elected from legal consultation offices participate in it.

A general meeting (or conference) of the members of a college of advocates shall be convoked either on the initiative of the presidium of the college of advocates or upon the proposal of the Council of Ministers of the autonomous republic, executive committee of the territorial, regional, or Moscow or Leningrad city Soviet of Working People's Deputies, or the RSFSR Minister of

Justice, as well as upon demand of not less than one third of the members of the college.

A decision of a general meeting (or conference) of the members of a college of advocates, in the event of its nonconformity to law or to the present Statute, may be annulled by the Council of Ministers of the autonomous republic or by the executive committee of the territorial, regional, or Moscow or Leningrad city Soviet of Working People's Deputies.

Article 18. The presidium of a college of advocates and the inspection commission shall be elected by secret ballot for a term of 2 years.

The number of members of the presidium and of the inspection commission shall be determined by a general meeting (or conference) of the members of the college of advocates.

Candidates who have received more than half the votes of those advocates present at the meeting (or conference) shall be considered elected.

In the event that one of the members of the presidium or inspection commission departs from membership in the presidium or inspection commission, supplementary elections to replace those who have departed shall be held at the next general meeting.

Article 19. The presidium of a college of advocates shall:

(a) convoke general meetings (or conferences) of the members of the college of advocates;

(b) organize legal consultation offices and direct their activity, conduct inspections of the work of legal consultation offices;

(c) handle admission into the college of new members and of probationers, organize their probationary periods, assign advocates to consultation offices, and expel members from the college and from the corps of probationers;

(d) appoint and remove from [their] work heads of legal consultation offices by agreement with the executive committee of the appropriate district [or] city Soviet of Working People's Deputies;

(e) confirm the staff structure and budgets of legal consultation offices;

(f) carry out measures to raise the ideological and political level and legal qualifications of members of the college, organize participation of advocates in the propaganda of Soviet legislation, exercise supervision over the quality of work of advocates, summarize and disseminate the positive work experience of legal consultation offices and advocates, work out and publish methodological aids on matters relating to advocates' activities:

(g) study and summarize, through materials on hand in the college, the causes of criminal acts and other violations of legality and submit appropriate proposals to state and social organizations;

(h) exercise supervision over observance of the procedure for payment for legal assistance rendered by advocates;

(i) exercise supervision over observance of the rules of internal order of the college of advocates, consider cases of disciplinary offenses of members of the college, and impose disciplinary penalties on guilty persons;

(j) disburse funds of the college in accordance with the budget;

(k) represent the college of advocates in state and social organizations;

(l) keep statistical and financial accounts on the established forms and present reports on the activity of the college of advocates to the Council of Ministers of the autonomous republic or to the executive committee of the territorial, regional, or Moscow or Leningrad city Soviet of Working People's Deputies, and to the RSFSR Ministry of Justice.

Article 20. The presidium of a college of advocates shall conduct its sessions if not less than half the members of the presidium are present. Decisions shall be adopted by a majority of the votes. If the votes are evenly divided, consideration of the question being discussed shall be carried over to the next meeting of the presidium, and members of the presidium who were absent shall be called in.

In the event of its nonconformity to law or to the present Statute, a decree of the presidium of a college of advocates may be reviewed by the presidium itself or annulled by a general meeting (or conference) of the members of the college of advocates, or by the Council of Ministers of the autonomous republic or executive committee of the territorial, regional, or Moscow or Leningrad city Soviet of Working People's Deputies, or by the RSFSR minister of justice.

Article 21. The presidium of a college of advocates shall elect from its number by open ballot a president of the presidium and vice-presidents, with subsequent confirmation of them by the Council of Ministers of the autonomous republic or executive committee of the territorial, regional, or Moscow or Leningrad city Soviet of Working People's Deputies.

Members of the presidium who hold staff offices in the college of advocates shall receive wages in accordance with the staff schedule and shall have the right, in addition, to engage in an advocate's practice.

Article 22. The president of the presidium of a college of advocates shall:

(a) preside at session of the presidium;

(b) organize and plan the work of the presidum and prepare questions for consideration at sessions of the presidium;

(c) prepare for consideration at sessions of the presidium questions of admission into the college and expulsion from it of advocates and probationers;

(d) disburse credits within the limits of the budget which has been confirmed;

(e) organize the verification of complaints and of other materials concerning the actions of advocates and submit appropriate proposals for consideration by the presidium or transfer materials of verification for resolution by a meeting of advocates of the legal consultation office in order that measures of social pressure may be taken;

(f) direct the work of the staff of the presidium of the college of advocates, appoint and dismiss staff personnel of the presidium and accountants of legal consultation offices.

Article 23. The inspection commission of a college of advocates shall elect from its number by open ballot a president and vice-president of the inspection commission.

The inspection commission of a college of advocates shall conduct inspections of the financial and economic activity of the presidium of the college of advocates and of legal consultation offices.

FOURTH CHAPTER

Legal Consultation Offices

Article 24. Legal consultation offices shall be created in order to organize the work of the members of a college of advocates.

The composition and location of a legal consultation office shall be determined by the presidium of the college of advocates by agreement with the executive committee of the appropriate district [or] city Soviet of Working People's Deputies.

A legal consultation office shall be directed by a head appointed by the presidium from among the members of the college.

Article 25. The head of a legal consultation office shall:

(a) organize the work of the legal consultation office;

(b) allocate work among advocates, taking into account their qualifications and personal requests to them [by clients], and not allowing too great a work-load for some or too light a load for other advocates;

(c) establish in accordance with an instruction the amount of payment for work performed by advocates;

(d) exercise supervision over the quality of work of advocates and carry out measures directed at improving their work;

(e) ensure observance by advocates of the rules of internal order;

(f) keep statistical and financial accounts on the established forms.

The head of a legal consultation office shall act as trustee for the presidium of the college of advocates.

The wages of the head of a legal consultation office shall consist of a salary based on the staff schedule and of sums received for activity as an advocate.

Article 26. In necessary instances a legal consultation office shall have the right to request from state and social organizations information, references, and other documents related to the rendering of legal assistance by advocates.

Article 27. A legal consultation office shall have a current account in the State Bank or in a savings bank [of the State Bank], and a seal and stamp containing a designation of its name.

FIFTH CHAPTER

Rights and Duties of Advocates

Article 28. An advocate shall have the right to elect and to be elected to agencies of the college of advocates, as well as to take part in the discussion of questions connected with the activity of the college.

Article 29. The rights and duties of advocates at the stage of preliminary investigation in criminal cases, as well as during consideration of criminal and civil cases in court, shall be determined by criminal-procedure and civil-procedure legislation, respectively.

Article 30. An advocate must be a model of strict and undeviating observance of Soviet laws, moral purity, and irreproachable conduct, and shall be obliged to improve his knowledge constantly, to raise his ideological and political level and professional qualifications, and to participate actively in the propagandizing of Soviet law.

Article 31. An advocate shall be obliged to utilize all means and methods specified by law to defend the rights and legal interests of citizens, enterprises, institutions, organizations, and collective farms that have turned to him for legal assistance.

Article 32. An advocate shall not have the right to accept a commission to conduct cases in instances:

(a) when an official who is a relative of the advocate is taking part in the investigation or decision of the case;

(b) when he earlier rendered legal assistance in the given case to a person whose interests are contrary to the interests of the person who has requested that he conduct the case, or when he earlier participated in the case as a judge, investigator, procurator, person conducting the inquiry, witness, expert witness, translator, or witness of investigative actions.

Article 33. An advocate must not disclose information communicated to him by a client in connection with legal assistance rendered in the given case.

An advocate may not be interrogated as a witness concerning circumstances of a case which have become known to him in connection with fulfillment of the duties of defense counsel in the given case.

Article 34. An advocate shall not have the right to withdraw from the defense of an accused once undertaken.

Article 35. The labor of an advocate shall be paid from funds received by the legal consultation office from citizens, enterprises, institutions, organizations, and collective farms for rendering legal assistance to them.

Article 36. An advocate shall enjoy the right to support-payments for temporary loss of ability to work, as well as to pension insurance, in the usual manner.

Article 37. Members of a college of advocates may not serve in institutions or organizations or at enterprises. An exception may be allowed by the presidium of a college of advocates for persons engaged in pedagogical or scholarly work.

SIXTH CHAPTER

Incentive Measures for Advocates

Article 38. The presidium of a college of advocates shall have the right to reward advocates who have especially distinguished themselves for exemplary fulfillment of their duties or for long-time and irreproachable work.

Article 39. Incentive measures shall be:

(a) an expression of gratitude;

(b) a monetary bonus;

(c) the awarding of a valuable gift.

SEVENTH CHAPTER

Disciplinary Responsibility of Advocates

Article 40. Advocates shall be subject to disciplinary responsibility for violation of the rules of internal order, a careless or unconscientious attitude toward discharge of their duties, and other acts which discredit the title of advocate.

Article 41. Measures of disciplinary sanctioning shall be:

(a) a reproof;

(b) a reprimand;

(c) a severe reprimand.

As an extreme measure, if the presidium of a college of advocates considers the measures of disciplinary sanctioning insufficient, expulsion from the college of advocates shall be applied.

Article 42. A disciplinary sanction may not be imposed if more than one month has passed from the day the offense was exposed or more than one year from the day the offense was committed.

Cases of disciplinary offenses shall be considered by the presidium of a college of advocates either on its own initiative or upon the proposal of the Council of Ministers of the autonomous republic or the executive committee of the territorial, regional, or Moscow or Leningrad city Soviet of Working People's Deputies, or of the RSFSR minister of justice.

Prior to consideration of the case of a disciplinary offense, the presidium of a college of advocates must demand a written explanation from the advocate, carefully check the grounds for bringing him to disciplinary responsibility, and familiarize [him] with the materials of the disciplinary case.

Consideration of the case of a disciplinary offense shall be conducted in the presence of the advocate being brought to responsibility. An advocate's repeated failure to appear without valid reasons shall not be an obstacle to consideration of the case of a disciplinary offense.

In the event of commission by an advocate of an offense for which he may be expelled from the college, the presidium shall remove the advocate from work until the matter is finally resolved.

A decree of the presidium of a college of advocates imposing a disciplinary sanction may be appealed by the advocate within two weeks from the day it is rendered to the Council of Ministers of the autonomous republic or to the executive committee of the territorial, regional, or Moscow or Leningrad city Soviet of Working People's Deputies.

Article 43. If during one year from the day of imposition of a disciplinary sanction an advocate does not commit a new offense, he shall be considered as not having been subjected to a disciplinary sanction.

If an advocate has proved his correction by a conscientious attitude toward his work and irreproachable conduct, the presidium of the college of advocates may remove the disciplinary sanction from him ahead of time.

Removal of a disciplinary sanction ahead of time may be done upon the motion of the head of a legal consultation office, of a general meeting of advocates, or of social organizations of the consultation office.

EIGHTH CHAPTER

Funds of a College of Advocates

Article 44. The funds of a college of advocates shall be formed from sums deducted by legal consultation offices. The amount of deductions shall be established by a general meeting (or conference) of the members of the college of advocates, but shall not exceed 30 per cent of the sum total of the honorariums received by the legal consultation office.

22. MODEL STATUTE ON THE JURISCONSULT

Introductory Note

Jurisconsults (<u>iuriskonsul'ty</u>) in the Soviet Union are legal advisors employed by enterprises and other institutions and organizations. Only the larger enterprises, institutions, and organizations in fact employ full-time jurisconsults, the smaller ones either sharing a jurisconsult with other organizations or retaining advocates from legal consultation offices.

Most of the union republics have enacted statutes on the jurisconsults in the last decade. While the majority have adopted ordinary statutes, a few (among them the RSFSR) have adopted so-called "model statutes." In the decree which confirmed the Model Statute, the RSFSR Council of Ministers required ministries, departments, and soviets to adopt statutes based on the Model Statute. This system is designed to allow individual ministries, departments, and soviets to take local differences into account in regulating the work of their jurisconsults.

The statutes adopted in the various union republics are by no means identical to each other. Some republics, for example, permit the director of an enterprise, institution, or organization to hire and dismiss jurisconsults at will, while others (e.g., the RSFSR, Article 8) require the director to obtain the consent of the director of his superior agency.

Although the Model Statute is directed primarily at the activities of jurisconsults in state economic enterprises, it applies as well to those employed in other state, cooperative, and social enterprises, institutions, and organizations.

MODEL STATUTE ON A LEGAL (OR CONTRACT-LEGAL)
SECTION, CHIEF (OR SENIOR) JURISCONSULT, OR JURISCONSULT
OF AN ENTERPRISE, INSTITUTION, OR ORGANIZATION

(confirmed by a decree of the Council of
Ministers of the RSFSR, March 29, 1963)

Article 1. The basic tasks of a legal (or contract-legal) section, chief (or senior) jurisconsult, [or] jurisconsult shall be to strengthen socialist legality in the work of enterprises, institutions, and organizations and actively to foster by legal means the improvement of their activity and the safeguarding of the integrity of socialist ownership.

Article 2. A legal (or contract-legal) section, chief (or senior) jurisconsult, [or] jurisconsult shall be charged with:

(a) verification of the conformity to legislation in force of drafts of decrees, decisions, regulations, orders, instructions, and other legal acts issued by the enterprise, institution, [or] organization;

(b) participation in preparation of opinions on drafts of normative acts transmitted to the enterprise, institution, [or] organization for approval;

(c) rendering legal assistance to the respective structural subdivisions of the enterprise, institution, [or] organization in presenting claims and drawing up drafts of contracts on the basis of materials [submitted] by such subdivisions;

(d) giving opinions, consultations, and information on legal questions which arise in the activity of the enterprise, institution, or organization;

(e) placing before the director of the enterprise, institution, or organization questions of changing or annulling legal acts issued by the enterprise, institution, [or] organization which contradict legislation in force;

(f) conduct of judicial and arbitrazh cases upon authorization from the directorate of the enterprise, institution, [or] organization;

(g) systematic analysis and summarizing of the results of the consideration of judicial and arbitrazh cases and of the practice of concluding and performing economic contracts, and placing before the director questions of improving the activity of the enterprise, institution, [or] organization;

(h) periodic verification of the state of legal work in subordinate enterprises, institutions, [and] organizations;

(i) instruction of jurisconsults of subordinate enterprises, institutions, [and] organizations and giving them advice on legal questions;

(j) keeping a record of legislative, governmental, and other normative acts and making notes of the annulment, modification, or amendment of such acts;

(k) informing personnel of the enterprise, institution, [or] organization concerning current legislation and rendering legal assistance by giving advice to the FZMK [factory-plant local committee], comrades' court, and other social organizations.

Article 3. If the draft of a document presented for verification contradicts legislation in force, the chief of the legal (or contract-legal) section, chief (or senior) jurisconsult, [or] jurisconsult must append to it a note which indicates in what way the draft does not conform to the legislation in force and sets forth proposals for a legal means of resolving the questions specified in the draft.

Article 4. The chief of a legal (or contract-legal) section, chief (or senior) jurisconsult, [or] jurisconsult shall be obliged to refuse to conduct judicial or arbitrazh cases if there are no grounds for the given enterprise, institution, [or] organization to commence a suit or to object to a suit commenced with good grounds against it.

Article 5. In the event that violations of legality are exposed in the activity of the enterprise, institution, [or] organization, the chief of the legal (or contract-legal) section, chief (or senior) jurisconsult, [or] jurisconsult shall be obliged to inform the director of the enterprise, institution, [or] organization to such effect and, in those instances when the director does not adopt measures to eliminate the violations, [to inform] the director of the superior organization.

Article 6. The chief of a legal (or contract-legal) section, chief (or senior) jurisconsult, [or] jurisconsult shall be present at sessions of the Council of the National Economy, or collegium of the ministry [or] department, or executive committee of the local Soviet of Working People's Deputies, as well as at assemblies convoked by the director of the enterprise, institution, [or] organization, and shall give opinions on legal questions which arise.

Article 7. The chief of a legal (or contract-legal) section, chief (or senior) jurisconsult, [or] jurisconsult shall receive from all structural subdivisions of the enterprise, institution, [or] organization documents and information neces- sary for carrying out the duties with which he is charged.

Article 8. The chief of a legal (or contract-legal) section, chief (or senior) jurisconsult, [or] jurisconsult shall be appointed and dismissed in accordance with the labor legislation in force — in ministries and departments of the RSFSR in the procedure established by the decree of the Council of Ministers of the RSFSR of February 26, 1960, No. 287; in councils of the national economy, Coun- cils of Ministers of autonomous republics, territorial executive committees, re- gional executive committees, the Moscow city executive committee, [and] the Leningrad city executive committee, by decree of the council of the national ec- onomy [or] Council of Ministers of the autonomous republic [or] by decision of the territorial executive committee, regional executive committee, Moscow city executive committee, [or] Leningrad city executive committee; in other institu- tions, organizations, and enterprises, by order of the director of the enterprise, institution, or organization by agreement with the superior organization.

Article 9. Persons having a higher legal education shall be appointed to the offices of chief of a legal (or contract-legal) section, chief (or senior) juriscon- sult, [and] jurisconsult.

In individual cases persons with secondary education may be appointed to these offices if they have not less than five years' work experience as a jurist.

Article 10. The chief of a legal (or contract-legal) section, chief (or senior) jurisconsult, [or] jurisconsult shall be directly subordinate to the director of the enterprise, institution, [or] organization.

Article 11. Utilization of personnel of a legal (or contract-legal) section, a chief (or senior) jurisconsult, [or] a jurisconsult in work not related to their direct duties shall not be permitted.

Article 12. The administration of an enterprise, institution, [or] organiza- tion shall be obliged to provide the legal (or contract-legal) section, chief (or senior) jurisconsult, [or] jurisconsult with normative acts and other materials on legal matters (reference books, aids, etc.).